Managing——
Banking
Risks

Eddie Cade

Managing
Banking
Risks

Eddie Cade

Glenlake Publishing Company, Ltd.
Chicago • London • New Delhi

AMACOM
American Management Association
New York • Atlanta • Boston • Chicago • Kansas City • San Francisco • Washington, D.C.
Brussels • Mexico City • Tokyo • Toronto

This book is available at a special
discount when ordered in bulk quantities.
For information, contact Special Sales Department,
AMACOM, an imprint of AMA Publications, a division of
American Management Association,
1601 Broadway, New York, NY 10019.

This publication is designed to provide accurate and authoritative
Information in regard to the subject matter covered. It is sold
with the understanding that the publisher is not engaged in
rendering legal, accounting, or other professional service. If
legal advice or other expert assistance is required, the services of
a competent professional person should be sought.

Printing number

10 9 8 7 6 5 4 3 2 1

'There is a tide in the affairs of men,
Which, taken at the flood, leads on to fortune . . .'

(William Shakespeare, *Julius Caesar*)

'Fools rush in where angels fear to tread'

(Alexander Pope, *An Essay on Criticism*)

Contents

Foreword

Risk management in banking is not a new activity. Since banking began managers of banks have spent at least some of their time worrying that a failure of borrowers to repay their loans or some other disaster would prevent the bank from being able to remain profitable or, in extremis, from repaying the bank's depositors. Cynics might say, however, that such worrying has too often not resulted in satisfactory risk control, since the history of banking in both developed and developing countries contains too many instances of bank losses and failures, usually at a time of economic recession in the country concerned. At a more personal level, today's bank chief executives and risk directors are aware that even if their bank survives their own careers are at risk should unusually high loss levels appear.

Against this background, risk control was nevertheless regarded as more of an art than a science until the last two decades when, aided by computerised calculation and database techniques, the use of quantitative and calibrated controls has steadily spread, first through the market risk arena and more recently through credit issues.

There are extremely promising developments, which offer the real possibility of a less volatile performance from banks in future, to the benefit of both themselves and the communities within which they operate. However, perhaps inevitably at this stage, these new techniques have spawned a patchy proliferation of learning possibilities concerning banking risk management, ranging from university and business school texts to highly tailored courses and seminars and a plethora of risk management periodicals. All of these have their place but there is a paucity of accessible introductory texts which span the full range of risk management issues and emphasise the need for a combined use of business sense and quantitative methods. Eddy Cade's book, which benefits both from his wide UK and international banking experience and his clear style, is therefore a very welcome addition to the risk management library.

Alan Brown
Director Credit Policy
Barclays PLC

Preface

Why write another book on risk; or, more precisely, why *this* book now? Because I wanted to try and fill something of a gap in the literature by offering a practising banker's overview of the full spectrum of risks that a modern bank needs to manage. Experience tells me that a lot of people could benefit from a wide-ranging primer based on inside knowledge of the subject: certainly there have been many times when I myself could have done with just such a guide.

Following years of setbacks in the late 1980s and early 1990s, in the longest economic recession that most of us can remember, 'risk' is a topic very much in vogue. Yet it is honoured more often by invocation than by classification, being a word that apparently means all things to all people. With few exceptions, banking literature on risk remains highly compartmentalised, and much of the newer thinking resides in specialist magazines, in unpublished theses, or in confidential reports rendered by consultants.

Literary fragmentation is not surprising as, in many aspects, risk management is a science still in its infancy. Risk maps are sometimes offered at financial seminars and symposia, but these visions tend to suffer from their own exclusivities, circumscriptions, gaps, and discontinuities of approach and authorship. Often they are too abstract to shed any light on the specific problems of banking.

This book is for generalist reading and will not qualify any of us to be a specialist risk manager (a little learning can be a dangerous thing, as Alexander Pope warned). For greater depth of study in particular areas, it is necessary to resort to the compartmentalised literature or to seek guidance from experts in the relevant discipline. But aren't generalists a dying breed anyway? Actually no, far from it. Outside our own specialisms, we are *all* generalists who need to find a common language if the business is not to disintegrate. One of the dangers of modern specialisation is that it can lead to a form of moral hazard: the presumption that 'I no longer have to understand things outside my field, because other people will look after them.'

As Chapter 9 points out, a single financial instrument may embody a number of different types of banking risk, and a good banker should be aware of them all in a general sense even if only one of them is his special responsibility. It is a sobering moment when a lending banker, having purchased a debt security with the canny idea of enhancing the rate of return on a particular corporate credit relationship, discovers that he has simultaneously incurred an interest rate risk requiring daily revaluation.

Board directors and top management in banking need to come to terms with the whole gamut of risks over which they preside, as must those aspiring (or being groomed) to succeed them. Territorial heads of banking operations in foreign jurisdictions are 'top management' locally, and carry analogous responsibilities. Internal auditors or inspectors are still required to deploy a versatile under-standing of the various risks being run in the organisation: they, after all, have to sanction and monitor many of the safeguards put in place. An overarching perspective, spanning blinkered specialisms, is of value to anybody with an interest in how his or her piece of the picture fits into the whole.

Outside the banking industry itself, one could go on to list regulatory authorities, bank auditors, rating agencies and manage-ment consultancies – all of whom need to know their way around the landscape of risk. Finally, there are all manner of students, investment analysts and commentators on the banking scene, for whom little introductory literature on risk management exists.

On the one hand, risk analysis nowadays can be akin to a discourse on nuclear physics, barely accessible to the most educated reader. On the other, there remains a populist tradition in commercial banking which equates the concept of 'risk' with credit risk alone. Renaming the credit function 'risk management', as this school of thought has been known to do, seems a recipe not so much for risk awareness as for confusion. Some fuzziness is a natural legacy of branching structures where almost the only financial risk in sight *was* credit risk, the others being largely hidden away in head office; however, it is time to widen the horizons and sharpen the focus.

The 'wooden spoon' performance of credit risk management in recent years may also have given rise to the perception that if credit risk is not the only risk, it is the one that matters and that line management can do something about. Moreover, the hubris of identifying credit risk with risk *per se* sometimes carries with it the unspoken premise that if there *is* anything else out there (apart from credit risk) the same 'risk manager' can pick that up as well; but, as should become clear in the space of a few chapters, such a pious hope is out of touch with reality.

In short, risk management theory in banking has historically been patchy and incoherent, lacking in consensus. That is not to deny that bankers have appreciated the need for rules and regulations, audits and inspections, without recognising them under a caption of 'risk management'; rather like Molière's Monsieur Jourdain, who discovered that he had been 'talking prose for the last forty years and never known it'. This book aims to achieve a balanced synthesis of the obvious and the esoteric, the old and the new, and thus provide a conceptual framework for a rational approach to the subject.

Risk management is not merely about *reducing risks* (although that is in many cases a necessity), but essentially about *taking risks* in an intelligent manner. Banking can no more be riskless than life itself.

As to the definition of 'banking', I am taking it simply to comprise the core activities of licensed banks, more or less anywhere, such as:

- Intermediation (taking deposits and lending money).

- Disintermediation (relinquishing the intermediary debtor/creditor position, whilst retaining a 'broker' role).

- Collection and payment system, money transmission.

- Foreign exchange, foreign trade services.

- Participation in the money and capital markets.

I do not, however, include some of the newer services which have been brought within the fold for marketing synergy, but which are separate and distinct businesses for regulatory and risk management purposes; notably insurance and investment management.

The prescription 'licensed banks' formally debars near-banks and the like (for example, mutual building societies) but, to the extent that their activities approximate to those of banks, the considerations and disciplines set out in this book are applicable also to them. The principle is: if the cap fits, wear it.

Whilst readers are assumed to be broadly conversant with modern banking practice, a glossary of financial terms is provided.

Acknowledgements

I am indebted to both Professor Harold Rose and John Hargreaves for much general advice and encouragement, as well as specific guidance on the theoretical foundations of risk and reward (Chapter 1), capital adequacy (Chapter 3), and portfolio management (Chapter 6). Any residual errors are mine alone.

On the subject of credit risk management (Chapters 5 and 6 in particular), earlier comparative research by Bob Brice, of National Australia Bank, provided a wealth of information and ideas.

Gary Purtill, of Bank of Western Australia, supplied another Antipodean perspective on a wide range of financial risks.

I received excellent advice on aspects of solvency, liquidity, and systemic risk (Chapters 3 and 4) from central banking sources who prefer to do good by stealth and remain anonymous.

Above all, the task of compilation and analysis throughout would not have been possible without the extensive help of many friends and colleagues in Barclays Bank. They know who they are. To spotlight individuals here would be either invidious or impractical (by reason of sheer numbers); except perhaps to say that Matthew Bullock originally opened all the doors for me.

I am grateful to all these mentors, both for primary source material and for critical comment. It is only fair to add that the views expressed in this book are ultimately my own and not necessarily theirs.

Eddie Cade

CHAPTER ONE
Risk and reward

This chapter provides a grounding for the rest of the book, outlining:

- A banker's definition of risk.

- A statistical framework for assessing risk.

- A discipline for measuring return on economic risk capital.

- Market-based criteria for a minimum required rate of return.

Banks are highly geared financial risk-takers. When things go awry the results can be spectacular. In 1987 Merrill Lynch lost $377 million through trading mortgage-backed securities in an innovative form. In 1989 the junk bond market collapsed, and with it the fortunes of Drexel Burnham Lambert. In 1989 also, Midland Bank lost a reported £116 million by guessing wrong on interest rate movements.

In 1991 Bank of New England made massive bad debt provisions, suffered a run on deposits and had to be supported by government to the tune of some $2 billion. In 1992 Barclays Bank provided £2.5 billion for bad and doubtful debts and declared the first loss in its history. In 1993 Crédit Lyonnais succumbed to similar troubles and registered a net loss of FFr6.9 billion (say £834 million), precipitating a state rescue package of FFr44.9 billion: this proved to be merely the prelude to a further and much larger bail-out in 1995. In their financial year to March 1996, the major Japanese banks wrote off a total of some ¥6000 billion (say £36.5 billion) of bad debts accumulated from the preceding boom years.

In 1995 Barings, London's oldest merchant bank, was brought down by losses of £830 million on a speculative proprietary position in Nikkei 225 stock index futures. In the same year, Bankers Trust was sued by two dissatisfied customers for sums totalling $200 million in respect of disastrous swap contracts which the bank had arranged for them: these claims were settled for lesser amounts out of court.

Meanwhile, over a period of years, London banks have been counting the cost of marketing what turned out to be unenforceable interest rate swap contracts to local authorities with defective contractual powers; and police and public prosecutors have continued to unravel the skeins of massive internal fraud at the defunct Bank of Credit and Commerce International.

These are just a few examples from a long list of prominent accidents and failures in risk management, a science replete with hindsight but less endowed with foresight or consensus on preventive measures. Risk management scandals in banking are more reliable than buses: you can be sure that there will be another one along in a little while. But first things first: what exactly *is* 'risk'?

1.1 A definition of risk

This is a happy hunting ground for linguistic philosophers, mathematicians and actuaries, and we have to accept that no single definition of 'risk' will serve all purposes. Dictionaries, and much of common parlance, dwell on jeopardy, potential loss and disaster, whereas a business perspective needs to be more balanced. Business perspectives in turn differ, so that it is unsafe to apply insurance industry terminology, for example, to banking.

A suitable definition of risk in banking is: *exposure to uncertainty of outcome.*

Exposure, often omitted from risk definitions, denotes a position or a stake in the outcome, without which our interest is merely academic – we are not *at risk*, any more than is a racegoer who has refrained from placing a bet.

An *outcome* is the consequence of a particular course of action.

How and when we can recognise an 'outcome' will become clearer as we examine the various categories of risk in banking.

Uncertainty can be reflected in the *volatility of potential outcomes* plotted on a probability distribution curve, for which the normal measure of dispersion would be either the *variance* or the *standard deviation*. The wider the standard deviation, the greater the volatility; and thus, in theory, the uncertainty and the risk. 'Volatility' is the term in common currency, but it is perhaps too closely associated with a complacent belief that past fluctuations are the full key to future uncertainty: some experts therefore prefer to use the near-synonym 'variability' to revive the *frisson* of unpredictability.

The standard deviation shows the dispersion of values (in this case potential outcomes) around the arithmetic mean outcome (often called the 'expected outcome'). The appendix to this chapter explains and illustrates the methodology, which can be studied in greater depth in suitable textbooks on statistics, and can of course be streamlined by the use of a scientific calculator or a purpose-written computer program.

If deviation from the expected is the determinant of risk, and volatility or variability (encapsulated within standard deviations) is an index of 'how risky?', it follows that an expected outcome, no matter how dire, is not a risk. An adverse expected outcome (representing, say, normal bad debt experience) must be counted as a cost of doing the business, justifiable only within the context of the reward otherwise earned (and therefore the net return). The bank should position itself to accommodate the expected outcome within profits and provisions, leaving equity capital as the final shock-absorber for the unforeseen catastrophe.

1.2 A statistical definition of risk?

The attractions of this established mathematical approach are obvious. It offers a quantified picture of our risk, and a basis for decisions on altering the profile, engaging in or disengaging from exposures, hedging the risk, seeking commensurate rewards, setting prudent provisions for inevitable losses and planning capital adequacy geared to riskiness; in short, for managing our risk at a global portfolio level.

Not surprisingly, some commentators adopt volatility, conveyed in the standard deviation, as their *definition* of 'risk'. There are, however, a number of objections to doing so. In the first place, such confident analysis of potential outcomes is practicable only in trading and portfolio applications where there is a reliable historical database (granted that its use is modified if appropriate by expectations of changing outlook). In other words, it is a counsel of perfection still ahead of its time in many areas of operation.

Secondly, the use of the variance or the standard deviation as a principal measure of portfolio risk is only valid if 'skewness' of potential outcomes is not a problem – which it so often is in real life.

The statistical methodology is also open to outright challenge on the ground that it relies on the future resembling the past. This resurrects the age-old conundrum of *induction* (learning from experience), a principle which the greatest philosophical minds have struggled in vain to validate, but which in practice is the foundation of all rational thought, education and conduct. The objection, taken to its ultimate conclusion, can only win a Pyrrhic victory by disqualifying *all* history (statistical or otherwise) as 'bunk' (to quote Henry Ford). Most of us prefer to give some value to past experience, as a useful though not infallible guide.

A modified challenge, however, might target not induction (the learning principle) itself, but simply the *degree* of reliance on historical statistics of volatility – e.g. contending that such a record cannot capture the modern accelerating pace of change. This line of argument is not without validity, as mentioned earlier: risk implies the capacity to surprise. But pushed too far, the criticism effectively rules out the established body of portfolio management theory and practice, whilst leaving us short of sensible alternatives. However, far from denying the claims of volatility (or variability), it reaffirms them in its own way.

A more direct objection to volatility as the definition of risk is that a concept (such as risk) should not be confused with the means of measuring its dimensions. 'Distance' is not a synonym for 'miles', for example, and in the same vein it is worth preserving the full 'future unknown' flavour of 'uncertainty' as distinct from the statistical terms by which we seek to capture it.

To put this in another way, the problem of risk is not volatility *per se* but rather the uncertainty of the potential outcomes as reflected in that pattern of volatility. In other contexts, it is possible to imagine patterns of volatility that are quite predictable: e.g. climatic fluctuations in some countries. Conversely, a lack of volatility in outcomes might just catch everybody by surprise.

To discard volatility as itself the definition of risk is not to reject modern science, but to reassert the claims of experience, pragmatism, and indeed residual ignorance alongside it.

For our purposes, then, risk is exposure to uncertainty of outcome.

1.3 It is not always risk of loss

If a risk crystallises, in the shape of an outcome which deviates from the expected, that outcome is not necessarily a loss: in some circumstances it may be a gain. So-called 'pure' (or 'static') risk does extend only downside from the expected outcome (i.e. represents a possible loss), but 'speculative' (or 'dynamic') risk can produce either a better or a worse result (a profit or a loss). We shall see examples of both types, one-way and two-way, when we come to examine the broad classifications of banking risks in the next chapter. Regrettably, there is no known type of risk that is upside only.

1.4 What to do about risk

Several different courses of action are open to a banker faced with a particular source of risk:

- Avoid it, if in prospect.

- Accept and retain it on an economically justifiable basis.

- Increase, reduce or eliminate it by executive actions.

- Reduce it by diversification within a portfolio of risks.

- Hedge it artificially – i.e. counterbalance and neutralise it, to a degree, by the use of derivative instruments.

- Liquidate it by transfer without recourse to another party.

Which of these solutions is appropriate depends on the type of risk and the particular circumstances, as we shall see from many examples in the remainder of this book. The sections of this chapter that follow deal with the subject of reward, based on the assumption that some risk is retained. Risk is to be respected but not shunned. No enterprise can achieve anything without engaging in risk, and the business of banking is characterised by the way in which it underpins the financial risks of the community – too often, it must be admitted, at an inadequate rate of return.

1.5 Reward for risk

The proposal thus far is that risk is found in deviation from the expected, and that risk (equity) capital exists as the final shock-absorber for the unexpected outcome that cannot be accommodated within the buffer of provisions and profits. It follows that the amount of capital in a banking business should bear a rational quantitative relationship to the amount of risk being run. Capital adequacy requirements will be discussed in Chapter 3 on Solvency Risk: suffice it to say here that there is *regulatory* capital (a blunt instrument historically) and there is *economic* capital (the unofficial computation which attempts to adjust for risk).

According to the theory of expected utility maximisation, decision-makers seek a trade-off between the probability-weighted risks of an activity and the rewards to be gained from that activity. In banking, the reward for risk is the 'premium layer' of the return on the equity capital allocated to the risk. We shall first look at each of these components separately.

1.6 The return

The return is the net result of all direct and indirect revenues less attributable costs: a sophisticated incremental accounting and costing system is therefore essential. Costing is a vexed subject capable of halting management accounting progress in any bank for a prolonged period. Amongst the controversial aspects are *transfer pricing* (payment for procurement of funding) and *transfer charging* (payment for other services rendered) between different divisions or units within the bank. Leaving those aside, management accounting at division or business unit level ought to be relatively straightforward. Bigger problems arise when it comes to allocating notional costs to customer relationships and new business; yet no bank which is serious about the risk/reward trade-off dare shirk the task.

Another debate which has proved particularly intractable is that of fully-absorbed versus marginal costing. Fully-absorbed (all-inclusive) costing applies (with some qualifications) at business unit level, but it distorts the economics of a new business opportunity to the point where it may be wrongly turned away. Marginal costing, by contrast, assumes that a large proportion of the bank's central costs are 'sunk' and will not be affected by any new piece of business taken on. This approach can be perverted to such a degree that it puts out an indiscriminate 'welcome' mat for all new business because it is deemed 'cost-free'. Worse still, it can generate pernicious business volume imperatives in order to cover an imagined megalith of 'sunk costs'.

Dogmatic adherence to either extreme (fully-absorbed or marginal costing) is a vice, and it may be that the deadlock has to be broken by redefining the dichotomy as being between, say, 'fixed' and 'variable' costs, with new business bearing a realistic allocation of the latter.

The advent of hard-nosed 'performance-related pay' (PRP) schemes in these formative times puts extra pressure on people's objectivity, adding to the temptation to skew the measurement system in their favour. In an ideal world, the measurement of organisational performance would be well established and validated before the introduction of PRP into this numbers-driven framework.

At any rate, these battles are too important to be left to the accountants and the business developers alone. The bank's chief executive will need to follow the arguments closely and step in to deliver conclusive rulings when the occasion demands. There are no 'right answers' to some of these questions, only what is right for the organisation concerned.

1.7 Expected loss

Finally, a reminder that, under the philosophy of 'risk' expounded thus far, the expected outcome is not a risk: any expected loss (or conceivably gain) must therefore be included in the costs (or revenues) that go to make up the calculation of the expected return on the activity. This implies that risky assets (and derivatives) must in some sense be 'marked to market', or at least revalued according to best judgement. Whilst marking to market is an essential discipline in modern banking, it is not quite the panacea it is sometimes held out to be: when it is not violating respectable accounting standards, there are still problems over the depth of trading underlying alleged market prices – most notably in the secondary market for distressed debt. Too often the exercise will produce frivolous or masochistic results, which is why 'best judgement' (projecting a defined timescale of realisation) may sometimes be preferable.

Expected loss as a concept will be considered further in Chapter 6 on Analysing the Portfolio: mathematically its components are *probability of default* (or *expected default rate*) × *anticipated amount of exposure at time of default* × *severity*. *Severity* quantifies the damage in the event of loss: it is essentially a function of security offsets (if any) and the likely costs of administration and delay in finalising recovery/loss. The return adjusted for expected loss is sometimes referred to as 'risk-adjusted return', but that must be a misnomer if (as we have said) expected loss is a cost, not a risk.

Conventional accounting and taxation standards in many countries do not as yet accommodate the debiting of a statistically-based 'expected loss' at the time the business is written. Where it is normal practice to create a 'general provision', logic suggests that that provision should be wholly or mainly based on expected losses. If no such recognised solution is available, then it will be necessary to keep score unofficially, so that business development and portfolio management are not targeted on illusory profitability.

1.8 Equity capital allocated to the risk

The capital allocated in the risk/reward calculation is the *economic equity capital* – i.e. adjusted according to the particular risk that it is intended to cover. The adjustment will reflect contribution to group risk, of which the ingredients are: size of exposure, volatility of net returns and correlation with the bank's larger portfolio (we shall revert to this discussion in Chapters 3 and 6). Depending on these factors, economic (or risk-adjusted) capital may represent a higher or a lower percentage against a particular exposure than does the stipulated regulatory requirement.

1.9 Reward for risk: the synthesis

Supposing that we have quantified the expected return (including the expected loss), measured the apparent risk, and determined the economic capital to be allocated to the risk, where do we go from here? How do we judge between competing claims on the bank's capital featuring differing combinations of risk and return?

The obvious answer is to calculate the expected rate of return on the risk capital allocated to each activity. For convenience, let us call that formula 'return on risk-adjusted capital' – or RORAC for short. Be warned, however, that some people style the same calculation RAROC (risk-adjusted return on capital), and yet others refer to it as RARORAC (risk-adjusted return on risk-adjusted capital). From our standpoint, the latter two are technically misleading because in fact the return is not risk-adjusted but expected-loss-adjusted.

All such labels are to be treated with circumspection: the important thing is to be clear about what is in each formula, regardless of name prejudices. Many American bankers seem to have adopted a form of RAROC as their generic term and way of life.

An alternative to the foregoing ratio approach is to evaluate new business in terms of net present value (NPV) of future cash flows, applying a discount rate equal to the bank's minimum required rate of return (or 'hurdle rate'). The criterion then becomes the size of the positive NPV, if any. This technique, which overcomes certain ambiguities, is preferred by some of the best brains in the banking business.

1.10 Required rate of return: cost of equity

Having identified an approach to measuring reward for risk, we now need a standard that will tell us whether the reward (on economic equity capital commensurate with the risk) meets the bank's rate of return requirement. In a capitalist society, this calls for a shift in focus, bringing into play not only the solvency aspects that are implicit in the discussion up to now, but also the distinctly different postulates of shareholder value and standard capital asset pricing theory.

The minimum required rate of return on any company's equity capital is sometimes expressed as its 'cost of equity'. This may be broken down into an assumed 'risk-free rate' (usually represented by the three-month treasury bill rate for purists, or a medium term gilt rate for some pragmatists) plus a premium applicable to the equity market as a whole representing its non-diversifiable risk. The (somewhat leaky) underlying assumption here is that since 'the market' constitutes the total available equity portfolio, it is not possible to diversify equities outside it (for more on diversification of risk, see Chapter 6).

In the UK, the equity market risk premium above medium term gilts has ranged from as high as 17% in the 1920s and 1950s to as low as 0.2% in the 1970s. The average for the period 1919 to 1993 was 7.5%, and the present trend is downwards from the 7.2% of the 1980s.

The risk premium is indiscriminate as between different companies with widely disparate risk profiles. It therefore has to be 'customised'. This is achieved by multiplying it by the particular company's own 'beta' coefficient, which is a historically derived measure of the sensitivity of the return on that share to a general change in the return on the market (as represented by a relevant share index). If the share is more sensitive than average to the market, its beta will be higher than 1.0; if less sensitive, it will be lower than 1.0. For practical purposes, the beta may also be plotted by reference to share prices.

Once again it is necessary to warn against too easy an assumption that statistical history represents future risk. Historical beta is a useful indicator, but we need to look at trends and other portents of where future beta may be going.

Clearly a comprehensive database is required to track these figures back over five years or more in the equity market concerned. In the United Kingdom one of the best-equipped statistical sources is the London Business School.

By way of illustration, if the medium term gilt rate is 8% (say 6% net of mean marginal rate of income tax), the risk premium is 7%, and our beta is 1.1, the bank's cost of equity (minimum required rate of return on equity) is: $6\% + 7\% \times 1.1 = 13.7\%$ post-tax. That is the required weighted average of all its multifarious rates of return from different activities. In as much as an average is made up of lower as well as higher figures, it follows that the average is not necessarily a universal minimum requirement or 'hurdle rate', but it provides a basis from which such hurdle rates can be set in terms of RORAC for new business of various kinds – depending on their contribution to the business mix and even, some argue, their individual notional betas.

When we speak of a required return on equity, do we mean *book value* of equity ('shareholders' funds' in the bank's accounts) or *market value/market capitalisation?* The capital market thinks in terms of the latter, whereas the bank's management will find it more practical to cope with a formula based on book value. This discrepancy matters less than might appear at first sight since, although the two values of equity capital are often dislocated from one another in the short term, over the long run the leads and lags will tend to self-correct with a bias to convergence.

As may be seen, we have here an elegant and persuasive theorem which, in the present state of knowledge, can be applied only with a considerable degree of imprecision. There remains much scope for developing the science. Not everybody endorses the *capital asset pricing model*, but it still holds centre stage in management theory and a better rationale for required rate of return on capital has yet to be found.

Finally, as mentioned earlier, there is a technical case for new business evaluations to be rendered in terms not of rate of return but of net present value of future cash flows, in which the discount rate is the hurdle rate. The NPV approach resolves difficulties with respect to size, life and time profile of competing investments.

1.11 Warning on required rate of return

This is an 'all things being equal' approach and, as always, words of caution are necessary. Since the 'cost of equity' is based on a series of highly volatile and variable numbers, it is as well to attune all calculations (including also expected losses) to a full economic cycle of, say, six or more years' duration; in other words, to posit something of a steady state requirement irrespective of the highs and lows of the economy. On the one hand, competitive pressures undeniably rule out complete rigidity in pricing: on the other, we surely ought to have learned some lessons from the Rake's Progress of short termism and boom-and-bust banking which characterised the late 1980s.

Secondly, this orderly description of required rate of return assumes a sustainable rate of growth in risks. It will need to adapt to any marked change in the size or intensity of risks being taken on. In particular, when annual percentage growth in risk assets reaches double figures the required rate of return on the whole book starts to escalate steeply just to sustain capital ratios in addition to satisfying shareholders' demands. These dynamics, widely ignored or misunderstood throughout banking history, will be examined more closely in Chapter 3 on Solvency Risk.

1.12 Summary

This chapter rests on the following propositions:

1   Risk in banking is defined as exposure to uncertainty of outcome.

2   The scope of uncertainty is reflected in the volatility or variability of potential outcomes.

3   Where the volatility is capable of being quantified, its dimensions lie in the range of deviation from the expected outcome, which latter is taken for practical purposes to be the arithmetic mean of the distribution of potential outcomes. Where possible, measurement of volatility should be by way of either the variance or the standard deviation.

4   Expected loss, if any, is not a risk but a business cost which should be allowed for in the pricing at the outset.

5   Equity capital exists to cover unexpected loss. It can therefore be allocated (as risk-adjusted or economic capital) according to assessed risk.

6   The reward for risk is the excess of return on economic equity capital over and above the risk-free rate.

7   The required rate of return is founded not on solvency calculations but on a market-determined 'cost of equity'. This outline necessarily skates over great depths of complexity, and subtle academic controversy, on the question of how best to convert the bank's global cost of equity for practical application at business unit, portfolio, product, customer and transaction levels.

How far does this exposition represent current practice? The big

American banks are probably some five years ahead of the field in development. By comparison, most British banks are still at the starting gate; the only benefit of which may be that they can now model their systems on refinements of the early more primitive theories. Banks in some other countries have yet to understand or accept the arguments.

Appreciation seems to go hand in hand with national culture and the economic framework. A climate of political and regulatory paternalism does not foster independent thoughts of taking responsibility for one's own risks and earning a proper return on them; neither, on the other hand, does naive headlong competition for market share, which behavioural pattern is no stranger to the supposedly most mature markets.

Appendix: Volatility and the standard deviation

Figure 1.1 is a histogram showing a symmetrical example of a probability distribution curve, plotting default rates on a single-graded slice of an imaginary loan portfolio. The horizontal axis depicts annual percentage default rates, to each of which is assigned a probability weighting on the vertical axis. In this case, the probabilities have been assessed in terms of 'chances out of a hundred', and (we may assume) are based on cumulative statistical evidence sufficient to give an informed view of a full credit cycle. The arithmetic mean and expected outcome (which would be referred to as the expected default rate) in this particular exercise is known to be 1.0% per annum, and the standard deviation works out at approximately 0.175%.

To calculate the standard deviation, we first square each of the deviations of the individual values from the mean and multiply the squares by the respective probability weightings. We then add the answers together (total in our example: 3.06) and divide by the total of probability weightings (in our example, 100) to arrive at the variance. The square root of the variance will give us the standard deviation. The exercise would be slightly more complicated if (because of a more irregular pattern of values across the horizontal plane) we first had to guess and then find the arithmetic mean.

For a 'normal' symmetrical bell-shaped curve, approximately 68% of the values in a distribution will lie within one standard deviation on either side of the arithmetic mean, some 95% within two

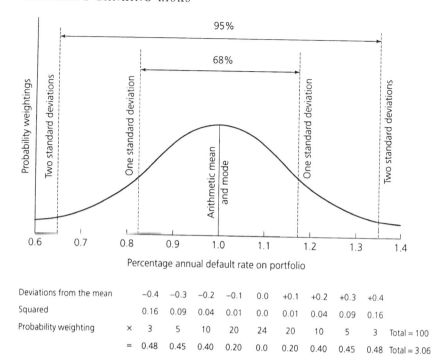

Deviations from the mean		−0.4	−0.3	−0.2	−0.1	0.0	+0.1	+0.2	+0.3	+0.4	
Squared		0.16	0.09	0.04	0.01	0.0	0.01	0.04	0.09	0.16	
Probability weighting	×	3	5	10	20	24	20	10	5	3	Total = 100
	=	0.48	0.45	0.40	0.20	0.0	0.20	0.40	0.45	0.48	Total = 3.06

$$\frac{3.06}{100} = 0.0306 = \text{Variance}$$

Standard deviation = $\sqrt{0.0306} = 0.1749285$

1.1 Volatility and the standard deviation.

standard deviations on either side, and in excess of 99% within three standard deviations on either side. However, many curves are not conveniently symmetrical, or normal.

If the distribution is asymmetrical, we may for some reason choose as our expected outcome the *mode:* that is, the single value with the highest chance of occurring. The mode is not the same thing as the arithmetic mean (which most people would call the average), although in a symmetrical distribution like Fig. 1.1 the two will coincide.

CHAPTER TWO

What are the banking risks?

This chapter surveys:

● The generic types of risk in banking.

● Which of them are 'pure' and which 'speculative'.

● Which categories of banking risk are the most dangerous.

Chapter 1 proposed a systematic approach to risk and reward, applicable to the business of banking. Not only is the word 'risk' open to varying interpretations and usages, but different industries encounter their 'risk' in different ways. The same frame of reference will not serve for an airline, a railway company, a nuclear power station, a pharmaceutical manufacturer, a supermarket chain, and Lloyds of London. Banking has its own set of risk priorities which this chapter will attempt to delineate.

If defining risk and reward is a rigorous intellectual exercise, classifying the broad types of risk found in banking turns out to be a much more subjective field of enquiry. Analysts sometimes forget that the purpose of such classification is not to elaborate an abstract theology but to enhance understanding of particular sources of risk, of their possible consequences, and of practical approaches to managing them. Writers typically identify between three and ten basic risk categories, depending on which traits they choose to regard as primary and which as secondary. Fortunately the result is not quite as anarchic as it may sound, for there are many common themes even though emphases differ.

2.1 Proposed framework

The following framework has proved robust, and has the advantage of being readily recognisable to bankers:

Type of banking risk	Definition
Solvency risk	Risk of ultimate financial failure of the bank through chronic inability to meet obligations.
Liquidity risk	Risk of the bank being unable to meet repayments, withdrawals and other commitments on time.
Credit risk	Risk of loss to the bank through default by an obligor.
Interest rate risk	Vulnerability of net interest income, or of portfolio present values, to changes in interest rates.
Price risks	Risk of loss/gain in value of assets, liabilities, or derivative contracts due to changes in market price; notably movements in exchange rates or share prices.
Operating risks	Risks arising from failures in operating processes, or the systems that support them, due to human error or omission, design fault, business interruption, fraud, sabotage, natural disaster, etc.

2.2 But what about all the others?

Where, you may ask, are the *derivatives* (swaps, options, futures, etc), and the *systemic risk* with which they are so closely associated in discussions between regulators and market makers? The answer is that derivatives, being exactly that, reflect the risk characteristics of the underlying instruments (i.e. from which they derive), albeit sometimes in more complex form. There is no separate 'derivative

16

risk', but the risks associated with derivative contracts will be found spread across the spectrum in the chapters that follow. Systemic risk is considered in the context of liquidity risk (Chapter 4). Some risk management guidelines for derivatives are contained in the appendix to Chapter 10 on Price Risks.

The umbrella term 'market/position risk', which bridges some of the interest rate and price risks mentioned above, has found favour in dealing and regulatory circles as a 'territorial patch' and conceptual counterpoint to credit risk (e.g. in the dialogues on capital adequacy emanating from Brussels and Basle). One is therefore tempted to adopt it as the lingua franca: the objection is that it is simply too sweeping as a title, that it oversimplifies and is likely to be misinterpreted by the general reader as embracing many things that it does not.

To the foregoing list some writers would add 'legal risk', 'regulatory risk', 'event risk', 'portfolio concentration risk', 'behavioural risk' and/or numerous other candidates which − it is argued here − can, to the extent that they are necessary constructs, be regarded as subsumed within the classes named above.

For example, 'legal risk' might seem to be a fearsome harbinger of woes like the UK local authorities swaps débâcle of the early 1990s, where the authorities were found to have lacked the contractual powers (*vires*) to be legally liable as swaps counterparties. On the other hand, it is equally arguable that ascertaining the contractual powers of counterparties is standard credit risk procedure, as stressed in every approved textbook and lending manual.

Granted that documentation needs to be unassailable, that laws and supervisory regulations have to be properly interpreted and then obeyed (so that 'compliance' has become a full-time preoccupation), that changes in laws and regulations may leave banks and their customers exposed, and that we live in a litigious society; are these sufficient reasons to give law and regulation generic risk categories of their own? The alternative is to treat the legal/regulatory problems as and when they come up within the relevant headings listed above, with credit risk being the most common field.

At first blush, 'event risk' sounds suspiciously like a simplistic 'bad luck' risk category for those who do not trust risk categories. However, two of the more intelligible versions relate to a sudden and unexpected relegation in credit grading suffered by (a) the bank, or (b) a major counterparty or issuer to whom the bank is exposed. Event (a) would undermine profitability by raising the bank's interest costs and perhaps curtailing its ability to transact certain deals (e.g. high grade swaps) at all. Event (b) could expose the bank to interest rate or price risks as defined above. 'Business event risk' also surfaces as a common subdivision of operating risks in Chapter 11. 'Event risk' is really too much of a chameleon to qualify as a primary species of banking risk.

'Portfolio concentration risk' will be discussed in Chapter 6 on Portfolio Analysis as an integral part of credit risk management. It has widespread disciplinary applications, but is not a necessary risk type in its own right. 'Behavioural risk' boils down to fraud, error and other human factors (e.g. 'key personnel risk'); all of which, for the purpose of this book, fall within operating risks.

These, at any rate, are the inconclusive kinds of arguments generated by the attempt to put banking risks in boxes. For the sake of progress, let us accept the framework of risks as set out above. These categories, however, do not exist in watertight compartments but can spill over into one another, causing multiple effects. When poor credit risks come home to roost, a liquidity crisis may ensue, exacerbated by a run on deposits precipitated by fears for the bank's solvency; a sequence witnessed in the failures of Continental Illinois (1984), Bank of New England (1991), and countless others throughout banking history. Similarly, defective credit appraisal may expose the bank to price risk losses on failed forward exchange contracts. Conversely, speculation on derivatives can turn an erstwhile creditworthy customer into a bad debtor (and possibly an aggrieved litigant against the bank).

2.3 'Pure' and 'speculative' risk

Chapter 1 made passing mention of a distinction drawn between so-called 'pure' (or 'static') risk and 'speculative' (or 'dynamic') risk. These terms are borrowed from the insurance industry, and bankers may find it more helpful to substitute for the former 'one-way risk' (all downside) and for the latter 'two-way risk' (possible upside as well as downside outcomes). In any case, the distinction has been modified by the relatively new concept of *expected loss*: this makes it possible by definition to do either *better or worse than expected,* which turns many negative risks into a two-way bet even if the upside is not always 'profit' as we once knew it. Subjecting our banking risks to this revised test, we can tabulate the findings as follows:

Solvency risk	One-way (downside). Solvency is 'par' and insolvency a disaster.
Liquidity risk	One-way. Liquidity is a necessary condition and not a bonus.
Credit risk	Hybrid. One-way in the sense that the obligor will not pay more than face value or what is legally due, and may pay less. Arguably two-way in the sense that expected loss may not materialise, in which case you 'win'. Loan trades could also produce winners as well as losers through revaluations. Conversion of hard core debt into shares changes the risk to a price risk, which is two-way.
Interest rate risk	Two-way. Risk is both upside and downside.
Price risks	Two-way. Gains or losses are possible.
Operating risks	Mainly one-way, apart from serendipity, the occasional fluke that can yield a windfall gain. Can arguably be classified as two-way in those cases where an expected loss does not materialise (as for credit risk above).

2.4 Which of these categories is most threatening to a bank?

Solvency and liquidity are the two irreducible conditions upon which society allows the banking industry to gear up (in American parlance, to leverage itself) 20 or more times on its equity capital base. Since both conditions are heavily exposed to *credit* risk, these three – solvency, liquidity, and credit – make up what may be regarded as a classical trio of banking risks.

Solvency risk is the ultimate risk, embracing the viability of the business: it differs from the others as life/death differs from health/sickness. You cannot, so to speak, go insolvent from insolvency, any more than you can die of death. By definition, insolvency is disqualified as a primary cause of bank failure. On the other hand, equally by definition, it is the almost universal secondary cause (through insufficiency of risk capital to cover the actual risks); a tortoise of a tautology scorned by those banking hares who chafe at the very existence of capital constraints.

Liquidity risk is structural in nature, and does not of itself entail loss entries or capital writedowns (although these may occur for other reasons). However, we should not thereby conclude that illiquidity is a mild disorder. It can be brought on by imprudent funding or deployment of funds: a comprehensive run on deposits, however, betokens a loss of depositor confidence in the bank (or, in mercifully rare times, the banking sector as a whole). The primary reason will then lie outside illiquidity (although the condition feeds on itself) in a depositor perception that repayment is not assured, because of losses, actual or impending, sustained by the bank.

Mention has already been made of Continental Illinois and Bank of New England in this context. It may well be that the secondary stage of chronic illiquidity was more fatal to their chances of independent survival than was the first stage of debt crisis. When a bank cannot fund itself normally but has to be propped up by the regulatory authorities over a prolonged period, there is no remedy but to close it down or induce a takeover by a stronger bank. Such a fate has even been known to befall innocent banks through nothing more than contagion: in 1985 two Canadian banks, Northland Bank and Continental Bank of Canada, suffered a run on deposits because of a credit crisis at Canadian Commercial Bank; the latter bank was eventually liquidated and the other two had to be rescued by takeover.

Credit risk has historically proved to be the most lethal hazard of all, in every continent. A study of bank failures in New England found that, of the 62 banks in existence before 1984 which failed from 1989 to 1992, in 58 cases commercial real estate loans were the dominant factor. Similar devastation (of profits at least) has occurred worldwide, from North America to Japan, Australia and New Zealand, the United Kingdom, Scandinavia, France and Germany. Previous waves of destruction involved Third World debt and overexposure to parts of the energy industry.

The immoderate enthusiasms underlying these surges point up a fundamental weakness in the banking industry: inadequate portfolio management. This is seen in disproportionately large exposures to fashionable sectors, and sometimes to individual names. Examples of the latter misdeed are to be found in: Continental Illinois, which suffered from the 1982 collapse of Penn Square Bank which it funded overgenerously; Schroder, Munchmeyer, Hengst, a German private bank which came to grief in 1983 after lending nearly eight times its own capital to the IBH building machinery group; and Johnson Matthey Bankers, whose two largest exposures had risen by 1984 (the year that the Bank of England stepped in) to 76% and 34% respectively of JMB's own capital.

Obviously credit risk peaks during and immediately after periods of recession which are not representative of the economic cycle as a whole. Even taking that into account, the evidence shows that this is perennially the most damaging of the banking risks. The advent of derivative instruments in no way challenges this primacy, since they themselves hinge on the credit risk of counterparties.

For *interest rate risk* there is the example of the US Savings & Loans sector, which ran into a calamitous interest rate crunch in the 1980s through funding 20-year fixed rate mortgages with short term deposits. Then we have the case of Midland Bank, which owned up to losing £116 million in 1989 by positioning itself incorrectly for changes in interest rates. This category of recorded mishap would doubtless be much larger if all banks were equally honest, *and* had the systems to quantify the effects. With net interest turn still contributing the bulk of total revenues in many banks, the risk of getting it wrong must be taken very seriously.

Turning to *price risks*, we can cite the classic case of Bankhaus Herstatt, which was closed down by the Bundesbank in 1974 following foreign exchange losses eventually put at some £200 million. What this bank is remembered for, however, is so-called 'Herstatt risk', a particular form of settlement risk (which this book examines under the headings of both liquidity risk and credit risk). At the time its final closure was announced (3.30 pm in Germany), Herstatt had still not completed its leg of a number of foreign exchange deals due for settlement. In the case of dollar/mark deals, some unfortunate counterparty banks in New York had paid out dollars irrevocably through the clearing house (CHIPS) system as the first leg of their deal, but were unable to receive marks in settlement because Herstatt had already closed at 10.30 am New York time and was never to reopen. Having been brought down by its own foreign exchange losses, Herstatt caused settlement losses exceeding $620 million to its counterparties.

More recently we saw the collapse of Barings, whose Singapore office took a huge proprietary position in exchange-traded Nikkei 225 stock index futures. A successful outcome depended on the index remaining stable; but it fell, leaving Barings insolvent with losses of £830 million. This disastrous sitation of price risk, accompanied by operating risk (the operation being out of control) overwhelmed an ostensibly solvent merchant bank within a matter of weeks.

The Barings case crystallised widespread anxieties regarding the safety of derivatives markets generally. With the continuing growth in investment banking and in the international capital and money markets, the importance of price risks in banking inevitably looms larger.

Operating risks are multifaceted, and a major source of complaints and claims on the part of customers, as well as disciplinary actions by regulators. The problems, which range from systems errors and breakdowns to armed robberies and bomb damage, can be extremely disruptive and costly. In 1985 Bank of New York suffered a collapse of its electronic entry system for trading in government securities. The fault was rectified within two days, but meanwhile the bank had run up an overdraft of $23.6 billion at the Federal Reserve at an interest cost of $5 million and had been suspended from trading for 90 minutes. In addition BNY had to undergo the humiliation of subsequent investigation by the US House Subcommittee on Domestic Monetary Policy, and was widely held responsible for single-handedly driving down short term interest rates by at least 1.5%.

The IRA bomb attack on the City of London in 1993 affected the National Westminster headquarters particularly badly, causing hundreds of millions of pounds worth of physical damage and loss of some documents. Staff escaped unscathed but the building had to be evacuated and all operations relocated elsewhere.

By far the most common cause of 'operating' loss, however, is internal fraud, the supreme example of which in recent years is seen in BCCI. In the annals of banking worldwide, fraud probably ranks second only to credit risk as a destroyer of profits, and third after credit and liquidity risks as a primary cause of banking collapse.

2.5 Conclusion

This chapter has surveyed the basic sources of risk encountered in the banking business, and has essayed some historical 'danger ranking'. Problems with credit, liquidity, and fraud are the most common primary causes of bank failures, and combinations of these misfortunes are often seen. Capital inadequacy for the risks being run is by definition an almost universal secondary cause, the prelude to banking insolvency. These four are highlighted, but in truth any of our other categories of banking risk is capable of precipitating a collapse; otherwise they would not merit a place on the generic list.

The chapters that follow will examine each of these risk categories in turn, suggesting how to monitor and manage them in the light of professional experience and scientific analysis. The aim always must be to optimise the risk/reward relationship, avoid shocks (from excessive exposure to particular sources of risk), and provide prudent cover for expected and unexpected loss. Getting this right is the key to survival and to consistent success in running a bank.

CHAPTER THREE
Solvency risk

This chapter explores:

- The place of solvency risk in banking.

- The role of risk capital.

- Economic capital adequacy.

- Regulatory approaches to capital adequacy.

- Capital allocation.

- The dynamics of sustainable growth.

- The problem of 'excess capital'.

Solvency is the capacity to meet external liabilities in full by realising assets at current value. It is ascertained by a *value* calculation, as distinct from liquidity which is a *cash flow* phenomenon (see Chapter 4). Solvency is always at risk because losses may be incurred which necessitate a writing down of the value of some assets, with the result that external liabilities may no longer be met in full. For the purposes of this chapter, solvency risk is a bank's exposure to the possibility of becoming insolvent. Once the latter condition is recognised, the bank's creditors or (more likely) its regulators will compel it to cease trading until it is recapitalised, taken over, or wound up.

In theory, solvency may be maintained without any capital, so long as losses or expenses can be absorbed by current undistributed profits and provisions; but that would be an imprudent and impractical way of operating, leaving no safety margin for the unexpected. The bank would be in constant danger of sudden death, and would be an unacceptable risk for depositors unless backed by government guarantee or the like. The necessary buffer is equity capital (ordinary shareholders' funds), a liability which in need is available to be written down in a going concern so as to avoid writing down external liabilities (mainly public deposits in the case of a bank). Adequate capital is the final safeguard of bank solvency, being the third line of defence behind profits and provisions.

As we saw in Chapter 2, solvency risk is a secondary category, hinging on capital adequacy to accommodate unexpected losses emanating from the primary risks incurred in the business of banking. Perhaps because the primary problem is always something else (e.g. credit risk, price risk, operating fraud), there is a fallacious tendency to deny the relevance of capital levels in banking failure. How often have we heard the assertion: 'No bank ever went bust because of its capital ratios'? On closer analysis, however, it would be truer to say that capital inadequacy *in relation to the risks being run* is behind virtually every bank failure: a proposition oddly dismissed by some writers as hardly worth consideration.

Let us compare two cases. During the 1980s and 1990s many leading banks around the world declared annual losses stemming from primary (mainly credit) risk mismanagement, but most of those survived without the need for external support because their capital cushion was adequate (and their solvency risk management thus intact). By contrast, in 1995 Barings collapsed as an independent entity after derivatives trading losses that exceeded its capital and reserves (and would have wiped out part of its deposits as well). The moral is clear: other risk categories may occasion the unexpected losses, but the level of solvency protection then determines whether the bank continues in business or goes under. Solvency is hardly an irrelevant risk category.

Walter Bagehot, the nineteenth century banker, journalist and political commentator, is said to have coined the question-begging aphorism that 'a well managed bank needs no capital, whilst no amount of capital can save an ill managed bank.' There is a grain of truth in this, at the extremes, but an all-or-nothing conclusion is far too absolutist to be practical. How 'well managed' and how 'ill managed', and what about all the intermediate conditions? It is a truism that 'good management' is the key to everything, but who is to be the infallible judge and guarantor of management quality? Most banks are a mixture of good and not so good management and, as circumstances and top teams change, are managed better in some eras than in others; not that we can always tell the difference at the time. The admired banks of one decade so often fall from grace in the next.

Bagehot wrote in an age when the concepts of probability distributions and standard deviations, expected and unexpected losses had not been formulated, and when attempts to link bank capital to the quantum of risk would have seemed a good deal more questionable. We have less excuse for the same scepticism today.

To dismiss the place of capital in banking is tantamount to denying the rationale for risk capital in business generally: bankers are not so quick to accept such an outrageous piece of special pleading from their borrowing customers. The community similarly is entitled to a measure of protection from banks' follies and misfortunes: capital which makes only a partial contribution in insolvency is better than nothing, even if it is insufficient to save the bank.

That said, it is important to keep things in perspective. A bank's primary risks are not taken care of solely by throwing more capital at them. It is even more necessary to control and curb risk-taking to an acceptable level where stable and economic returns can be made (as outlined in Chapter 1). 'Strong' capital ratios *alone* will never tell you whether a bank is well managed or headed for destruction: in that limited sense, Bagehot was right. Sustained profitability is the first line of defence, which in practice absorbs nearly all losses, and is the only long term guarantor of a bank's viability.

3.1 Economic equity capital: a historical perspective

Equity capital (ordinary shares and reserves, or 'shareholders' funds') is the fundamental building block and the vital element in a bank's capital base: we shall come to subordinated loan capital and other elements later.

How much equity capital does a bank need for the conduct of its business? The economic principle established in Chapter 1 is that equity capital exists to absorb unexpected loss – to the extent that current profits fall short of that capacity – and thus to minimise the probability of insolvency.

One rational exercise might therefore be to examine the bank's historical rates of return on total assets over 20 or more years, and use these as a guide for imaginative extrapolation of probability distributions of rates of return over, say, the next 20 years. Past annual results will be too sparse, and too subject to artificial effects, inconsistencies and distortions, to give a reliable statistical base. Furthermore, it is essential to take account of the pace of change in banking. Projections of the future should therefore be influenced by scenario modelling, relating external effects to the bank as a whole and to its various parts (e.g. to lending and to capital markets operations).

Given a more or less 'normal' (symmetrical) distribution curve of perceived possible outcomes (rates of return on total assets), we could then begin to assess the ratio of equity capital needed to cover unexpected losses – bearing in mind the useful rule of thumb that three standard deviations from the mean will encompass more than 99% of the possible outcomes depicted within the curve (see Chapter 1, appendix).

Let us take an illustrative example. For a British bank in the decade of the 1980s, average pre-tax return on assets was approximately 1% per annum with a standard deviation of 0.5% per annum (source: London Business School). Three standard deviations below the mean of 1% would be a subtraction of 1.5% (i.e. 3 × 0.5%), making a negative return on assets of 0.5%. On the face of it, we might therefore be content with an equity capital ratio of 0.5% of total assets, which would cover three standard deviations and thus almost all single-year unexpected loss eventualities.

However, a single year is arguably too short a period to do justice to the cumulative effects of a run of bad years. Perhaps we should project three years in a row. Assuming (simplistically, for the moment) that successive period outcomes are independent of one another, in a statistical sense, standard deviation increases with the square root of time. Our annual standard deviation of 0.5% is therefore multiplied by 1.7 (the square root of 3) to produce a three-year standard deviation of 0.85%. Three standard deviations below the mean would be a subtraction of 2.55% from 1%, making a return of minus 1.55%. On this view, an equity/assets buffer of 1.55% might be considered sufficient to absorb almost all potential unexpected losses. A four-year precautionary view, based on the same formula, would produce an equity/assets requirement of 2%.

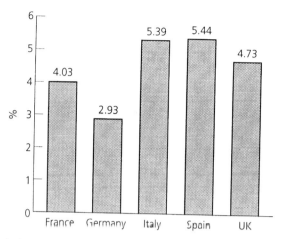

3.1 Tier 1 capital as percentage of total assets, banks in European Union, 1995 (Source: *The Banker*)

How do these estimates compare with actual levels of equity capital in the banking industry? Figure 3.1 shows that in 1995 European banks were maintaining Tier 1 (mainly equity) capital/assets ratios much higher than our notional 1.55% or 2% equity/assets: at 4.73% in the case of the UK. There could be several explanations for this disparity, including differences in quantified risk assessment and/or additional (less self-evidently 'economic') motives for holding capital:

1   Covering a mere three standard deviations may be deemed insufficient, implying as it does that a bank with a normal probability distribution of results faces insolvency on average once in every hundred or so years.

2   Furthermore, our methodology is rough and ready, based upon too small a statistical sample and upon assumptions that will not be universally valid. With changes in business mix, and growth in complexity of banking risks, future outcomes may depart significantly from the statistical past. Maybe the world is becoming a riskier place. If the distribution curve of possible outcomes displays a 'long/fat tail' (associated with large but rare events), or is otherwise seen as asymmetrical, a different mathematical technique may be needed which could well produce a higher economic capital requirement.

3   Prudence would dictate an overshoot in actual capital ratios, to allow for imprecision in risk assessment, and to ensure that if unexpected loss occurs some capital is left over for the future that lies beyond the dismal event.

4   In banking, confidence is all-important: the *perception* of capital adequacy is as essential as objective adequacy. Banks may be pitching their capital ratios at a higher level that is calculated to inspire public/counterparty/rating agency confidence and to stabilise funding, rather than at a lower one guided by probability criteria. Perhaps an 'arms race' of sorts is taking place, with a possibility of consensual reductions later on.

5   Historically, banks have generally been obliged to carry extra capital in order to accommodate various prudential deductions from the capital base, such as

   ● goodwill and other intangible assets;
   ● investments in unconsolidated subsidiaries and associates;
   ● connected lending of a capital nature;
   ● investments in the capital of other banks;
   ● other trade investments and infrastructural fixed assets (no longer a deduction under the Basle regulatory guidelines).

6   The most potent influence in boosting capital ratios has been the Basle framework itself (see section 3.3 below). Banks now have no choice but to maintain capital ratios possibly higher than economic need might otherwise suggest.

Why might regulators have a tendency to impose 'overcapitalisation' on the banking system? First, because until recently very little analysis could be brought to bear on what was an appropriate level of capital in relation to risk: present science has still some way to go; meanwhile, best to err on the side of caution. Secondly, because Procrustean ('one-size-fits-all') standards will have a natural bias towards the capital needs not of the average but of the least competent banks (even though in some countries the regulator also has the power to add differential risk premiums to the minimum base).

It has been said that a primary motivation among regulators is to avoid being blamed (and who, indeed, could blame them for such solicitude?). To be fair, however, modern regulators have declared that it is not their business to eliminate losses or failure in financial institutions, but rather to mitigate the damage and limit the spreading of instability.

3.2 Does overcapitalisation matter?

There is unfortunately no inconsistency between the following two propositions: that banking insolvencies will continue exceptionally to occur; and yet that the average bank under the Basle regime is probably compulsorily overcapitalised, on the basis of historical experience as opposed to external received opinion. It all depends, of course, on how much insurance against insolvency you think it is reasonable to take out. Bank insolvency will always occasion outrage and derision, whether we reduce the actuarial probability in any one name to an event 'once in five centuries' or 'once in several millennia'. Rating agency criteria tend to load the argument in favour of the latter.

Overcapitalisation is generally held to imply economic inefficiency, waste and opportunity cost, for shareholders and society alike. That is something of an oversimplification, as a higher capital ratio should logically be compensated by a lower beta coefficient and therefore a lower cost of equity (required rate of return – see Chapter 1). This self-levelling relationship is discovered in the formula:

Geared share beta = ungeared share beta $\times \dfrac{D+E}{E}$

Where D = debt (i.e. non-equity liabilities) and E = equity, with non-quoted debt at book value and quoted debt and equity at market values.

What this means in essence is that shareholders demand a minimum rate of return on the bank's assets, governed by 'ungeared share beta' (otherwise known as 'asset beta'), which is multiplied into a 'geared share beta' via the balance sheet gearing (leverage). Therefore higher equity capital ratios (lower gearing) make for lower geared betas. Comparison of bank share betas provides some empirical evidence that market participants accept this logic, although there may prove to be a limited appetite for reductions in bank betas below 1.0 (not common at time of writing).

That aside, it is still possible to argue that overcapitalisation penalises borrowers and economic progress through reduced availability of credit. As we shall see later in this chapter, sustainable growth in banking business becomes significantly more difficult to manage under a high capital ratio regime. Common sense suggests that unnecessarily high capital requirements cannot, and should not, be justified solely in terms of compensating beta movements: otherwise the equity capital requirement might as well be 100% rather than the much lower percentages normally proposed.

3.3 Capital adequacy regulation: the Basle approach

Capital adequacy is regulated in every country in the interests of maintaining a solvent (and, by psychological association, a confidently liquid) banking system and protecting the depositor. With the growth of international banking, national regulators have sought common standards to insure against cross-border contamination of local banking systems and to establish fair competition (the so-called 'level playing field').

One system of capital adequacy regulation now dominates the international scene: that known as the 'Basle Accord', endorsed in December 1987 by the Group of Ten countries meeting as the Basle Committee on Banking Regulation and Supervisory Practice, under the auspices of the Bank for International Settlements. The proposals were formalised in a paper published in July 1988 ('International Convergence of Capital Measurement and Capital Standards'), and phased in by 1992 in all signatory countries.

The European Union's capital adequacy framework, subsequently enacted, conforms closely to the Basle pattern.

Like most of its divergent predecessors, the Basle formula recognises a numerator (capital base), a denominator (in this case, weighted risk assets), and a resulting ratio (numerator expressed as a percentage of denominator). The Bank of England's version of these elements is summarised in the appendix to this chapter.

A bank's capital base consists of two tiers, as shown in the appendix. Tier 1 consists mainly of equity capital (ordinary shareholders' funds), the only kind available to be written down to absorb losses in a bank as long as it is a going concern. In large international banks, equity capital accounts typically for 80–90% of

Tier 1 capital. The second most important element is perpetual non-cumulative preference shares, on which dividends may be passed when a bank is in difficulty, and which are subordinated to all other liabilities except equity capital in a bank liquidation.

Tier 2 capital consists mainly of various types of term loan capital which cannot be written down in a going concern but offer protection (via subordination to creditors) in a bank liquidation. Such secondary capital has an important advantage, in that it can be issued in a number of different currencies to hedge foreign currency asset risks. Other components of Tier 2 include fixed asset revaluation reserves, a debatable concession which reflects investment stakes and dependencies in some countries.

Some British bankers have argued for general provisions to be classified as Tier 1 rather than Tier 2· however, if (as advocated in Chapter 1, though contrary to accounting conventions in many countries) these provisions were to represent a portfolio view of expected loss, they would not actually belong in *any* part of the capital base, which by definition exists to cover unexpected loss.

A bank's risk assets and other credit exposures are divided into five basic classes according to perceived ascending credit risk, as outlined in the appendix. Netting of individual counterparty exposures is permitted under defined conditions (see Chapter 5). Exposures are multiplied by their respective risk weighting and summated to produce total weighted risk assets (WRAs).

Off-balance sheet items such as guarantees and commitments are multiplied by credit conversion factors in order to arrive at credit equivalent exposures (CEEs). Interest- and foreign exchange-related instruments (derivatives) have to be converted to CEE by a process of marking them to market (valuing at current market price) and then adding a prescribed percentage of the notional principal amount to allow for future volatility during the remaining life of the contract. Each CEE is then multiplied by the appropriate risk weighting for the type of counterparty concerned, so as to arrive at a WRA value.

The regulatory requirement is that the total capital base should be not less than 8% of the value of weighted risk assets, with any surplus of Tier 2 above the value of Tier 1 being disallowed (thus Tier 1 cannot be less than 4%). Those are universal minima, with the proviso that a country regulator may impose higher requirements on individual banks. The Bank of England sets individual 'target ratios' (norms) and 'trigger ratios' (floor levels calling for corrective action) above the basic 8% for each bank. The

Federal Reserve publishes a supplementary definition of a 'well-capitalised bank', and then leaves it to each bank to decide for itself whether it wants the recognition that goes with attaining that more stringent standard.

Since in practice a spread of differently weighted risk assets will always add up to a lower *weighted* figure than their combined *book* value, a Basle Tier 1 ratio of 4% could equate to a straight equity/assets ratio of, say, 3% (i.e. in a case where total WRAs happen to work out at 75% of their own book value, ignoring off-balance sheet items for simplicity's sake).

A prudent bank will aim not for precise compliance but for an extra safety margin calculated to ensure that regulatory target levels are never under threat: for example, maintaining Tier 1 at 6% instead of the minimum 4%, and total ratio at 10% or better. The Tier 1 surplus, being intentionally usable as a buffer rather than a more or less untouchable regulatory ornament, has some of the characteristics of economic equity as discussed earlier.

The Basle consensus represents a triumph of negotiation and co-operation on the part of the national regulators (with help from the regulated). It is also a technical step forward in addressing credit risk (the biggest risk the banks face) in a more disciplined way than had been attempted by regulators before. There are, however, a number of well-aired criticisms, of which the following are a representative sample:

1   There is room for some misgiving over the treatment of the bank's physical infrastructure: its owned (including long leased) property, equipment and other fixed assets. These items tend to be specialised, of limited tradability and of greater worth to the bank than to a potential purchaser (as any banker may know who has tried to dispose of second-hand automated teller machines). Depreciation rates on equipment are geared to expected internal life rather than external saleable value. It is therefore questionable whether infrastructural assets should be allowed into a bank solvency calculation. By classifying them as risk assets with a 100% weighting (underwritten by 8% capital), the Basle formula implies that for solvency risk purposes they are equivalent to legally enforceable claims on non-bank private sector counterparties; surely a dubious proposition.

Prior to Basle, it was considered prudent practice to deduct infrastructural assets from the equity base in order to arrive at 'free equity' or 'free capital' forming the numerator of a capital ratio (in which the usual denominator was non-capital liabilities). The mathematical difference in treatment produces a substantial divergence in outcomes: it takes little modelling to show that a bank can be in perfect compliance with the Basle rules, yet technically 'insolvent' under the old 'free equity/free capital' methodology.

When the 'free equity' concept disappears, no prudential constraint except liquidity remains to govern the 'affordability' of capital expenditure. This realisation has led some banks to continue to monitor free equity as an internal safeguard against capital budgeting extravagance.

Similar reservations apply to the Basle decision to allow fixed asset (and, as applied in some countries, also equity investment) revaluation reserves to count in Tier 2 of the capital base. In practice this means that property investments will introduce their own brand of volatility into the capital base. Some would argue that banks should not be encouraged to think and behave like property companies: professional competence in the management of their properties is a necessity, but speculation is another matter.

2   There is a structural oddity in that most of the substantive deductions (e.g. investments in unconsolidated subsidiaries and associates) are taken off the total capital base, instead of Tier 1 where common sense would suggest they belong. As a result, Tier 1 is overstated and loses authenticity, whilst the two tiers as ratio percentages do not add up to the net capital percentage.

3   The Basle process (in its initial phase) implies that credit risk is the only risk occasioning unexpected loss, and for which capital therefore needs to be held: this is simply not true (see Chapter 2). The Basle and EU regulators have recognised that credit risk is merely the first to be captured, and are working on extending the scope (see section 3.4).

4   Even within the confines of credit risk, the methodology assumes that all risks are linear and additive, or else that they are perfectly positively correlated, and thus ignores the portfolio realities of correlation and diversification of risk (covered in Chapter 6).

5   The rule-of-thumb risk weighting bands lack statistical validity, both internally and *vis-à-vis* one another. The bread-and-butter 100% risk weighting band, in particular, pays no regard to differential credit *quality*, as measured in terms of highly variable default rates (see Chapter 6 on credit grading).

6   There are numerous other quibbles over points of detail and boundary lines; for example, the rule that committed lines of credit attract a nil credit conversion factor (and derived risk weighting) if up to one year, but a 50% credit conversion factor if longer than one year. This particular step change was apparently designed to accommodate the overdraft system, but also lends itself to unworthy gamesmanship in respect of other facilities. All the poachers have to do to escape a capital requirement imposed by the gamekeepers is to write their committed lines for 364 days, subject to review and rollover thereafter (the so-called 'evergreen' facilities).

3.4 Further evolution: the European capital adequacy directive

At time of writing, the European Union has leapfrogged Basle in extending the scope of the capital adequacy computation to certain non-credit exposures described collectively as 'market risks'. The new requirements came into effect from January 1996.

'Market risks' are what are classified in this book as 'interest rate risk' (trading exposure, see Chapter 9) and 'price risks' (Chapter 10), and the Bank of England's defining document refers specifically to:

●   Foreign currency risk, including derivatives.

●   Repos (repurchase agreements) and stock lending.

●   Reverse repos and stock borrowing.

●   Interest rate position risk (i.e. the potential for price movements in interest-bearing debt instruments consequent upon interest rate changes), including derivatives.

- Equity position risk, including derivatives.

- Underwriting.

The framework divides a bank's business into 'the trading book' and 'the banking book'. The trading book consists essentially of: (a) proprietary positions taken in financial instruments, in the hope of gain or through broking operations, plus trading book hedging positions, and (b) other exposures due to unsettled transactions, over-the-counter (OTC) derivative instruments, repos and reverse repos.

As well as market risks, the trading book will naturally contain some counterparty credit risks (e.g. relating to OTC derivative contracts), which are subject to the pre-existing capital adequacy rules for credit exposures.

All positions in the trading book must be marked to market (revalued) daily. By default, any position not defined as part of the trading book falls within the banking book and is subject to the earlier credit-based capital adequacy rules (as described in section 3.3 above). Under a *de minimis* provision, banks with a 'trading' level below a defined threshold are deemed to have all their activity in the banking book. However, the rules applying to foreign currency risk uniquely apply across the board, without distinction between the two books.

Having defined a 'trading book', this new supplementary approach goes on to propose a methodology for risk-adjusting net open positions and applying a capital requirement. The broad outline is as follows.

For *foreign currency risk*, the basic method imposes an 8% capital requirement on the overall net foreign exchange position. Alternatively, by agreement with the Bank of England, a 'back-testing' method can be used which draws on a historical database and calculates the 'losses' applicable to the net open position(s) in rolling 10 working day holding periods for the past five years. The capital requirement is based on either a 99% confidence level for the past three years or a 95% confidence level for the past five years.

For *interest-bearing debt instruments*, there is a capital requirement in respect of both specific risk and general market risk. Specific risk capital requirements are based largely on the perceived credit quality of the issuer, falling into three categories:

● 'Government', principally 'Zone A' (OECD) countries, attracting a nil requirement.

● 'Qualifying', attracting 0.25% to 1.6% depending on maturity.

● 'Non-qualifying', attracting 8%.

General market risk refers to price changes caused by parallel and non-parallel shifts in the yield curve, rather than by specific risk (issuer) factors. Capital requirements are calculated, per currency, by reference to either a weighted maturity band method or a modified duration method (for explanation of these concepts, see Chapters 8 and 9).

Further complex rules are applied to the various types of derivative instrument. A special dispensation allows banks to use 'recognised' software models in interest sensitivity 'pre-processing' calculations for derivatives and amortising bonds.

For *equity position risk*, there is a similar distinction between specific risks (individual positions relative to the market) and general risks (movements in the market as a whole). The basic method is to allocate equity positions to the country in which each equity is listed. The specific risk calculation sums the individual net positions for each country, irrespective of whether those positions are long or short, to produce an overall gross equity position for that country. For 17 'qualifying' Zone A (OECD) countries, the capital requirement is 4% of that gross position (reduced to 2% for equity portfolios meeting a prescribed test of being highly liquid and well diversified): for other countries, it is 8% of the gross position.

The general risk calculation nets off the individual long and short positions for each country so as to produce an overall net equity position for that country. The capital requirement is then 8% of the overall net position. Subject to certain criteria, offsets are allowed between country portfolios where the national markets are recognised as highly liquid.

Again, detailed rules are spelled out for different types of derivative instrument.

The new directive naturally takes a fresh look at 'own funds' (i.e. a bank's capital base). For the banking book, capital requirements continue to be expressed as a percentage of weighted risk assets. For items allocated to the trading book, the level of required capital is determined as an absolute monetary figure (jocularly known as a 'haircut'). For the purpose of calculating an overall risk asset ratio spanning the banking and trading books, total haircut capital is multiplied by 12.5 to produce notional grossed up weighted risk assets (i.e. supported by haircut capital at 8%).

A new third tier of capital is introduced, styled as 'trading book ancillary capital'. This consists of short term subordinated debt and daily mark to market profits calculated by approved methods. The subordinated debt must have a minimum original maturity of two years plus one day and will not be notionally amortised as is the case with Tier 2 subordinated debt. Tier 3 capital is subject to a 'lock in' clause: it cannot be repaid before or even at maturity without supervisory consent. At the consolidated level, a bank's Tier 2 and Tier 3 capital combined are not normally permitted to exceed 100% of its Tier 1.

3.5 Regulation versus self-assessment

Clearly the direction of regulation is towards an ever more intricate set of capital adequacy requirements, necessitated in part by continuing innovation in the risk-taking activities of the banks. However, the complex reporting and compliance framework outlined in section 3.3 above, with expansions and elaborations described in section 3.4, can only be justified if the methodology is aligned with, or superior to, best 'in-house' practice in the industry. Such a claim would be difficult to substantiate, not least because most of the criticisms listed in section 3.3 remain untouched by the reforms discussed in section 3.4. For example, portfolio management theory on diversification of risk and hedging (see Chapter 6) is to some extent catered for in the market risks of the trading book, but continues to be ignored in the measurement of credit risk in the banking and trading books.

Best practice in the banking industry takes a more holistic view, currently favouring an assessment of 'value at risk' or 'earnings at risk' in the trading context (further discussed in Chapters 9 and 10). These internal disciplines focus on the present and future value of the bank, as enhanced or diminished by prospective profits or losses. They represent in fact a rigorous modelling of an economic capital requirement (see section 3.1), based in detail on a bank's present risk positions and associated statistical probabilities. There are, admittedly, problems of aggregation in proportion to weakness of correlation between different activities.

The European Union's capital adequacy directive makes a preliminary gesture towards this kind of self-assessment, in allowing banks with recognised simulation and sensitivity models to use them in calculating exposures in respect of foreign exchange risks and interest rate products. The Basle authorities have now come forward with a proposal which (for sophisticated banks) goes further, away from the 'building block' syndrome and in the direction of value at risk self-assessment. A rapprochement between the Basle/EU regulatory schemes for market risks is inevitable: both, however, have a limited application, mainly in a 'trading book', and thus fall short of a comprehensive scope. The 'banking book', if it is to remain a separate concept, is a retarded segment in the intellectual framework and certainly needs to be revisited by the regulators.

The dangers of a wide divergence between regulation on the one hand, and industry best practice on the other, are obvious. Substantial extra costs would be incurred in maintaining two disparate information and compliance systems ('regulatory' and 'prudential' respectively), the regulatory and the public eye might be on the wrong ball, and parts of the banking industry might become artificially lamed or economically distorted in other ways.

One final observation: expanding the scope of regulatory risk measurement (a doubtless desirable process, and still by no means complete), without any offsetting reductions, increases a capital requirement which by economic criteria would appear to be already on the high side (see sections 3.1 and 3.2 above and 3.8 hereafter). This suggests in turn that regulatory zeal needs to be tempered by realism: there must be more to the evolution of capital adequacy science than piling layer upon layer and tier upon tier.

3.6 Moral hazard

'Moral hazard' is a loose and fashionable term for a collection of behavioural distortions which may arise out of widespread dependence on banking regulation and safety nets. Thus banks that see themselves as 'too big to fail' may take irresponsible risks in the expectation that, for the sake of the public interest, the authorities will underwrite their liquidity and their solvency. Banking sectors as a whole may adopt the compliance mentality or even the gamekeeper/poacher charade, to the detriment of their independent risk awareness.

The banks' counterparties and depositors may be ensnared by similar complacency. In countries with a formalised system of deposit guarantees, depositors may feel encouraged to place their money in the riskiest banks with the highest interest rates, thereby exacerbating unsound banking practices.

The loser in these scenarios is the public purse which subsidises bank shareholders and the other players in the market. Critics of moral hazard are calling for the abolition of safety nets and for revised forms of bank regulation, including perhaps the 'hands-off' approach favoured in New Zealand. Some Janus-faced commentators, of course, are never satisfied and like to have it both ways (complaining alternately of too much regulation *and* too little, the only constant being that what we have is the wrong kind).

There is a difficult balance of interests here, as well as a philosophical confusion which remains to be resolved. But one does not have to subscribe to the abolitionist school to concur with them on one cardinal principle: that banks are morally responsible for their own risks and their own solvency, and cannot shuffle off prudential accountability onto their regulators, no matter how intrusive, demanding, or indeed passive the latter may be.

3.7 Capital allocation within a bank

In practice, a bank will have to maintain its capital base at a level which meets an economic or a regulatory requirement (plus operating safety margin), whichever is the higher. A risk/reward discipline, as outlined in Chapter 1, will lead the bank naturally to allocate capital notionally to internal units, activities and product lines, customer relationships and facilities. This enables the bank to measure performance and potential by effective rate of return, and to select its portfolios and set its pricing according to risk/reward criteria guided by cost of capital.

Should the bank make such allocations by reference to the full capital base (now to be three official tiers), or just equity capital? No doubt there are arguments both ways, but the weight of instinct and logic favours 'required equity capital' as the fundamental denominator of risk/reward. The *cost* (i.e. interest or dividends) of non-equity capital needs to be allocated out in some fashion, but no particular benefit or insight accrues from allocating out the non-equity capital itself: more likely a conceptual confusion.

Chapter 1 proposed that equity capital be notionally allocated on a risk-adjusted basis – and thus, as far as possible, an *economic* basis. The adjustment should reflect contribution to group risk, of which the ingredients are: size of exposure, volatility and correlation with the bank's larger portfolio. The basic formula, discussed further in Chapter 6, is:

$$wA \times c \times \frac{sRA}{sRP} = \text{Proportionate contribution to portfolio variance}$$

where wA = weight of specific asset (size proportionate to portfolio), c = correlation, sRA = standard deviation of return on specific asset (including net losses), and sRP = standard deviation of return on portfolio.

Thus an item that contributes, say, 2% of the variance (volatility) of the portfolio should be allocated 2% of the capital underpinning that portfolio. If the item contributes 3% of the volume and 2% of the variance, and the overall equity capital requirement is deemed to be 4%, then the equity capital requirement for the specific item is:

$$\frac{2}{3} \times 4\% = 2.67\%.$$

This notional risk-adjusted capital allocation can then be used to calculate actual, potential, and required rates of return on the lines indicated in Chapter 1. In the comparatively rare event that the correlation (denoted by c) is *negative* (see Chapter 6), then the contribution to portfolio variance will emerge as a minus figure. Negative capital should accordingly be allocated, reflecting the item's beneficial influence in reducing overall portfolio risk (and with it the need for positive risk capital). Such an effective hedge usually has to be paid for: the cost therefore generates a negative return on negative capital, cancelling out the two minus signs and producing a normal measurement of return on capital. In the providential case where a natural hedge with a negative correlation earns a positive return, the conventional rate of return calculation breaks down and has to be replaced by a net present value methodology of the kind touched on in Chapter 1.

3.8 Capital adequacy and sustainable growth

As we saw in Chapter 1, in a capitalist society the required rate of return on equity is determined by market criteria ('cost of capital'). A necessary adjunct to this pronouncement is that the rate of return (after expected losses) should also be sufficient to maintain capital ratios (via retentions) at required prudential and regulatory levels. Stated conversely, growth in risks must pay due regard to the organic growth capabilities of the equity base (i.e. as augmented by retained earnings). A rights issue is economically justifiable only in terms of cost of capital, not to plug a gap created by otherwise unsustainable business growth. Too often we see banks which can neither earn their cost of capital nor organically sustain the rate of growth in risks that they have chosen to pursue.

Banks have been slow to accept the dynamics of sustainable growth, but have been saved from the consequences of their neglect by the lack of sophistication of the capital market itself, as well as by the periods of stagnation in the economy when wounded capital ratios had a chance to recuperate. The Basle 'compliance' mentality has also diverted attention away from pure equity capital (the true core in a living bank) towards the development of near-equity substitutes and secondary (and now tertiary) capital with weaker credentials. Nevertheless the issue cannot be ducked.

By way of illustration, assuming that a bank is in a state of compliance/adequacy (by whatever criteria), and all other things being equal:

- If balance sheet footings (as a rough proxy for risk assets, and indeed for risks generally) grow by, say, 20% per annum, the equity capital base will need to grow similarly in order to maintain the equity/asset ratio at a constant level.

- Assuming this equity growth *is* from retentions alone, and if a dividend is paid out on the basis of three times cover (i.e. two-thirds retained), the bank will have to earn a *post-tax* return of 30% on its opening equity capital; or 25% on its closing equity, 27.27% on the straight average of year-opening and year-closing equity. *Pre-tax* return might therefore have to be roughly in the range of 40–50%, depending on the above-mentioned formulaic choices, tax rates and other factors.

- If, alternatively, the dividend is covered only *twice* – i.e. if half of post-tax earnings are paid out in dividends – the required post-tax return on average equity rises to 36.36%.

- If the bank is geared up 25 times (i.e. has a not untypical equity/asset ratio of 4%), the required post-tax return on average equity of 27.27% translates into a post-tax return on average assets of 1.09%, whilst an ROE of 36.36% implies an ROA of 1.45%.

All these required rates of return, remember, are after providing for bad debts. Any banking analyst will recognise how formidable (not to say improbable) such performance targets, demanded by an asset growth rate of 20% per annum, would be.

The logic may of course be reversed, starting with expected rate of return and constraining balance sheet growth accordingly. Figure 3.2 is a ready-reckoner showing some of the other possible permutations related to post-tax return on average equity, depending on whether dividends are covered four times, three times, twice, or one-and-a-third times. Figures 3.3 and 3.4 render the same dynamics in terms of return on *assets* at equity/asset ratios of 4% and 3% respectively.

The equity/asset ratio is convenient for illustrative purposes, but is not necessarily the most meaningful yardstick: for example, within limited periods it is feasible for weighted risk assets to fall while asset volumes are rising, and vice versa. This modelling exercise could in principle be replicated using Basle/EU ratios, or

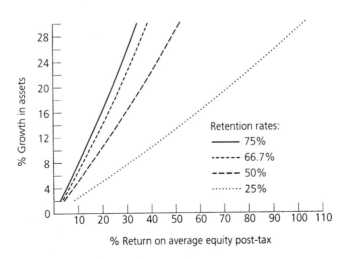

3.2 Maximum sustainable growth rates.

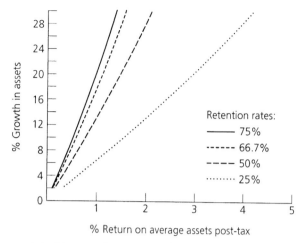

3.3 Maximum sustainable growth rates – equity/asset ratio 4%.

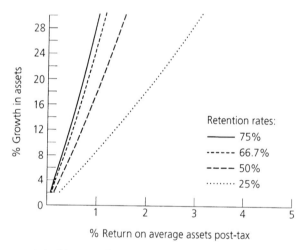

3.4 Maximum sustainable growth rates – equity/asset ratio 3%.

other more 'scientific' formulae (weighted risk assets themselves being unscientific, as pointed out earlier). But the same finding will emerge in every instance: the higher the volume growth rate, the higher the required *overall* rate of return. This is by definition logical, but it contradicts common misconceptions (a) that growth takes care of its own capital requirements, so that a single target rate of return will suffice for all business growth scenarios, or (b) that the higher rate of return requirement will apply only to incremental business rather than to the whole book. Most well-run banks following a sensible dividend policy will find that they can cope comfortably with single-digit annual volume growth, but that capital strains begin to set in at the 10–15% growth range.

How realistic, then, is our chosen example of 20% asset growth, and its required rate of return? An annual asset growth rate of 20% or more is not unknown in boom conditions, and was fairly widespread in several countries at various times during the 1980s. In the late 1980s, the UK 'big four' clearing banks notched up domestic advances growth within the following ranges:

	1987	1988	1989
Highest %	21.4	32.1	19.6
Lowest %	13.2	23.0	13.7

On the line of reasoning we have been following so far, and on the evidence of Fig. 3.2 to 3.4, we may deduce that the rates of return required to support the upper growth rates tabled above were never in prospect *even if there had been no resultant tidal wave of bad debts*. If we look at one of the most profitable banking years in recent memory, 1994, the UK 'big four' (with HSBC inheriting Midland Bank's mantle) recorded post-tax returns on average equity ranging from 23.7% down to 18.7%. We may call such results historically exceptional or 'obscene', depending on our philosophical standpoint; neither adjective alters the fact that these returns would still be nowhere near sufficient to support the pace of advances growth quoted above for the three consecutive years 1987-89 . . . not that such a juxtaposition comes naturally to mind when memories are short and subsequent growth has decelerated to vanishing point.

A decline in equity/advances (and hence equity/asset) ratios was inevitable, exacerbated later by unprecedented levels of bad debt provisions: it is only the ebbing of that tide, accompanied by a stagnation of asset volumes, that has enabled bank equity ratios to recover in the 1990s without resort to rights issues. Clearly the 'dash for growth' of the late 1980s had more to do with deregulation, competition and market share than with enlightened financial calculation: today's hindsight is missing half the point if it imagines that only the bad debt aftermath spoiled or invalidated the strategy.

Figure 3.5 shows the profitability of the 1000 largest banks in the world, measured by pre-tax return on Tier 1 capital (not the same as on equity, but close enough as a proxy) and on assets. As will be clear from the preceding discussion, such low average rates of return at the pre-tax level (compared with all our examples above at the post-tax level) could justify no more than low single-digit annual percentage growth in risk assets. How many of these banks

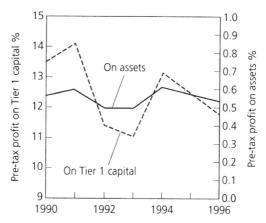

3.5 Pre-tax profit ratios of 1000 largest banks in the world (Source: *The Banker*).

are earning their cost of capital is a matter between them and their shareholders.

Perhaps the synthesis is that banks should plan their rate of return on equity to meet or exceed their cost of capital, and in the process should gear their volume growth to a self-sustaining pace taking, say, a three-year view. Such a discipline would have saved banks much grief in the past. A bank can sometimes afford to exceed the sustainable pace for a purely temporary period (say, one year), so long as it recognises the need to return to normal housekeeping thereafter; but it should always address the question: 'to what end?' The problem comes when volume expansion (business development) is seen as an end in itself.

The fact that double-digit lending growth has been taken almost for granted as the banks' public and competitive duty in buoyant economic conditions, and yet that it is so hard to sustain organically (by means of a retention-enhanced equity capital base) may be one further reflection of an enforced regulatory overcapitalisation of the banking system. The higher the capital requirement, the more difficult sustainable growth becomes, as illustrated in Fig. 3.3 and 3.4.

3.9 When capital overshoots regulatory/prudential requirements

The economic cycle tends to produce periodical swings in capital adequacy, from famine to feast and back again. In times of low asset growth, well-managed banks often accumulate an excess of equity capital above regulatory and prudential needs, in accordance with the dynamics outlined in section 3.8. A similar overshoot can occur through disposal of investments, or sale or securitisation of other assets. The problem then is seen as what to do with the surplus, rather than how to cope with sustainable growth. Historically, banks in this frame of mind have often been a danger to themselves and everybody else, and several cautionary notes must be sounded:

- As section 3.2 shows, the market beta should self-adjust so perhaps the capital surplus need not burn a hole in the pocket after all.

- The surplus will be exaggerated if the bank has not made adequate provision for expected losses.

- It is shortsighted to dispose of the full excess during a slump, only to incur an immediate shortage when more rapid growth resumes (as it undoubtedly will).

- The worst solution is to lower risk/reward standards and throw excess capital at speculative investments or at growth for growth's sake.

If it is nevertheless felt that something must be done, the best corrective may be to distribute the surplus directly back to shareholders by way of dividend, or else to buy in a portion of the bank's own shares in the market and then cancel them.

3.10 Capital adequacy and monetary inflation

Some bankers in many countries would like to believe that double-digit (or worse) inflation entitles them to *pari passu* balance sheet growth just to stay in the same place, and that the austere laws of sustainable growth may be somehow suspended or flexed for inflation. Disappointingly, the dynamics make no such concession. No matter what the rate of inflation may be and how it serves to pump up the nominal value of risk asset demand, a 20% volume growth still requires a commensurate overall rate of return (allowing also for the dividend), and inflation does not hand you that compensation on a plate. Unless society is prepared to sanction indexation of a bank's assets and liabilities (including paid-up capital), the hard lesson is that following a path of capital rectitude may at times cause a bank's business to shrink in real terms. Society's proper response is not to debase prudential standards but to combat inflation.

3.11 Cross-currency effects

Where a bank has risk assets (and risks) in a number of different currencies, it will have to do what it can to hedge the positions so as to maintain its capital ratios in reasonable equilibrium regardless of currency fluctuations. The shareholders' funds are in the home currency, but preference shares and secondary capital can be issued in major international currencies to underpin some exposures pro rata. The use of currency swaps can further help to balance the position.

If the bank has operations in other countries, capitalised in local currency mismatched against the parent's home currency capital, a 'structural open position' can provide a hedge, subject to approval by the regulator and compliance with applicable accounting standards. Regular valuations of the foreign currency investment (an asset) will simply produce equal fluctuations in the parent's home currency capital base (a liability). The remaining question then is not currency risk but whether the foreign subsidiary operation itself is adequately capitalised and earning its cost of capital.

In Basle terms, a bank with multicurrency exposures and operations will tend to have a substandard Tier 1 for most foreign currencies individually, balanced by a possibly overweight individual Tier 2. This is because the possibilities for issuing foreign currency capital are greater in Tier 2 than in Tier 1. The regulatory authorities tend to judge each case on its merits, generally paying more attention to the bank's total (merged currency) capital ratios.

3.12 Book capital versus market capitalisation

The discussion of capital adequacy in this chapter has been based on the conventional book value of a bank's equity capital. There is, however, an arguable case for preferring the market value as a guide to a bank's net worth (assuming, of course, that the bank is quoted on a stock market). Briefly, this case is based on the grounds that:

- If other book items are marked to market, it is inconsistent not to do the same with equity capital (but its book value is the balancing factor).

- Market value must be a truer reflection of the bank's risks, prospects, and current net worth (debatable).

- Management can manipulate or distort book value but not market value.

- Market value gives a 'truer' (and sometimes very different) picture of a bank's gearing (leverage).

- Market value gives a good indication of the terms on which fresh capital can be raised in need.

Collectively these arguments may have their investment merits, but by the same token they take the capital base out of the control of the bank's management. Moreover, they create a false picture of the size of the buffer available to absorb losses by book entries in a going bank or ultimately in a gone bank (by which time market capitalisation will have collapsed anyway). From a *solvency* perspective, it is difficult to see that market value capital can yet replace book value capital as the numerator of a meaningful capital adequacy measurement.

As mentioned in Chapter 1, the two values of equity capital will in any case tend to regress towards one another intermittently, albeit by a perpetual process of leads and lags.

3.13 Summary

Solvency risk is the almost universal secondary cause of banking failure. The adequacy of the solvency buffer (risk capital) is hard to measure economically, and depends at all times on how well the bank's other risks are being managed. 'Strong' capital ratios alone are no guarantee of survival: rather, sustained and soundly based profitability at 'required' levels is the key.

International capital adequacy regulation stands at a crossroads as it extends its range beyond credit risk and attempts to assimilate its approach more closely to industry best practice, whether of the 'value at risk' school or of other variance/covariance-based methodology.

Equity capital should be the substance of capital allocation within a bank: a risk-adjusted formula is offered.

Modern bankers need to take to heart the principles governing sustainable growth. Whilst it is natural for management to feel almost irresistibly driven by external economic forces, including competition, that is actually not a sufficient rule of conduct. Business expansion is not a birthright but has to be earned. This dynamic is logically separate and distinct from the deterioration in credit quality that bedevils rapid growth strategies anyway.

The problem of 'excess capital' is a historical danger zone, and any corrective action needs to be well considered.

Appendix: Main elements in Basle/Bank of England capital adequacy formula, first phase

A. Definition of capital

Tier 1: Core capital

Paid up ordinary share capital
Perpetual non-cumulative preferred shares (including convertible)
Disclosed reserves
Published (externally audited) interim retained profits/losses
Minority interests
less
Goodwill and intangibles
Current year's unpublished losses

Tier 2: Supplementary capital

Undisclosed reserves and unpublished current year's retained profits
Reserves arising from revaluation of tangible fixed assets and of fixed asset investments, and shares issued by capitalisation of property revaluations
General provisions held against latent but unidentified losses
Perpetual cumulative preferred shares
Perpetual subordinated debt (including convertible)

Dated preferred shares

Subordinated term debt with minimum original term of over five
years; subject to straight line amortisation in the last five years,
leaving no more than 20% outstanding in the final year

Minority interests applicable to Tier 2

Deductions from total capital

Investments in unconsolidated subsidiaries and associates

Connected lending of a capital nature

Guarantees of a capital nature on behalf of connected companies

Holdings of other banks'/building societies' capital instruments
(subject to specified market makers' exemptions); also Zone A
investment firms subject to the European capital adequacy
directive or an equivalent regime

Derivatives of a capital nature (e.g. forward purchase of a bank
capital instrument)

Limits and restrictions

Tier 2 not allowable above the value of Tier 1

Subordinated term debt (in Tier 2) not allowable above 50% of the
value of Tier 1

General provisions (in Tier 2) not allowable above 1.25% of
weighted risk assets

B. Risk asset weightings

0% Cash, and claims collateralised by cash placed with the
lending bank

Claims, excluding tradable securities, on Zone A central
governments and central banks

Claims, excluding tradable securities, on Zone B central
governments and central banks denominated and funded
in local currency

10% Loans to discount houses, gilt-edged market makers,
institutions with a money market dealing relationship with
the Bank of England, Stock Exchange money brokers in
the gilt- edged market, where the loans are secured on
gilts, UK treasury bills, eligible local authority and eligible
bank bills, or London CDs

Holdings of treasury bills and fixed interest securities (including index-linked) issued or guaranteed by Zone A central governments and central banks with a residual maturity of one year or less, and similar floating rate securities of any maturity

Holdings of Zone B central government and central bank securities with a residual maturity of one year or less denominated in local currency and funded by liabilities in the same currency

20% Holdings of Zone A central government and central bank fixed interest securities (including index-linked) with a residual maturity of over one year

Holdings of Zone B central government and central bank securities with a residual maturity of over one year denominated in local currency and funded by liabilities in the same currency

Claims on multilateral development banks

Claims on banks (and investment firms subject to the European capital adequacy directive or an equivalent regime) incorporated in Zone A countries

Claims on banks incorporated in Zone B countries with a residual maturity of one year or less

Claims on Zone A public sector entities

Loans to discount houses which are unsecured or secured on assets other than specified in 10% above

50% Loans to specified Housing Associations

Mortgage loans to individuals

Loans to special purpose mortgage finance vehicles

Mortgage subparticipations

Mortgage-backed securities

100% Claims on the non-bank private sector

Claims on banks incorporated in Zone B countries with a residual maturity of over one year

Claims on Zone B central governments and central banks (unless denominated in their national currency and funded by liabilities in the same currency)

Claims on commercial entities owned by the public sector

Claims on Zone B public sector entities

Premises, plant, equipment and other fixed assets – i.e. the reporting bank's physical infrastructure

Real estate, trade investments other than banks and building societies

Notes:
(i) Zone A comprises the membership of the Organisation for Economic Co-operation and Development (OECD), currently: Australia, Austria, Belgium, Canada, Denmark, Finland, France, Germany, Greece, Iceland, Ireland, Italy, Japan, Luxemburg, Netherlands, New Zealand, Norway, Portugal, Saudi Arabia, Spain, Sweden, Switzerland, Turkey, United Kingdom, United States of America.
 Zone B consists of all countries not in Zone A.
(ii) Where an exposure is guaranteed or collateralised by a superior category of obligor/asset named in this list, the risk weighting assigned is generally that of the guarantor/asset concerned.

C. Credit conversion factors for off-balance sheet risk

Credit conversion factors (CCF) should be multiplied by the weights applicable to the category of the counterparty for an on-balance sheet transaction.

CCF

100% Direct credit substitutes, including general guarantees of indebtedness, standby letters of credit serving as financial guarantees, acceptances and endorsements (including *per aval* endorsements)

Sale and repurchase agreements and asset sales with recourse where the credit risk remains with the bank

Forward asset purchases and any other commitment with a certain drawdown

50% Transaction-related contingent items not having the character of direct credit substitutes (e.g. performance bonds, bid bonds, warranties, and standby letters of credit related to particular transactions)

Note issuance facilities and revolving underwriting facilities

20% Short term self-liquidating trade-related contingent items (such as documentary credits collateralised by the underlying shipments)

0% Standby facilities, credit lines, etc, with an original maturity up to one year, or which can be unconditionally cancelled at any time

Endorsements of bills (including *per aval* endorsements) which have been previously accepted by a bank

D. Risk asset ratio %

$$\frac{\text{Net Capital Base (A)}}{\text{Total Weighted Risk Assets (B)}} \times 100$$

Basle minimum: 8%. The Bank of England imposes 'target' and 'trigger' ratios above that level for each bank individually.

CHAPTER FOUR

Liquidity risk

Banks must be capable of meeting their obligations when they fall due. Such obligations mainly comprise deposits at sight or short notice, term deposits and commitments to lend, including unutilised overdraft facilities. The mix of these obligations and their incidence in any period of time will vary between banks, but the maintenance of an assured capacity to meet them is an essential principle of banking which is common to all.

'The Management of Liquidity', Bank of England, July 1982

This chapter discusses:

● Liquidity management and regulation.

● Systemic risk.

● The impact of derivatives on systemic risk.

● The process of asset and liability management.

'Liquidity' is a term used by different bankers in different ways. Traders have in mind market depth and the relative ease or difficulty with which they can encash/liquefy/liquidate their positions. Other observers speak of liquidity risk as applying to nothing less than a tidal run on deposits, caused by loss of market confidence in the bank; in other words, as an extreme symptom of some other problem rather than a risk that can exist in its own right. Bank treasurers have to take a more comprehensive view: that liquidity risk has its sources on both sides of the balance sheet, and that management of the risk has to address normal as well as stressed conditions.

Liquidity risk, the potential for running short of cash in hand to settle debts and commitments when due, has some kinship with solvency risk (Chapter 3). Both are crystallised in an inability to meet financial obligations in full; but illiquidity is temporary, and insolvency permanent. Insolvency in a normally capitalised bank is the direct consequence of massive losses, whereas illiquidity is not necessarily associated with losses or writedowns but results from incoming and outgoing cash flow relationships. However, failure to control liquidity risk adequately can, uncomfortably quickly, turn a temporary difficulty into a permanent one.

Liquidity risk may also be seen as something of an obverse or reciprocal of credit risk (Chapter 5). My liquidity problem may cause me to be unable to pay you: that is your credit risk as my creditor. My default may precipitate your liquidity shortage which prevents you from paying your creditors, who may then have difficulty paying theirs . . . . The potential for such a bilateral or multilateral chain reaction of alternate credit and liquidity failures is known as *systemic risk*, which we shall come to in a later section.

In one sense or another, it is true to say that liquidity is bought *at a cost* and is thereby intimately bound up with interest rate risk (Chapter 8). Some analysts take this logic to the extreme of classifying liquidity risk as a branch of interest rate risk. Whilst not endorsing such reductionism, this chapter recognises the need to co-ordinate the management of these classes of risk in a treasury-led asset and liability management (ALM) process, as outlined in section 4.11.

4.1 Liquidity management

Liquidity management is a matter of balancing cash flows within forward rolling time bands – e.g. next day, next week, next month – so that, under normal conditions, the bank is comfortably placed to meet all its payment obligations as they fall due. The immediate focus is essentially short term because, as assets and liabilities run off and are replaced, the pattern of the bank's more distant cash flow engagements will be reconstituted many times over before their settlement time draws near.

That does not mean that the bank has no long term perspective, however. In a positive yield curve environment (see Chapter 8), the classical route to a self-induced liquidity crisis is to 'borrow short and lend long' in pursuit of enhanced interest turn. Granted, this practice of maturity mismatching (or *transformation* in French parlance) is, in moderation, an accepted function of a banking intermediary; but house disciplines are needed to ensure that it is not carried to excess.

In addition to scheduling smooth flows in normal conditions, the bank will want to keep something in reserve for hiccups and limited emergencies arising out of its business (e.g. counterparty defaults and/or unexpectedly high levels of deposit withdrawals). But it will not expect to hold sufficient liquidity to survive (much less help others to survive) a prolonged crisis in the national monetary system as a whole, where remedial action is the responsibility of the central bank. Contingency plans will therefore accommodate an estimated survival capability of, say, one week without recourse to central bank support. This is buying time for the emergency to recede, or else to be recognised as chronic and beyond the unaided power of self-cure. Rescue by the central bank is no soft option but an embarrassment to be avoided if at all possible.

Three elements make up a bank's liquidity profile: its expected cash flow, its capacity to borrow in the market, and its stock of readily available high quality liquid assets.

4.2 Expected cash flow

Cash *inflows* will be estimated, within defined time bands, mainly from existing contractual maturities (including scheduled loan repayments) on the assets side of the balance sheet, and from sales proceeds and revenue receipts. The expectation is that scheduled payments to the bank will be honoured in full and on time, unless there is reason to believe otherwise. Some assumptions, based on past experience and seasonal factors, will have to be made regarding the behaviour of amount-uncertain and maturity-uncertain items such as overdrafts (theoretically repayable on demand but in practice rather longer term in nature). A bank which ties up its short term funding in long term loans cannot look to loan repayments for much of the cash inflow needed to meet its frequently recurring outflow obligations: the balancing factor will be a heavy dependence on inflow from new replacement deposits and/or rollovers.

Estimated *outflows* will include deposit repayments, interest payments on deposits, staff salaries, bank dividend payments, drawdown of loans, overdrafts and other already committed credit facilities, investments and purchases by the bank, and other known expense items. It is prudent to assume that all *wholesale and institutional* contractual payments must be discharged in full – e.g. that institutional depositors will withdraw their money rather than roll it over on maturity. Large depositors are sensitive to credit risk and pricing, and are active shifters of money.

On the *retail* side, however, behavioural adjustments can be made to the schedule to reflect loyalty, inertia and stability in the customer deposit base. Most retail deposits in a commercial bank are formally repayable on demand or at short notice, but there is a pronounced tendency in normal times for them to stick with the bank (although in abnormal times this funding could prove to be the most fickle). Statistical analysis can identify trends in the net movement of retail deposits, including seasonal influences, with a high degree of confidence.

Some assumptions are also necessary regarding likely drawdown of unutilised loan and overdraft facilities.

A cardinal principle for the funding book is to maintain a diversified deposit base in terms of numbers of wholesale and retail depositors, geographical distribution, types of account or instrument, and spread of maturities. This affords better behavioural stability, and avoids excessive frequency and concentration of potential cash outflows in any one day or period. To state the obvious, a policy of raising one-week money requires 52 visits to the market every year whereas six-months money entails just two sorties.

These projections of cash inflows and outflows, within defined time bands, are based primarily on the bank's existing book, which naturally is destined to shrink as maturities run off on both sides. Some prudent allowance, however, can be made for short term replacement business not yet contracted, on a steady state basis or adjusted for perceived growth prospects and seasonal factors. But too much flexing is self-defeating as it distances us from the present realities of the book that need to be addressed.

When the expected inflows and outflows are put together, a picture of net cash flow emerges as illustrated in Fig. 4.1. In the first hypothetical case, there are sufficient positive net cash flows within

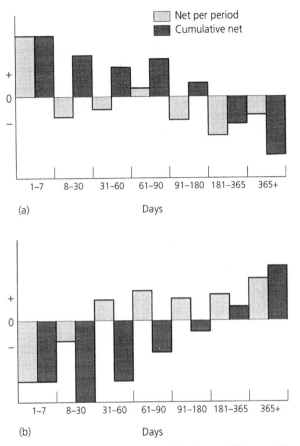

Net per period
Cumulative net

(a)   Days

1–7   8–30   31–60   61–90   91–180   181–365   365+

(b)   Days

1–7   8–30   31–60   61–90   91–180   181–365   365+

4.1 Examples of expected cash flow reports: (a) early cash flow positive; (b) early cash flow negative.

the next week and the next month to meet the bank's needs: the more distant time bands are of less significance at this moment, because their make-up will undoubtedly change as their remaining life shortens. The lower chart in Fig. 4.1 shows a contrary (and perhaps more typical) example, where natural cash flow falls short of full needs in the early positions and the bank must look to its next line of defence, namely its capacity to borrow extra funds in the market.

4.3 Capacity to borrow in the market

Borrowing in the money market to supplement funding is a normal activity, but few banks really know the limits of their own borrowing capacity. The question should not be left open-ended: each bank ought, by reference to past history and its internal criteria, to establish realistic ceilings to its market borrowing requirement (equating to its acceptable cash flow deficit) within cumulative time bands up to, say, one-month maturity. This self-imposed limitation recognises the vulnerability of funding plans that are overreliant on the money market fall-back; moreover, the orderly progress of the bank's business (including possible capital raisings) will not be helped by overexposure of its name in the market place.

That much said, there is also a maxim that we should accumulate liquidity when the market offers it rather than when we have to go looking for it. There is no prohibition on dealers occasionally exceeding the internal limit on market borrowing, provided that the excess has not been actively sought and represents no new structural 'requirement', and that the funds can be profitably employed.

The bank should maintain an extensive range of counterparties in order to diversify its dependencies. However, granting committed standby lines of credit to other banks is an indulgence that should be strictly limited and controlled. Such lines could end up being drawn in extreme and inappropriate circumstances, when the drawer bank has become a bad risk or when a systemic crisis has arisen which calls for comprehensive management by the central bank.

Natural cash flow, supplemented by the bank's capacity to raise wholesale funding as and when needed, should suffice to meet a normal range of business conditions. Normality, however, cannot be taken for granted, and the possibility of abnormal conditions calls for a third line of defence in the shape of a stock of encashable assets.

4.4 Stock of readily available high quality liquid assets

The stock of liquid assets is held solely as a reserve, to be turned into cash in crisis conditions when the bank cannot meet all its payment obligations from normal cash flow and from borrowing in the money market. The assets must be of high quality so that, in need, immediate sale/realisation is assured with minimal losses. Such items, apart from cash itself, might include:

- Operational balances with the central bank.

- Treasury bills and bonds.

- Short and medium dated gilts.

- High grade bank and local authority bills.

- Secured overnight deposits with discount houses and other market makers.

- Certificates of deposit issued by other first class banks.

No exact science governs the recommended size of this emergency portfolio, which must depend to some extent on the nature of the bank's business. Regulatory requirements (of which we shall speak later) do, of course, provide a quantified answer of sorts to the conundrum. In principle, the stock of liquid assets can be geared to a percentage of the bank's public liabilities. Alternatively and more rationally, the size can be approximated to the bank's potential net cash outflows (market borrowing requirement) over a chosen 'survival period' of, say, one week; the theory being that in crisis conditions the liquid assets may have to be turned into cash to replace funding that cannot be obtained from the money market.

Beyond that short term survival period, the problem must have either abated or been consigned to some other form of adjustment or work-out. A favourable outcome should be possible provided that other difficulties accompanying or precipitating the illiquidity do not tip the balance over into insolvency: illiquidity by itself (a rare but feasible occurrence) would not do that.

If, as is likely, the portfolio has predominantly short term maturities, there will be a constant turnover of liquid assets (which also helps to keep counterparties 'warm'); but this in itself is no source of general liquidity, since realisation proceeds must be used to purchase replacement assets so as to maintain the required stock level. In normal times, the paradox is that nothing is more illiquid than a 'liquid asset' which makes no contribution to the bank's cash flow. Fifty dollars kept in your pocket 'for emergencies only' is not fifty available dollars for shopping purposes. Consequently, if the bank expects to trade assets to generate everyday cash flow, it must carry a surplus of such instruments (possibly of lower quality) quite separate from the prescribed stock of liquid assets.

Not only are liquid assets immobile for normal uses, but their high quality/low yield status implies an opportunity cost compared with other commercial uses of the deposit moneys thus tied up.

Liquid assets limit the profitable deployment of each unit of funding raised. UK banks therefore tend to pass this opportunity cost of liquidity on to their borrowing corporate customers by means of a standard formula advised in the facility letter, cross-referring the average liquid asset yield to a London interbank offered rate. The underlying assumption, readers will notice, is that the balance sheet is asset-driven: were it to be liability-driven, logic and justice would teasingly suggest that this charge be levied on the depositor.

4.5 Cross-currency, cross-border

Globally integrated liquidity, combining all currencies and all countries in which an international bank operates, is not a practical proposition. There is no way that surplus cash flow, borrowing capacity, or liquid assets in sterling in London can meaningfully be set off against naira deficits in Lagos.

The general rule is that each currency must be self-balancing for liquidity purposes, even if that is achieved by earmarked switches of liquidity between readily exchangeable currencies managed in the same centre (with due care to avoid double-counting the same liquidity). Domestic currency positions must be managed within their national borders. Global banks may manage internationally traded currencies like the dollar globally if they have the information systems, control mechanisms, and time zone continuity to do so. Otherwise each centre must fend for itself day to day.

4.6 Regulatory approaches

Liquidity risk is regulated for much the same reasons as capital adequacy: to protect depositors and the financial system. The Basle Accord, recognising the impracticality of global prescriptions, assigns responsibility for liquidity regulation to the host authority in each country.

In days gone by, regulators in many countries did little more than require the holding of fixed ratios of approved liquid assets to total deposits or specified liabilities. This 'last ditch' focus ignored maturity relationships, cash flows, and day to day management of the liquidity profile in each bank. In some cases (e.g. the UK's now defunct Reserve Asset Ratio), the distinction between *liquidity regulation* and the aims of *monetary policy* (quite a different consideration) became somewhat blurred. As the science has progressed, however, banks and their regulators have increasingly come to converge on a more analytical appreciation constructed around the principles set out in the preceding sections of this chapter.

The Bank of England concentrates its attention mainly on the volatility of deposits. The key requirement is that banks should hold a stock of readily liquefiable assets that can be mobilised to replace funding which has been withdrawn owing to some perceived problem with the bank. The size of that stock is geared primarily to a nominated survival period of five business days without recourse to the money market, as determined by each bank's potential net outflow of wholesale funds. In addition, the stock must cover 5% of the gross retail deposit base. This formula confirms the verdict that wholesale deposits are in principle volatile and retail deposits stable.

The approved liquid assets are similar to those listed in section 4.4 above, except that other bank certificates of deposit (CDs) are allowed as a partial offset against net wholesale outflow (up to a maximum 50% of outflow) rather than as liquid assets proper. Moreover, CDs are subject to a 15% discount to reflect forced sale value in a troubled market.

In addition to these stipulations, the Bank of England monitors liquidity data submitted by each bank. Treatment of other commitments and contingent liabilities is still under consideration. These rules apply initially to sterling liquidity only, but a similar system is being developed to cover foreign currency liquidity.

There are some exceptions to this mainstream approach. The Bank of England monitors what are deemed to be 'non-retail banks' almost entirely on a mismatch ladder basis, setting maximum cumulative mismatch limits for eight days and one month for each bank individually. Branches of foreign-based banks should in theory be required to be self-sufficient for liquidity, but UK supervision will have a pragmatic eye to the background of parent pedigree.

UK-based banks (and branches of banks based outside the European Union) are required to contribute to a statutory deposit protection scheme which underwrites 90% of sterling deposits (excluding interbank) up to a maximum payout of £18 000. Other EU banks are governed by their home scheme. Any insurance payout, however, only comes into play after a bank's illiquidity has deteriorated into insolvency.

In contrast to such prescriptive controls, the regulatory bodies in the United States apply a qualitative and less structured approach suited to their large and varied market. A highly developed philosophy on liquidity risk is pursued through the agency of bank examiners. The regulatory guidelines lay great stress on the individual bank's 'funds management', linking liquidity risk with interest rate risk, and on the supervisory role of the bank's own asset and liability committee (ALCO – see section 4.11 below).

To cite another interesting example, the South African Reserve Bank has adopted a supervisory mission focusing on 'the quality and effectiveness of financial risk management in the banking system'. Direct responsibility for protecting depositors is expressly disclaimed by this regulator, although a healthy banking system will help to achieve that end.

The Reserve Bank monitors liquidity mismatches in maturity time bands and keeps a watch on trends, including diversification of funding sources. There is also a statutory requirement for a buffer stock of approved high quality liquid assets to be maintained at a minimum of 5% of public liabilities.

The Reserve Bank of New Zealand, which supervises an essentially foreign-owned banking system, has taken the concept of deregulation to new lengths by abolishing almost all prudential requirements, retaining only its allegiance to the Basle capital adequacy rules. Instead of the usual confidential returns to the regulator, there is a mandatory system of quarterly public disclosure statements containing balance sheet and income information, together with analyses of capital adequacy, asset quality and provisioning, credit exposures and market risks. This *caveat emptor* regimen makes no attempt to prescribe or monitor liquidity, although the Reserve Bank is ready to intervene in the markets if necessary to minimise systemic dislocations.

4.7 Systemic risk

'Systemic risk' puts a name to the market's collective nightmare: the possibility that default or failure by one financial institution could cause knock-on effects (direct or indirect) among its counterparties and others, spreading by chain reaction to threaten the stability of the financial system as a whole. An apposite analogy is that of an epidemic, requiring safeguards for public health. Systemic risk in banking embraces the interaction of counterparty credit risk with liquidity and solvency – depending on how severe and lasting the damage may be.

Risks that threaten the integrity of the financial system are by definition a central focus of attention for bank regulators. Such concern, however, is bound to be in a state of tension with the 'moral hazard' school of thought which holds that regulatory safety nets merely encourage wrongdoers and entail an unjustified charge to the public purse (see Chapter 3 on Solvency Risk). Obviously regulators with an eye to this censorious constituency are going to be keener on prevention than on guarantee or cure.

Responsibility for 'systemic risk management' is beyond the remit of individual commercial banks, but they can manage their own exposures so as to minimise their vulnerability. Each bank should control and limit its counterparty exposures in accordance with best credit practices and modern portfolio techniques – as described in Chapters 5, 6 and 7. In so doing, it will take care to avoid over-exposure to any one name or sector: that includes the banking sector, which merits no special favours but often receives them, thanks in part to low regulatory risk asset weightings (see Chapter 3 appendix) and liberal exposure ceilings (see Chapter 6). There is no good reason to suspend normal critical judgement, and the temptation to bid up interbank limits on grounds of reciprocity is one to be resisted.

The individual bank should also avail itself of the collective initiatives that regulators and the industry have launched to scale down burgeoning interbank transfer and settlement risks, in both domestic and foreign currencies. Structural improvements in these areas address two dimensions: *length of time* and *size* of exposures respectively. Complete success in eliminating either axis would automatically dispose of the other. As regards length of time, most countries have accelerated their wholesale payment systems by switching from paper-based to electronic processing. Electronic intra-day clearing house systems like CHAPS in the UK have undergone or are undergoing further conversion to real time gross settlement (RTGS), thereby eliminating some daylight risks (for further discussion of daylight/settlement risk, see Chapter 5 on Credit Risk).

In the securities market, settlement risk (and thereby systemic risk) resides in the potential time gap between delivery of securities by a seller (or lender) and payment for them by the purchaser (or borrower of the securities). Either party, having fulfilled its side of the bargain (by irrevocably paying away money or by releasing securities), can be left in the lurch by default of its counterparty. The industry aspiration is to construct real time depository and settlement mechanisms which close the gap and provide assured delivery versus payment (DVP).

A similar situation exists in the foreign exchange market, where amounts in two different currencies are exchanged on due date – with definitive settlement of each taking place in its respective home currency base. 'Herstatt risk', highlighted in Chapter 2, is emblazoned on bankers' memories. In this case, the risk-elimination remedy sought is simultaneous payment versus payment (PVP), overcoming the problem of differing time zones. This solution might be attained bilaterally by establishing a private sector co-ordinating institution, or by co-ordination between central banks, or multilaterally by setting up a dedicated clearing house on the lines proposed by the Group of 20 banks (see Chapter 5 on netting).

A corollary of all these impending developments is the need for linkage and a degree of integration between bank payment/clearing systems; and between them and the securities and other settlement systems which depend on final payment in 'good funds'. This demand poses formidable legal and logistical difficulties (extending cross-border and cross-currency), and international studies have been under way for some time under the auspices of the Bank for International Settlements, the Group of Ten Countries, and the European Union.

So much for the attack on the time dimension of credit and liquidity exposures. Collective initiatives to curb the size of exposures revolve around a separate but complementary theme: the netting of mutual obligations between active counterparties. This topic is covered at length in Chapter 5 on Credit Risk. Suffice it here to stress that the validity of netting schemes depends on legal enforceability under the relevant jurisdiction(s), and that any capital benefit depends on official recognition by the competent regulatory authority. In the absence of these preconditions, purported netting would be a chimera, powerless to reduce risk and likely to increase it by masking true exposure. Effective, approved netting, on the other hand, is a key element in the struggle to contain systemic risk.

How far these collective trends will lead to a permanent scaling down of counterparty exposures is an open question. Do we seek condensation because the risks are too high for comfort, or because we want to free up capacity to do more business (e.g. in the relatively new trade in derivatives products)? Motives are mixed, and entrepreneurial spirits may choose to regard any shrinkage as a case of *reculer pour mieux sauter* (regrouping in order to advance the better). Experience in other fields of human endeavour suggests that when an activity is made systemically less risky, the respite is short-lived: rather than accept the safety dividend in full, people have a habit of rebuilding risks towards accustomed adrenalin levels. Design safer skis, and skiers simply go faster. This phenomenon is known as 'risk compensation', and may also be viewed as an aspect of 'moral hazard'.

4.8 Derivative instruments and systemic risk

'Derivatives' are synthetic instruments which *derive* their value from that of an underlying type of asset, liability, reference rate, or index (see the Glossary for further description, and Chapters 3, 5, 9 and 10 for aspects of exposure measurement and risk management). As 'a natural extension of traditional risk intermediation' (in the words of the Washington-based Institute of International Finance), they partake of systemic risk in the same way as other counterparty exposures. There is an obligor (one or other counterparty) who may, at worst, default on due date (or become prematurely insolvent), with possible knock-on effects. The issues of payment, settlement, and netting are operationally identical.

Derivatives are, however, seen by many as escalating the threat of 'payment gridlock' or 'systemic melt-down' (in the hyperbolic language of the debate) because:

- Leverage is high: large volumes of potential counterparty exposure may be created for modest cash outlay and low capital impact.

- Over-the-counter derivative positions are customarily 'closed out' (where necessary) by entering into another contract, creating yet more counterparty exposure in the process.

- Exposures tend to be laid off in a multiplicity of 'sub-underwriting' interconnections which themselves could have far-reaching systemic implications in the event of default.

● Derivatives activity links different financial markets in such a way as to transmit systemic damage between them.

● Derivatives facilitate proprietary speculation as much as hedging (witness Barings).

● They can exaggerate market swings and price volatility.

● Derivatives exposures are subjected to inconsistent accounting treatment and inadequate disclosure in company accounts, thereby frustrating normal credit evaluation.

● Commercial experience of derivatives is relatively short: the combination of rapid market growth with product complexity, and with untested moral, legal and behavioural aspects, leaves practitioners exceptionally vulnerable to the law of unintended consequences.

The statistics of market volumes and growth, as portrayed in Table 4.1, are indeed spectacular. Global outstandings of over $27 trillion (i.e. thousand billion) are, by way of comparison, more than twice the gross domestic product of the USA. However, the aggregates are misleading, being based on the *notional principal* (the total value

Table 4.1 Financial derivatives: markets for selected instruments (notional amounts outstanding $billion)

	1990	1991	1992	1993	1994	1995
Exchange-traded instruments	2290	3519	4634	7771	8863	9185
Interest rate futures	1456	2157	2913	4959	5778	5863
Interest rate options[1]	600	1073	1385	2362	2624	2742
Currency futures	17	18	27	35	40	38
Currency options[1]	57	63	71	76	56	43
Stock market index futures	69	76	80	110	127	172
Stock market index options[1]	94	133	159	230	238	327
Over-the-counter instruments[2]	3450	4449	5346	8475	11 303	17 990
Interest rate swaps	2312	3065	3851	6177	8816	na
Currency swaps[3]	578	807	860	900	915	na
Other swap-related derivatives[4]	561	577	635	1398	1573	na

[1]Calls and puts. [2]Data collected by the International Swaps and Derivatives Association (ISDA) only; the two sides of contracts between ISDA members are reported once only. [3]Adjusted for reporting of both currencies; including cross-currency interest rate swaps. [4]Caps, collars, floors, and swaptions.

(Source: *The Banker*)

of the 'underlying') in each derivative contract as opposed to what is at risk, most commonly measured by its current *replacement value*. The latter represents a movement in rates or prices (interest, exchange, index, etc) since the start of the contract, and usually equates to a small percentage of the notional principal. In 1995 the International Swaps and Derivatives Association and Arthur Andersen conducted a survey of over-the-counter business outstanding in 67 leading dealers at year-end 1994. After elimination of double-counting for counterparties to the same contract, the survey found that:

- Notional principal totalled $8.5 trillion, whereas mark to market gross replacement values came to only $172.6 billion (2.03% of the notional).

- Netting under master agreements reduced the replacement values to $77.9 billion (0.92%), and counterparty pledged collateral further reduced them to $71.0 billion (0.84%).

In 1995 the Bank for International Settlements compiled statistics on derivatives markets in 26 member countries, in conjunction with its triennial survey of foreign exchange trading. This wider-ranging investigation found as at March 1995 a total of $16.4 trillion of notional principal outstanding on exchange-traded instruments, and $47.5 trillion over-the-counter. Compared with the combined notional total of $63.9 trillion, mark to market gross replacement values were estimated at $2.2 trillion (3.4% of the notional). Had information been available on netting agreements and counterparty pledged collateral, the replacement values could probably have been halved to around $1 trillion. Derivatives statistics are thus uniquely flawed because the bottom-line replacement variable does not lend itself at this stage to standardised statistical compilations, leaving notional principal as the only (inflated and much-quoted) alternative measurement.

We have, then, a sizeable addition to the cash markets, but not as overwhelming as appears at first sight. The argument that proliferation of counterparty linkages increases systemic risk is a curious inversion of the normal perception that depth of market and spread of risk-bearing is advantageous. Do we prefer to confine the activity to only a few big players, and is that systemically less risky?

Some say that derivatives encourage speculation as well as hedging of risks, and that the statistics indicate usage to be higher than the market's authentic hedging needs (however computed). A common rejoinder is that most companies make insufficient use of hedging techniques: both hypotheses could be true, though not overlapping. The distinction between hedging and speculation is, in any case, less clear cut than might be supposed: people's expectations of, and provisions for, the future differ, and one person's flutter may be another's prudent insurance policy (conjugation: I hedge, you speculate, he/she is an out-and-out gambler). The justification for particular derivatives engagements can only be assessed through careful scrutiny (dependent on adequate disclosure) and 'knowing your counterparty'; principles which are reflected in a steady migration to quality among active counterparties in the swaps market.

A standardised accounting and disclosure framework has yet to be willed into being, although various proposals have been put forward by such bodies as the Basle Euro-currency Standing Committee, the Group of Thirty (G30) Global Derivatives Study Group, the Institute of International Finance, the US Accounting Standards Board, and (jointly) the British Bankers' Association and the Irish Bankers' Federation.

On the *accounting* side, an emerging theme is on the need to distinguish between 'trading' and 'non-trading' transactions for purposes of valuation and income/balance sheet recognition. According to the BBA/IBF 1995 Statement of Recommended Accounting Practice (SORP) on Derivatives, 'trading' transactions consist of all customer and proprietary deals, and hedges thereof. These should be measured at 'fair value', defined as the amount at which the instrument could be exchanged in a current transaction between willing parties. 'Non-trading' transactions, by contrast, comprise derivatives held for hedging purposes against assets, liabilities, and positions arising from the bank's activities measured on an accruals basis; in other words, where the bank is an 'end-user' hedging its portfolio risks. In this case, valuation of the derivative should be on an accruals basis equivalent to that used for the underlying asset, liability, position or cash flow. Transactions are normally presumed to be 'trading' unless proved otherwise.

Not only do these classifications introduce a stark contrast in treatment between trading and non-trading: they also differ in turn from the G30 Study Group definitions, from the European capital adequacy directive (Chapter 3), and from in-house methods of exposure measurement described in Chapter 5. 'Fair value' now takes its place alongside such close relatives as 'credit equivalent exposure' and 'replacement value'. 'Accruals value' for non-trading items, whilst following an undeniable logic of accounting parity between the hedge and the thing hedged, represents a radical break with the market-based formulae. Whatever may be the arguments and the respective merits, there is a clear and urgent need for international convergence of accounting standards.

As regards *disclosure*, a broad measure of agreement exists on several features. Most interested parties envisage a format of financial accounts incorporating a 'qualitative' commentary on the bank's policies and practices with regard to derivatives trading and hedging. However, the Basle Euro-currency Standing Committee has added the memorable rider that qualitative disclosure can become 'meaningless boilerplate' if it is not linked to quantitative data on risks and realised outcomes.

Quantitative disclosures, it is widely agreed, should address credit, liquidity and market risks. They might take the form of a series of tables covering: trading and non-trading activities respectively, broken down into derivative types; counterparty analysis (e.g. by financial institutions vs others, by geographical location, by grade) on a net exposure footing where legitimate; maturity analysis based on net present values of future cash flows; and some assessment of the interest rate and/or price risks to which the bank is exposed by reason of its positioning (e.g. stress analysis).

4.9 'Derivatives angst'

This expression, coined by the President of the Federal Reserve Board of New York, neatly evokes the generalised worry that derivatives are novel and complex, inadequately understood (particularly at top management and board levels), and bristling with booby-traps. One of the most basic of risk management rules must be: if you don't understand the deal, the business, or the risks, don't do it. This seems to have received scant attention in a number of highly publicised mishaps.

In 1991 the UK Parliament's House of Lords ruled that swaps contracts entered into by the London Borough of Hammersmith and Fulham were void for want of legal capacity (*vires*). Losses consequently sustained by the counterparties of this and other similarly affected boroughs were estimated by Arthur Andersen and the International Swaps and Derivatives Association to amount to more than half of all losses from swap defaults worldwide since inception of the activity; not that that represented a large percentage of exposure (total 0.46% measured on a mark to market basis) compared with default losses regularly suffered in the conventional credit field (twice as high, or worse, over an economic cycle). We may perhaps concede that, in falling foul of the law in this particular instance, the banks were more unlucky than careless as they had in fact taken copious legal advice.

As we have seen, the collapse of Barings in 1995 was occasioned by losses in the Singapore office of some £830 million on proprietary speculation in Nikkei 225 stock index futures. Senior management in London apparently had no true understanding of, or control over, what was going on during a period of more than a year. Similarly, several end-user corporates and institutions have burnt their fingers, ostensibly on derivatives positions: in recent times notably the German company Metallgesellschaft, Orange County in California and Charles County in Maryland. Bankers Trust has been sued by two of its dissatisfied derivatives customers, Procter & Gamble (claiming $200 million under anti-racketeering laws) and Gibson Greetings (a $20 million claim): both suits were settled out of court for upwards of 70% of the amounts claimed. The same bank has also been disciplined by three US regulatory bodies in respect of quality control deficiencies.

4.10 But do derivatives increase systemic risk?

Derivatives exist in the first place to help *reduce* risk, but in so doing they create additional exposures and dependencies of their own. Is it fair to describe these as unduly onerous and predominantly systemic?

Derivatives afford a prudent company or bank unparalleled scope for hedging (containing) its financial risks, granted that there is no perfect hedge and no infallible counterparty. They are equally available for speculative position-taking, which itself can range from the canny to the reckless. Sometimes the distinction between hedging and speculation becomes confused, as in the example of Metallgesellschaft where long term fixed price supply contracts were unwisely hedged with short term exchange-traded derivatives. When people do irrational things with derivatives, some of the mud sticks to the reputation of the instrument as well as the user.

Default by one party liable on a derivative contract undoes a hedge or a speculation relied on by the counterparty: this is by no means equivalent to default on a loan, except for unrequited settlement of currency swaps (and also foreign exchange forward contracts, which are derivative in nature though not always counted as such) where gross amounts are due to be exchanged. In the case of sensational bank collapses like British & Commonwealth Merchant Bank, Drexel Burnham Lambert, Bank of New England and Barings, substantial derivatives portfolios were liquidated without shock waves; demonstrating, if anything, that fears of *systemic* risk emanating from derivative sources are exaggerated. We need to keep a sense of proportion: it is illogical to strain at the gnat of *feared* derivatives contagion whilst swallowing the camel of *known* credit loss severity in the cash markets. The G30 Global Derivatives Study Group, in its authoritative 1993 report on 'Derivatives: Practices and Principles', concluded that derivatives do not appreciably aggravate systemic risks.

That is not to say there is nothing at all to worry about. The derivatives market needs to find answers to its systemic weaknesses in top management control (of which more in Chapter 10 on Price Risks) and in accounting and disclosure standards. Correction of these shortcomings will help to demystify the activity and allay the angst. In the long run, there may be some migration from over-the-counter activity towards exchange-traded contracts. On the face of it, that would help to improve discipline, transparency and liquidity in the markets. It is worth noting, however, that Barings got into trouble in precisely this exchange-traded area.

4.11 Asset and liability management (ALM)

ALM is the recognised term for the process by which a bank's treasury department makes its contribution to the organisation's profit objectives and co-ordinates the trade-offs between liquidity risk, interest rate risk and price risks. Concentrating on any one of these risks at the expense of the others could be extremely costly. For example, maximising liquidity can minimise interest turn, and vice versa. Price risk positions carry liquidity and interest rate risks, and so on.

ALM impinges on everything, and everything impinges on ALM. The boundaries of ALM's jurisdiction can be set broadly or narrowly, but most banks prefer to confine the treasury department's discretion to issues involving liquidity, interest rate risks, and price risks (notably foreign exchange and equity trading). Discharge of this responsibility involves, *inter alia*:

- Managing funding mismatches and attaining desired levels of liquidity in the terms described in this chapter.

- Managing rate-sensitive assets and liabilities and the effects of rate, volume, and mix changes so as to preserve and optimise the interest turn.

- Managing various portfolio price sensitivities.

- Liaison with other parties regarding financial plans and budgets, business development and new products, portfolio management, capital adequacy and sustainable growth.

On the universal principle that war is too important to be left to the generals, it is common practice to establish an asset and liability committee (ALCO) as the top level forum which agrees ALM policy, and reviews its implementation by the treasury department. The constitution of this committee must be treated with some care, so that it is integrated within the management structure and the strategic planning process, and not seen as a law unto itself. An ALCO is not a substitute for the chain of command, but rather a consultative solution to a community of (sometimes conflicting) interests. Its duties and authorities need to be spelled out, and endorsed by the bank's board of directors. Membership should include such officers as:

- The bank's chief executive, or his deputy.

- The finance director.

- The treasurer.

- The chief dealer.

- The chief lending officer.

- The heads of planning and marketing.

- The economic adviser.

Meeting perhaps monthly, the ALCO will receive and debate reports from treasury on the liquidity profile, the interest rate turn, interest/ exchange rate/equity price sensitivities, balance sheet structure, regulatory considerations, market and economic intelligence. On the basis of the forecasts, projections, scenario modelling and recommendations placed before it, the ALCO will affirm the ALM policies to be followed, actions to be taken, and prudential limits applied pending its next review; and will convey the necessary instructions, with the chief executive's authority, to line management. It is, of course, essential that adequate minutes of the proceedings be recorded and distributed.

Even those with limited faith in 'management by committee' generally find that the ALCO system makes sense in the control of these treasury risks (liquidity, interest rate and price risks), conferring special benefits in the form of involvement and educational spin-off at senior management level. A more detailed examination of what is entailed in managing interest rate risk is to be found in Chapters 8 and 9, whilst price risks are the subject of Chapter 10.

4.12 Summary

The elements of liquidity management are the bank's expected cash flow, its capacity to borrow in the market, and its stock of high quality readily liquefiable assets. In a crisis, even the soundest risk management precautions within an individual bank cannot be expected to cover more than a survival period of a few days, as the regulators recognise.

In the modern era, systemic risk is more of a folk memory than a current event. However, interbank and other counterparty credit exposures are historically high and continue to grow. Strenuous efforts are being made to condense daylight and settlement risks by means of conversion to real time payment and simultaneous exchange systems, and through the adoption of netting between active counterparties in an increasing number of countries. Purpose-built clearing houses and depositories have an important contribution to make.

Derivatives add complexity (not to say perplexity) to the market place, with controls and accounting/disclosure standards as yet leaving much to be desired. Banks and their customers are still in a learning phase, and accidents are to be expected. Nevertheless, it seems clear that the impact of derivatives on systemic risk has been greatly exaggerated by the critics.

Liquidity, interest rate and price risks are closely interrelated and should be the subject of co-ordinated asset and liability management (ALM) in the treasury department, overseen by a top level asset and liability committee (ALCO).

CHAPTER FIVE

Credit risk: policy overview

This chapter introduces some of the fundamentals:

- Credit culture.

- Authority and decision-making.

- Types of exposure and their quantification.

- Credit risk of derivatives.

- Daylight/settlement risk.

- Netting.

- Lenders and environmental liability.

- Confidentiality and conflicts of interest.

Credit risk is the risk of loss to the bank through default by an obligor. *Default* is any material breach of the contractual obligation to pay (or repay) principal or interest. The most common form of default is failure to pay in full and on due date, but various other acts, omissions, or events (e.g. insolvency) may be defined as 'default' within the terms of the loan agreement or other contract. An *obligor* is one who binds himself to make payment, either as principal debtor or as surety: in other words, the one to whom the bank is looking for settlement.

A partial synonym for obligor is *counterparty*, meaning the opposite party in a credit-based contract: somebody likely at some stage to owe the bank money in terms of that contract. Where the net obligation can swing either way, as in a swap contract, the bank itself is also a 'counterparty' in the eyes of the other   side.

Credit risk has at times been mistaken by commercial bankers for the sum total of risk, to the extent of their appropriating the title of 'risk management' for the credit function. Chapter 2, whilst giving the lie to any such oversimplification, identifies credit as the single most damaging category of risk in banking. This is not surprising, as it permeates a wide range of services and exposures: not just loans and overdrafts, but also forward exchange contracts, swaps, options, futures and other derivatives, and daylight/settlement positions.

According to one indicator, credit risk must have become steadily more perilous for banks over the years: the rate of company insolvencies in the UK has roughly quadrupled since 1950 (see Fig. 5.1). Banks as financiers will not have been left unscathed by that deterioration in company fortunes.

There are many excellent textbooks on the theory and practice of lending money and getting it back. This chapter takes the corpus of technical literature as a given, and will concern itself only with panoramic issues of policy and approach to credit risk. Chapters 6 and 7 will deal more comprehensively with the newer science of portfolio management.

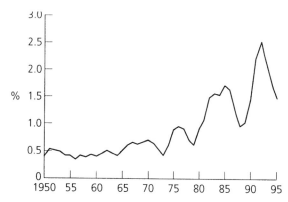

5.1 Insolvency rate of UK companies.

5.1 Credit culture

The first requirement for success in managing credit risk is a strong credit culture, something which cannot be taken for granted in an age of disintegrating values. Like an elephant, credit culture is easier to recognise than to define in so many words.

Credit culture, overtly or implicitly, embodies the psychology and beliefs of a bank's management. No two cultures will be identical, because each reflects a particular franchise and a balance between different imperatives, experiences, and personalities. Values and emphases will differ, with some banks exhibiting heightened (maybe creative) tension between, say, business development and portfolio selectivity. A culture can be painted in contrasting primary colours or in harmonious pastel shades: the one is not necessarily better than the other.

The begetters and custodians of this philosophical framework are the chief executive and the chief credit officer (or equivalent), but the teaching needs to permeate downwards and be supported by force of example at every level of management. In a strong credit culture, top management will have a good understanding of: the trade-off between risk and reward, the concept of expected loss, the required rate of return (Chapter 1); the economic limits of sustainable growth (Chapter 3); and the principles of portfolio management (Chapters 6 and 7). Senior credit officers will have long memories, and lending experience of at least two business cycles.

The bank's time horizons for attainment of its goals will be medium and long term rather than short term: there will be a decided preference for stability and predictability of results as opposed to rootless variability, unprincipled opportunism and 'luck'. The bank's business impulses will not be continually oscillating between the twin polarities of greed and fear.

A strong credit culture will achieve a prudent equilibrium between business development and quality control, and not merely a sales bias that pays lip service to such checks and balances. Performance incentives geared to turnover of deals must be tempered by considerations of quality and outcome. Staff in quality control functions need rewards, status, training and career prospects that do not make them poor relations of the sales people; otherwise regard for their role, and for any credit culture, is fatally undermined. Respect for the calibre and experience of credit officers will ensure that even their 'decline' verdicts are accepted with good grace, an essential condition in a well-ordered bank.

A strong credit culture takes the trouble to prescribe *risk appetite*, in terms of sectors, grades, types of financing, and individual customer/counterparty names. This pre-empts the situation where exposure is piled on exposure merely because, in the absence of preconception or policy, nobody can think of a reason on the spot not to do it (a real enough situation, incredible though it may seem to non-bankers).

Sound credit culture requires comprehensive and coherent written credit policies, and no condoning of habitual disparities between policy and practice. Few exceptions to policy or norms will be countenanced. Urgent requests should be highlighted as a danger zone, since they can prompt a spirit of either panic or extra helpfulness and bounce the unwary banker into assent when denial would be the more judicious response. There is still something to be said for the now unfashionable adage that 'if an answer is wanted in five minutes, the answer is "no".'

A bank that demands high standards of itself is likely to expect the same of its corporate customers. It will look askance at the appearance of dishonesty or accounting trickery on their part, or refusal to divulge financial figures to their bankers. This latter can be a special problem with private companies and wealthy families, but mere 'name lending' should not be part of the bank's vocabulary. Some international entrepreneurs, rather than give up their secrecy, are willing to provide full cash cover: this can be an acceptable solution, if the bank is satisfied as to legal, country and exchange risks.

In general, however, security is no substitute for an informed analysis of the customer's business and prospects. Lending without properly identified means of repayment, other than realisation of the security taken, is vulgarly known as 'pawnbroking'. It is not the safe bet it is sometimes taken to be, but is a high risk area; the more so when the security also forms the purpose of the advance (e.g. property development, acquisition finance, equipment purchase). It is worth repeating here a principle enunciated in Chapter 4: if you don't understand the deal, the business, or the risks, give it a miss.

A strong credit culture is committed to investing in its people, technology and systems. It is aware of the costs of the credit process, and keen to eliminate waste, but on balance it is planning to spend more, not less, on credit risk management in the 1990s.

If all this sounds like so much piety, consider by contrast the credit boom of the late 1980s and its aftermath of bad debts. Then, too few bankers anywhere had an adequate understanding of the risk/reward trade-off, expected loss, the required rate of return, the economic limits of sustainable growth, or the principles of portfolio management. Memories of past business cycles were submerged by bullish sentiments, whilst salesmanship and short termism were in the ascendant. Meanwhile, the devalued credit control function was under continual pressure to soften rules, accept property security as a panacea, give quicker (favourable) answers, cut its own costs and otherwise get out of the way. Investment in credit training and systems had too low a priority.

In brief, credit culture in the 1980s fell short (in some cases, fell apart), with results that we have all seen. This catalogue does not apply in full to every bank, but the industry generalisation is true enough to have contributed to a major credit crisis spanning continents: 'contributed' because the principal cause, economic expansion followed by recession, was by no means entirely of the banks' making.

When credit culture breaks down, credit philistinism reaps its own reward. It is an open question whether the credit culture in most banks will have been rebuilt sufficiently to withstand the next cyclical boom in lending.

5.2 Authority, sanctioning and decision-making

Sanctioning (credit approval) procedures tend to bring out extremist opinion. One school of thought regards sanctioning as the essence of credit risk management: another believes that credit risk management is what happens *after* sanctioning. In fact, sanctioning is the primary safeguard of credit quality and a vital component (not the totality) of credit risk management.

Every bank has its own administrative structure and hierarchy. To what extent does this need to be varied to cater for the management of credit risk? In the past, commercial bank managers from the branch upwards were generalists, but that core has been steadily eroded in favour of specialisation. Apart from the benefit of expertise which specialisation confers, banks now recognise an inherent conflict of interest between business development and credit evaluation. Separating the two functions (commonly dubbed 'state' and 'church' respectively), as far as practicable, helps ensure objective judgement in the sanctioning (approval) process. Too much separation, on the other hand, can cause alienation, to the detriment of the common effort.

At branch or business unit level, rigid segregation between developers and sanctioners is neither practical nor desirable, but second opinions and initials (whether before or after the credit decision) are a fairly normal balancing requirement within a management team. At regional office level there is the critical mass to create a specialist credit sanctioning and supervision team, answerable to the regional head and/or (via matrix management) to a central credit department in the head office.

Because of the claims of responsibility/accountability, such reporting lines tend to be controversial. Who controls the central credit department, and where do the two lines – business development and credit quality control – meet at the top of the organisation chart? They must converge at some upper level, assuming there is only one chief executive, but the bank may choose to close the gap at a point one or two tiers below that pinnacle of authority. Line heads will feel less excluded from the credit process if they are actively involved in the top sanctioning roster or credit committee. Even the best organisation chart is bound to be a compromise that can be made to succeed or to fail, according to the attitude of the participants.

Figure 5.2 illustrates a typical management structure in a multibranch bank, where graduated discretionary limits are allocated to the different levels of management engaged in the granting of credit. Similar principles could be applied within a more monolithic wholesale bank. In this escalating system, proposals above the powers of the branch manager are passed to the next level up, say the regional office; if too large for the regional office, they are dispatched to central credit (whether by a paper-based system or by electronic transmission). In the interest of speed of service, some element of leap-frogging may be introduced into this lengthening (and repetitious) chain; but, by the same token, that absolves those who are leap-frogged from collective responsibility for the decision.

The central credit department will itself have limited approval powers, above which a proposal will have to be forwarded to specified executive signatories in sequence (the 'crawling file' method) or else to a top level credit committee. Which of these two sanctioning structures a bank chooses depends on its perception of which best brings out the relevant features of credit proposals, mobilises the skills of its most experienced sanctioners, and renders

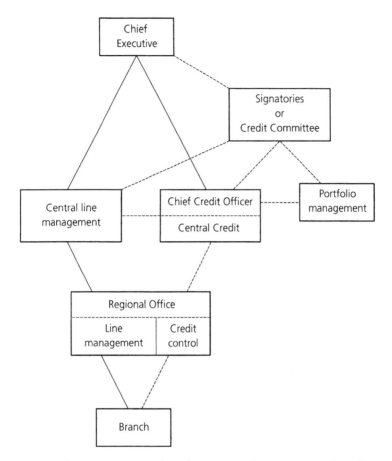

5.2 Example of separate decision lines for business development and credit.

the best service to the customers. Both need some sort of post-decision review system, if only by simple tabulation and report to the board. There is as yet no real body of evidence as to the relative effectiveness of crawling file versus committee decisions, and the preference will be part and parcel of the bank's credit culture.

The bank's chief executive officer should not have independent approval powers, and is best kept out of the processing of individual deals and names so as not to upset the balance of the machinery. Subject to the same caveat, he may, however, participate in top level credit committee meetings.

The bank will have to decide where it places the balance between centralisation and devolution of decision-making. Centralisation (which implies smaller discretions delegated to divisions, regions, and branches or business units) has advantages in the maintenance of tight control, consistency of standards, concentration of skills, synergy and economies of scale. Devolution (implying larger delegated discretions) favours accountability, integrated planning and a fuller sense of empowerment within line divisions: it has difficulty handling the centralised issues of policy and consolidation of cross-divisional exposures (which are common in large corporate relationships). Fashions in centralisation and devolution tend to be subject to tidal reversals every decade or so; but, at the very least, credit policy, credit grading, portfolio management, and supporting systems design will need to be led by a dedicated resource at the centre.

The advent of credit grading (discussed in Chapter 6) allows the possibility of flexing the system of discretionary limits by reference to customer grades as well as amounts. This goes some way to meet the objection that the smaller credits as a class are often the riskiest, yet are the sanctioning responsibility of the most junior and least experienced managers. A relatively modest grade 5 (weak) exposure, for example, might be lifted to regional office, rather than branch level, for approval; or from regional office to central credit. Staffing logistics, however, need to be borne in mind before we go overboard on this approach, and it may be that decision support systems (covered in Chapter 6) can achieve some of the same ends.

Conversely, some economies can be achieved in the processing of top grade credits without undue loss of control, by delegating larger than normal discretionary powers to regions and branches.

Facilities approved, by whatever system, are usually marked forward for review in 12 months' time. Frequent interim requests for increases or for excesses over limits are signs of indiscipline that strong credit culture will be at pains to discourage. This may sound rigid, but flexibility can be built in by including a justifiable element of 'headroom' in the limit sheet, at the disposal of the customer relationship officer under specified conditions, to accommodate additional facilities. There may also be a general dispensation allowing junior credit officers the finite power to increase a customer's total facilities by up to, say, 10% in between sanctioning/review dates without referring back to the higher sanctioning level.

A perennially vexed question is how much of a 'blaming culture' we should have when things go wrong. Too little, and business expansion can run amok; too much, and developers and sanctioners (who are occupationally exposed in a way that their critics often are not) will become excessively risk-averse. Within what time span is blame applicable: should there be a 'statute of limitations' concerning disciplinary action for alleged wrong decisions? At top executive level, arguably not.

Who is the more culpable for taking on a bad credit risk, leading to unexpected loss: the business developer or the sanctioner? That depends on the particular circumstances, and also partly on whether there is a standing arrangement in-house that unexpected loss is 'insured' internally by the one or the other. Hindsighted, simplistic, inquisition seeks a single identity on which to pin blame for loss apparently caused by faulty approvals or defective follow-up: this is part and parcel of the management philosophy of individual responsibility and performance-related pay. However, in the case of large exposures with collective handling such sharp definition is often impossible (or, if persisted in, unjust).

The fact that numbers tend to disperse blame may be a mixed blessing, but it is merely the corollary of a traditional (and, on the whole, wise) aversion to giving any single person the untrammelled authority to 'bet the bank'.

The approach to accountability and disciplinary action is important, but there are no magic answers and each bank has to find its own solution. In the field of corporate credit risk there is more than enough blame to go round, but true justice (as opposed to expediency and appearances) is an elusive ideal.

We now turn to selected key elements in the formulation of a commercial credit application.

5.3 The risk epitome

In addition to other standard information, the frontispiece of a written corporate credit proposal should spell out the facility limits (maximum recommended exposures), the sector, the customer's credit grade (which by definition implies the expected default rate at a portfolio level – see Chapter 6), and the prospective relationship return on risk-adjusted equity capital (RORAC or equivalent formula – see Chapters 1 and 3).

Exposures should be categorised by remaining life to final maturity: a convenient code is 'short term' (up to one year), 'medium term' (above one to, say, five years), and 'long term' (above five years). It offends banking sense to classify a 24-year aircraft financing as 'medium term', although that is a common enough solecism. Where there is a programme of amortisation, the *average* life of the exposure should also be shown.

Why the fuss over duration? Because the longer the exposure, the greater the potential for volatility, uncertainty of outcome, and therefore risk. This may or may not be adequately reflected in the economic capital allocation and the rate of return, but the sanctioner needs to know the length of the exposure and decide for himself if this is an acceptable risk within the bank's credit policy.

Exposure appetite for the customer name in question should be stated, both 'existing' and 'recommended', in terms of the respective time bands. There are basically four categories of bank appetite, hedged around with whatever rationale and conditions may be deemed appropriate to the particular case: 'grow', 'maintain', 'shrink', and 'exit'.

5.4 Types of exposure and their quantification

For limit-setting and monitoring purposes, credit exposure is measured by *maximum amount* at risk. The reasons for this lie in traditional accounting practicalities, together with a prudent belief that measurement of *probability-weighted* risk (a distinctly different concept which features increasingly in the chapters hereafter) has yet to be perfected. However, with a little effort, either system of quantification is translatable into the other.

Exposures come in different shapes which need to be reduced to a single monetary measure, so that the bank can see what is at risk (i.e. could be lost in the event of default) against a particular customer/counterparty name. The categories may be tabled broadly as follows, irrespective of whether the facilities are on or off the bank's or the customer's balance sheet:

(i) *Conventional* (or 'face value') exposures – where the principal amount at risk is directly represented by a balance recorded in the books of the bank.

(ii) *Credit equivalent* exposures (CEE) – where the contract between the customer and the bank has a fluctuating market replacement value, and exposure is therefore subject to continual revaluation during its life. This category is also known in some quarters as *presettlement* exposure.

(iii) *Daylight/settlement* exposures – where total transaction duration is intra-day, or where settlement day of a transaction included initially in (i) or (ii) above entails a different, uncovered, risk in the exchange of assets – e.g. stock for cash, dollars for pounds, etc. The risk resides in the potential gap between irrevocably paying away our side of the settlement and receiving recompense from our counterparty.

(iv) *Memorandum* exposures – where the bank's reliance on the name in question is indirect: e.g. where the customer owns 50% of a joint venture company to which the bank has direct exposure without parent guarantee (perhaps taking a 'letter of comfort', for what it is worth, instead). The bank has its reasons for wishing to record the offspring's facilities on the parent's limit sheet, if only in a non-additive mode.

From the foregoing brief description it follows that types (i) and (ii) are properly added together to arrive at a total exposure, either actual or contemplated (in the setting of limits). Type (iii), settlement exposure, is different in kind, representing the transitory endgame of bargains contracted within the first two categories. Some other types of daylight exposure (e.g. loans to discount houses) are simply independent of categories (i) and (ii). When an actual exposure (of whatever kind) is logged in category (iii), it is not simultaneously located in one of the first two categories: that would be double-counting, because the relationship is mutually exclusive; not *additive* but *alternative*. To avoid such confusion, it has become customary to table daylight/settlement exposure limits separately from the aggregate of the other direct credit limits, thus:

ABC Company limits

Conventional exposure	£1 000 000
Credit equivalent exposure	£500 000
Total	£1 500 000
Daylight/settlement exposure	£100 000
(Memorandum exposure	£50 000)

The illustrative limits expressed in this format imply the following rationale:

● The bank is prepared to tolerate outstanding credit exposures up to an aggregate of £1 500 000.

- It wishes to limit the bunching of daylight deals and/or other settlements to £100 000 in any one day: maturities of deals giving rise to settlement risk must be spread accordingly.

- The ABC Company has connections with, but is not directly liable for, other exposures in the bank's books totalling £50 000.

For sanctioning purposes, the level of sign-off will be determined by the largest aggregate of direct exposure: in this case, £1 500 000. With some financial institution counterparties, pure daylight (as opposed to term) exposures may form the bulk of the business and thus the 'daylight/settlement' aggregate could be the larger of the two.

Having glanced at the basic framework of quantification and aggregation, we can now examine the categories of direct exposure in greater detail.

5.5 Conventional exposures

These include the following facilities:

- Overdrafts and loans.

- Money market placings.

- Trade finance.

- Commercial paper purchases.

- Back-up or credit enhancement lines.

- Leases.

- Stock borrowing by the bank, secured by placing cash collateral with the counterparty.

- Stock lending by the bank, secured by cash collateral deposited by the counterparty.

- Customers' liability on acceptances, guarantees, and documentary letters of credit (note that in the case of guarantees there can be double-counting, erring on the side of prudence, if another customer is the bank's primary obligor).

This list is not exhaustive. The common characteristic is a face value readily ascertainable from an account balance in the bank's books. Dealers sometimes object to measuring conventional exposure by book value (for example in short term commercial paper trading), on the ground that this reflects only a worst case rather than a realistic risk. However, that argument, which would open many other floodgates and is anticipated in the introduction to section 5.4.

5.6 Credit equivalent exposures

This category of counterparty exposure includes all the modern derivative contracts such as:

● Exchange-traded futures and options.*

● Over-the-counter (OTC) products:
  – forward exchange contracts;
  – forward rate agreements;
  – interest rate swaps, currency swaps, commodity swaps, currency options,* forward rate agreement options,* swap options,* commodity options,* etc;
  – caps, floors, collars.

(*Bought options only: there is no *credit* risk in sold options, provided the customer pays the option premium up-front.)

A description of these instruments may be found in the Glossary to this book. The risk we are considering in this chapter is the *credit risk* that they entail, namely potential loss due to default by (or collapse of) the counterparty. The loss, if any, is the cost to the bank of replacing the failed contract with a new one at current market price. That replacement cost at the time of default is equal to the present value of expected future cash flows.

The amount in question depends on the direction and extent of price or rate movements since the contract was written. At initiation, the contract is priced at current rates, with no bias of advantage to either side: its value at that point is nil (if we ignore the profit margin normally priced in and taken up-front by the bank). Later, when rates move away from that equilibrium, the contract begins to have a positive value to one party and a negative value to the other. Given sufficient volatility of rates, these positions can reverse many times during the life of a contract.

From the bank's point of view, the contract is said to be 'in the money' if it has positive value – if, on balance, the counterparty owes money to the bank; 'at the money' if its value is nil; and 'out of the money' if the bank is indebted to the counterparty. The bank incurs credit risk only in the first case, when the contract is 'in the money'.

The exposure at any one time is quantified by the mark to market value (replacement cost) of the contract. However, since the exposure has a remaining life, a historically derived volatility factor needs to be added on so as to reflect potential further adverse movements in rates. The mark to market value plus the volatility add-on (VAO) constitutes the credit equivalent exposure (CEE). The VAO, normally calculated to give 95% confidence (two standard deviations from the expected), can be geared to either full remaining life of the exposure or, say, seven days. Full remaining life implies that the contract will not be liquidated prematurely, probably because the bank's counterparty is not an active trader in the financial markets. A seven-day (intrinsically lower) VAO is sufficient to allow the bank (at a cost) to trim its exposure to an active trader in the financial markets by:

- Settling (unwinding) the contract for a price negotiated with the counterparty.

- 'Recouponing' the contract by settling the mark to market amount due and then continuing the deal at prevailing mark to market rates (thus effectively resetting the present value to nil).

- Writing offsetting swaps with the same counterparty, where netting is legally permitted (as in the UK and USA).

- Obtaining cash collateral (which may be used for netting, where legally permitted).

- Buying options or futures to hedge further deterioration.

- Assigning the contract to a third party in the market.

Such corrective manoeuvres, most of which might give offence to an ordinary commercial customer of the bank, are accepted practice between active counterparties in the financial markets.

In summary:

- The bank marks exposure limits for the CEE category within its normal credit appetite and according to the customer's perceived need of derivative facilities.

- The exposures should be revalued daily on the basis of mark to market plus a VAO geared to seven days (for active financial market counterparties) or to remaining duration (for others): MTM + VAO = CEE.

- Where exposures so valued threaten to exceed limits unacceptably, corrective actions may be set in motion to cap or reduce the exposure as outlined above.

- However, in the case of counterparties not active in the financial markets, exit is less easy and hedging or other remedies may have to be sought.

5.7 Daylight/settlement exposures

Daylight and settlement exposures are not always accurately captured by bank systems, which are geared to 'end of day' accounting conventions. For similar reasons, they have never been included in recognised capital-to-risk ratios (even the Basle formula). This 'below-the-line' and uncounted status is sometimes wrongly deemed 'soft' exposure, because it is hardly noticed and goes away quickly, alleviated in need by regulators pumping in liquidity to avoid systemic risk. The 'soft' label is a misconception, the difference between intra- and extra-day being simply a matter of degree within a continuum: exposure durations of minutes or hours, as opposed to days.

Daylight and settlement exposures belong together for control purposes: both fall essentially within (or centre on) a single calendar day, although that timescale can be stretched into 'moonlight exposure' or worse by operational delays and different currency and time zones. Banking industry practice is for foreign exchange contracts to enter the 'spot' or 'settlement' mode two days ahead of due date; and where the bank is making an overseas payment, settlement risk can be measured from the moment when the payment instruction is transmitted until countervalue is known to have been received with finality. These confusing examples merely illustrate that settlement exposure is 'one day with extensions'.

Comparatively few bank losses historically can be traced to intra-day exposure, but Chapter 2 reminds us of the classic Herstatt case.

Bank or company collapses seldom occur conveniently after banking hours: in 1991, BCCI had its operations suspended at midday, catching out some bank counterparties in the process. Bankers also lost money in settlement failures caught up in the Maxwell group débâcle.

Daylight/settlement exposures include the following types:

- Interbank clearing systems (which are heading towards 'real time' settlement solutions).

- Foreign exchange settlements.

- Daylight overdrafts and money market loans.

- Securities dealing.

- Securities borrowing and lending.

Professional opinion is divided over settlement limits for derivative contracts generally. According to one school of thought, no settlement limits need be marked in respect of derivative contracts if the net settlement value by definition coincides with the mark to market (CEE) value on settlement day. There is, it is argued, no point in marking a settlement limit unless it denotes a heightened or in some way more naked exposure occurring on settlement day. Thus *interest rate swaps* are an example of a facility where the two values would be identical and a settlement limit superfluous. *Forward exchange contracts* and *currency swaps*, on the other hand, have a net replacement value during their life, but will have a much larger settlement value because gross amounts of the two currencies concerned are actually to be exchanged on settlement day: thus a settlement limit is necessary.

That piecemeal approach may be technically correct but the pragmatic counter-argument is that it omits to measure a significant part of the contract settlements that can fall due on any settlement day: namely most of the derivative maturities, including interest rate swaps which are the largest element. Thus, regardless of any ostensible limit marked for daylight/settlement exposure in a counterparty name, there will not in fact be comprehensive control over the bunching of settlements on any one day.

In the absence of any industry consensus or regulatory requirement, each bank will have to decide which measurement system best suits its control needs. At any rate, a bank that takes daylight/settlement risk seriously will want to:

- Inculcate a general awareness so that such potential exposures are always identified and properly sanctioned.

- Monitor the exposures accurately using real time systems that track and reconcile payments and receipts.

- Eliminate unnecessary exposures by active control and netting (within the bank and externally) where possible.

- Charge for the exposure wherever feasible.

- Take daylight/settlement exposure into account in managing the credit portfolio as a whole.

Most banks have yet to do full justice to these precepts.

5.8 Netting

With the expansion of the financial markets, notably in foreign exchange and derivative products, the quest for *netting* of single product obligations between active counterparties has assumed prime importance as a means of condensing exposures and thus utilising capacity to maximum economic advantage. English law permits netting (or set-off) for all mutual dealings, and indeed demands it under the Insolvency Act of 1986. US law provides statute support, depending on the agreements and entities involved. In France and Belgium, where the law traditionally favours the *pari passu* treatment of creditors (and opens the way to 'cherry-picking'), recent law changes protect the main types of financial institution in the interests of avoiding systemic risk. Most major jurisdictions have now shed their former hostility to netting.

Netting reduces counterparty risk and therefore, logically, the need for capital. The 1988 Basle Capital Accord (with subsequent amendments) recognises this in respect of most basic forms of netting, provided that:

- The practice is legally valid within all relevant jurisdictions, and changes in the law will be properly monitored.

- The netting contract contains prescribed provisions for the event of the counterparty's default, bankruptcy or liquidation.

The Bank of England has added that UK banks may not obtain relief

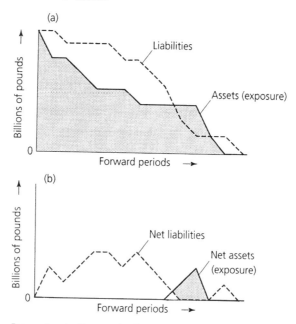

For most maturities, netting has reduced our exposure to nil.

5.3 Effect of bilateral netting with a counterparty bank: (a) before netting; (b) after netting.

from gross capital requirements unless they adopt net limits for internal risk management purposes.

Netting may be bilateral between counterparties (as illustrated in Fig. 5.3), or multilateral through a central clearing house. The difference in advantage may be seen from one observation taken in a UK bank on a typical day. A pool of 80 bank counterparties was considered and 331 deals which involved payment or receipt of a US dollar amount were identified. Counterparties with 5 or more deals were assumed to be natural candidates for bilateral netting agreements: there were 23 such names, accounting for 188 nettable deals. The possible reduction in number of settlements through bilateral netting was therefore 165 (i.e. 188 − 23), leaving a total of 166 settlements still to be made: approximately half the original 331 settlements. However, assuming that all 80 counterparties were members of a central clearing house, our bank's number of settlements would have been reduced from the original 331 to a *single* net payment to or from the clearing house. The monetary exposure would of course undergo a similar drastic reduction.

That example relates to bilateral or multilateral netting of settlement cash flows, but the same principles are applicable to replacement values (CEE exposures).

The two most common forms of netting are *novation* and *close-out*. Netting by novation offsets all deals having a common value (i.e. settlement) date, either (a) by matched currency pairs or (b) by cash flows irrespective of currencies. Either method, (a) or (b), achieves a netting of both replacement value exposures and settlement exposures per value date for the contracts concerned.

Close-out netting allows all existing contracts with future value dates to be marked to market, converted to a net figure in a single currency for each value date, discounted back to present value, and netted to produce a single amount either payable or receivable. The close-out 'single payment' assessment is not only the ultimate reduction of exposure within a product range, but is also consistent with the mechanics of insolvency legislation in those jurisdictions that are favourable to netting.

A further refinement would be to add on a volatility factor (VAO) as required in the CEE computation described earlier. However, this introduces a conceptual difficulty in as much as VAOs are normally tailored to individual contracts on a basis that is antithetical to netting. The bank therefore needs to adjust the methodology so as to project volatility consistent with a net close-out position.

Another problem is the phenomenon of *roll-off*, where the execution of individual lumpy settlements on due date can entail stepped changes in close-out exposure. The prospect of such volatility occurring in the risk measurement needs to be continually monitored from the perspective of a few days in advance, so that anticipatory smoothing can be put in place.

Once close-out netting is agreed as standard practice between the counterparties, the door is also open for *cash collateralisation* to be adopted as a further means of mitigating exposure. At recognised trigger points, the bank may receive or pay the required amount of cash collateral, depending on whether the close-out position is 'in' or 'out of' the money. The placement of cash with the bank's counterparty represents a credit exposure in itself only to the extent that it is not covered at any time by countervalue to set off against it; otherwise it is simply part of the netting balance.

At time of writing, a number of multibank and multi-institution co-operative ventures, well established or in course of development, point the way forward for the industry:

- FXNET, an interbank bilateral netting system serviced by Quotron Systems.

- ACCORD, a subsystem of SWIFT (Society for Worldwide Interbank Financial Telecommunication) with a bilateral netting facility known as Netting Advisory Service.

- IFEMA (International Foreign Exchange Master Agreement), a bilateral netting agreement set up by the British Bankers Association, the Foreign Exchange Committee of New York, and the Market Practices Committee in Tokyo; available for use by corporates as well as banks.

- ISDA (International Swaps and Derivatives Association), whose master agreements document the majority of derivatives trades.

- ECHO (Exchange Clearing House Limited), a multibank owned clearing house for the multilateral netting of foreign exchange contracts between banks.

- MULTINET, the North American equivalent of ECHO.

- The Group of 20 (G20), an association of international banks which between them handle some 30% of global foreign exchange trading. G20 plans to establish a clearing house featuring instantaneous settlement linked to national payment systems such as CHAPS in the UK and Fedwire in the USA.

Thus far the main thrust has been to extend the scope of netting within single product types and single jurisdictions. Cross-product netting, whilst in accord with insolvency rules in some jurisdictions, is not encouraged for the time being within the Basle capital requirement reliefs. Cross-border netting is allowed in principle, but encounters practical problems over differing national legal codes and market practices.

The development of netting is making a vital contribution to the management of counterparty credit risk, and hence of systemic risk, in the foreign exchange and derivatives markets in particular.

5.9 Lenders and environmental liability

With the parallel advance of scientific knowledge and public expectation, reinforced by comprehensive legislation, environmental liability has become a factor which the business world and its financiers have to take into account. Population growth and industrial activity have inevitably caused contamination of land and pollution of water and air in many countries. A 1993 estimate by the Confederation of British Industry put the cost of minimal treatment of contaminated land in England at about £20 billion: thorough rehabilitation would cost up to double that figure. In the United States, the US General Accounting Office suggested a 30-year clean-up cost to the government's Environmental Protection Agency and the private sector of $300 billion (1990 value), with further liabilities of $200 billion facing the defence and energy departments.

Debates on environmental damage centre on how much is acceptable, what preventive and remedial actions need to be taken, and who is responsible and liable. The principle that 'the polluter pays' is universally accepted, but recent years have seen a move to widen the net so as to include other deemed contributors. A bank therefore has to consider potential effects both on the financial condition of its business customers and on itself as lender to those customers. Broadly speaking, the customer's strength (and credit-worthiness) may be sapped by

- The cost of complying with legislation.

- Fines for non-compliance.

- The cost of decontaminating a polluted site.

- Reduction in land values due to contamination.

- Contingent liabilities for environmental warranties given on sale of land.

Under English law, the bank itself may be drawn into a position of direct liability in any of the foregoing respects if it is deemed to 'own', 'operate', or 'be responsible for' a site or facility. This can come about through taking possession of land held as security, or even through being adjudged to have 'participated' in the management of a borrowing company. The position in most of continental Europe is somewhat safer, in that realisation of property security is exercised by the courts rather than by the lender taking possession.

In the USA, the pioneering legislation that has cost bankers dear is the Comprehensive Environmental Response, Compensation and Liability Act 1980 (CERCLA, also known as 'Superfund'). The 1990 case of *United States* v *Fleet Factors Corporation* established an interpretation whereby a lender may incur environmental liability merely by being in a position to influence the environmental business decisions of an enterprise. A subsequent attempt by the Environmental Protection Agency to roll back that precedent by issuing its own clarifying rule was challenged and defeated in a Federal Appeals Court.

American public policy has therefore led to joint and several liability and the pursuit not only of the polluter but also of its friends and associates with the deepest pockets, notably the banks. The potential cost to a bank can far exceed the simple credit exposure. One bank in Montana with a loan exposure of $27 500 (incurred before CERCLA was enacted) was found liable for a real estate clean-up totalling $5 million. Another bank acting as trustee of a land trust, for a fee of $80, was pursued through the courts for clean-up costs of $80 million. Not surprisingly, more money has so far been expended on disputation and making the legal profession rich than on restoring the environment.

Of further significance is a 1991 survey by the American Bankers Association which disclosed that 62.5% of respondents now rejected some loan applications because of possible environmental liability; whilst 45.8% had discontinued lending to vulnerable sectors such as service stations, chemical industries, dry cleaners, and agribusiness. Thus one unintended consequence of the legislative thrust is a 'chilling effect' on availability of credit for companies that most need it to help clean up their own environment. Another is that small businesses generally find it harder to obtain bank finance, given that they have little to offer as security other than land and buildings.

In the United Kingdom, modern integrated regulation arrived with the Environmental Protection Act 1990 and the Water Resources Act 1991. The legal framework provides for a licensing system covering industrial processes, waste, water and air quality. Powers are given to Her Majesty's Inspectorate of Pollution, the Waste Regulation Authorities, and the National Rivers Authority which could result in enforcement of ground remediation, investment in improved pollution control techniques, the levying of fines, or imprisonment.

Liability falls on one or more of three categories, depending on the circumstances: 'the owner', 'the occupier', and 'the person responsible'. The bank may possibly stray into these categories by:

●   Foreclosing on property security and taking possession.

- Being 'the owner' in a leasing deal.

- Receiving assigned rents.

- Otherwise being seen to exercise direct control over a customer's environmental decision-making.

At time of writing, an Environment Act 1995, aimed at further consolidating and refining UK law, has received the Royal Assent but has yet to be implemented owing to consultative delays. A single new Environment Agency is to replace the existing three agencies. The Act will be supplemented by statutory guidance for the benefit of local authorities and other parties who have to make it work. It remains to be seen whether the banks can finally secure an unambiguous acknowledgement that the borrower/lender relationship does not entail any transmission of environmental liability from the former to the latter. Neither the banks nor their customers can afford a 'joint and several' future in which unlimited contingent liabilities for environmental damage are loaded on to the lenders, with devastating effect on their capital ratios, their commercial viability, and their willingness to support industry.

Public opinion, with no commercial stake in the outcome, may tend to regard banks as utilities with deep pockets, available to underwrite society's bills and to intermediate as environmental policemen or moral vigilantes. In reality, these are not tenable roles for private sector lenders.

Environmental regulation continues to evolve, with European Union action programmes also expected to exert increasing influence following the Maastricht Treaty of 1992. Meanwhile lenders should equip themselves with expert legal and professional advisers (both internal and external), raise the consciousness of their staff, and follow standardised procedures to take due account of environmental issues particularly in respect of:

- Vetting advances applications and reviews.

- Calling for environmental audits where appropriate.

- Taking land as security.

- Valuing or revaluing land held as security.

- Enforcing security, receiverships and liquidations.

Environmental concerns will undoubtedly present a major challenge to the banking industry in the years to come.

5.10 Confidentiality and conflicts of interest

This is an area where increasing regulation has been spurred by the growth of private enterprise and public sophistication. The development of investment banking has added to the complexity in the banking sector. The general rules of banking conduct will be much the same the world over and are set out below. Whilst each country will have its own particular legal, regulatory, and operational framework, the references hereunder are to English law.

At its simplest, a banker's fiduciary *duty of secrecy* regarding his customer's affairs is familiar ground, dominated in England by the legal precedent of *Tournier* v *National Provincial* (1924). In the nature of the relationship, a bank is privy to all manner of financial and trade secrets which a business customer does not want disclosed to its competitors (who may be with the same bank) or to the world at large. Here it should suffice for the bank's conduct to be guided by professional integrity and thorough staff training.

The next step up, however, introduces *conflicts of interest*, which call for the installation of 'Chinese walls' to restrict internal communications within the bank. For example, two customers may be in a contractual dispute with one another, and the bank will want to be in a position to demonstrate that it is not favouring either. Similar considerations apply where one customer is bidding to take over another. Beyond customer relations, the danger is that of being involved (perhaps unwittingly) in the crime of insider dealing – profiting, or helping privileged others to profit, from inside knowledge unavailable to the market as a whole. English law on insider dealing is governed by the Criminal Justice Act 1993.

A further layer of complexity is added if the bank has a corporate finance arm which is simultaneously advising either the offeror or the offeree on strategy towards the takeover bid. There may also be investment management operations advising other customers to buy and sell securities, or taking such investment decisions on the bank's own behalf. In all of these cases the bank has, or may be seen to have, a vested interest in the outcome which conflicts with its legal duties of secrecy and impartiality. The only practical safeguard is to establish permanent Chinese walls between the commercial (normally lending) bank, the corporate advisory arm, the investment managers, and the securities traders.

If the bank has credit relationships with counterparties who are market competitors of its own investment banking operation, they will constitute another reason for such a Chinese wall.

A conflict of interest can arise where the bank is lending to one customer against the security of shares in a publicly quoted company, and is also providing facilities to that company itself (commonly referred to as a 'pig on pork' situation). Often the first customer will be a director of the second, with the added complication of restrictions on directors' dealings in the shares (in the United Kingdom, covered by the Model Code of the London Stock Exchange). The conflict would occur if the bank should need to consider realising its share security.

The bank's position may be similarly compromised if it lends to a company of which it is part owner (the very situation in which the bank's lending role may be its chief commendation as a partner).

These are merely examples and not an exhaustive list. The guiding principle is that wherever there is price-sensitive information on a customer, or a conflict of interest within the bank, there is probably a need for some sort of Chinese wall.

So what is a Chinese wall? It is simply a notional barrier which prevents information known to persons in one part of the business being available (directly or indirectly) to those involved in another part of the business. In the UK, its detailed operations will conform to the requirements of the Financial Services Act 1986 as well as the rules of the Securities and Futures Authority, the Investment Management Regulatory Organisation, and the Personal Investment Authority.

Nominated bank officials are segregated in a team on either side of the wall, and they make their business decisions without knowledge of (or deference to) what is happening on the other side. The wall may be *ad hoc*, between two customer relationships, or *generic*, between conflicting interests in different arms of the bank. The teams (and therefore the wall) must go as high in the bank as is necessary to accommodate the sanctioning of advances on either side: this includes top executives and credit committee membership. The system calls for careful team selection, the husbanding of reserves, and the maintenance of precise and up to date records on who is allowed to see what.

Tight control must be exercised so that files, papers, and communications (whether oral, paper-based or electronic) do not stray to the wrong side of the wall. Code names are substituted for customer names as an extra precaution in case lists have to be circulated (e.g. to the bank's board). A central register should be maintained by an impartial unit, recording in date order each Chinese wall erected, with full particulars and names of staff involved on each side. This can be exhibited as evidence in the event of a subsequent inquiry by the Department of Trade and Industry, the Stock Exchange or the Takeover Panel.

Such an intricate system does not design or run itself, and some senior official in the credit function must be appointed to manage it day to day. In addition, a large bank will have a compliance officer who can arbitrate or advise on the finer points of law, regulation, and public image. From time to time, external law firms will also be consulted.

It is a seeming paradox that so much bureaucracy should be generated by the competitive and regulatory needs of modern capitalism. However, the driving factors include the expansion of banking into increasingly conflicting businesses, and a more demanding attitude as a quid pro quo on the part of customers, markets, and public opinion.

5.11 Summary

This chapter has outlined a conceptual and organisational framework for dealing with credit risk in the modern era. Credit culture shapes and pervades that framework and the decision-making within it.

Exposure is the most accurate possible quantification of maximum potential loss. It comes in different forms, some of which (derivatives) have to be translated into credit equivalent exposure values. Exposure should be neither understated by bogus 'risking' nor exaggerated by false aggregation.

Important developments are taking place in the areas of daylight/settlement risk and netting.

Banks must respond to new social and legal challenges posed by environmental liability and market-related conflicts of interest. It is beyond the scope of this book to catalogue the considerable differences in applicable law from country to country.

Chapters 6 and 7 will cover the issues and techniques of credit portfolio management.

CHAPTER SIX

Credit risk: analysing the portfolio

This chapter examines:

- Portfolio theory and diversification of risk.

- Sectoral analysis.

- Exposure ceilings.

- The key role of credit grading.

- Country grading for transfer risk.

- Expert systems.

- Credit scoring.

- Other artificial intelligence.

Portfolio theory applies equally to collections of credit risks and to equity and other investments. This chapter addresses credit risks, which traditionally are the core assets in a commercial banking business. History tells us that effective portfolio management must be one of the half-dozen most important disciplines for managing banking risks, a message that is only just beginning to be understood in the industry.

The purpose of having a portfolio of assets, instead of a single asset, is to reduce risk through diversification without to the same

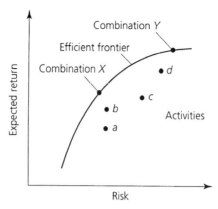

6.1 The efficient frontier.

extent sacrificing rate of return. An 'efficient' portfolio achieves a specified rate of return with the minimum possible risk *or* a specified level of risk for the maximum possible rate of return. This optimal trade-off of risk and return is sought by strategic positioning in the meeting ground known as the 'efficient frontier' (see Fig. 6.1).

Banks which have been in business for any length of time have gathered a portfolio of some kind: the question is whether they have the knowledge, the skills and the determination to manage it, as opposed to letting it manage them. Many banks, if they are honest, would admit that they have some way to go to prove themselves equal to the task.

The principle which underlies portfolio management is *diversification of risk*. In banking, this is illuminated by a number of analytical techniques such as: sectoral analysis, credit grading, country grading, expert systems, credit scoring and other artificial intelligence applications.

6.1 Diversification of risk

The use of diversification to reduce risk is widely understood, even by the large majority of people with no appreciation of its mathematical ramifications. Conventional wisdom concerning 'eggs in baskets', 'spreading the risk', 'strings to one's bow', and even 'safety in numbers' bears witness to the popular acceptance of this approach, which after all is confirmed by common experience.

Likewise banking lore and supervisory practice recognise the dangers of excessive industry concentrations and overexposure to individual borrowers. In short, there is nothing much wrong with the dictates of experience and good sense, as far as they go, when they can get a hearing; but modern professional portfolio management calls for more rigorous codification, in statistical terms first laid down by Harry Markowitz in 1952.

The starting point is *correlation*, which measures the linkage between the direction of changes in one variable (e.g. a component of a portfolio) and that of changes in another: it does not, however, refer to the *extent* of either changes or what causes them. If one variable always moves by a set proportion (no matter what) of the change in the other, and in the same direction, there is a perfect positive correlation denoted as '+1'. A similarly linked movement, but always in the opposite direction to that of the other variable, is a perfect negative correlation rendered as '–1'. In between the two extremes there are lesser degrees of positive or negative correlation, bisected by zero (no relationship at all).

Positive correlations are common, if only by linkage to the national and international economy. Negative correlations are harder to find (let alone *perfect* negative correlations), but might be exemplified by the fluctuating and somewhat reciprocal business fortunes of airlines, ferry companies, railways and buses. A zero correlation is encapsulated in the public mind as 'chalk and cheese'.

For risk-reducing purposes, a strong positive correlation is unhelpful, as the two variables under scrutiny would behave similarly, like two baskets of eggs crashing to the ground simultaneously (or two property development borrowers defaulting together). A weak positive correlation starts to supply the desired effect of reducing the risk, and the benefit improves as we move through zero to the negative end of the scale. Thus, to the extent that movements in variables differ or offset one another for whatever reason, including randomness, it is possible to achieve a portfolio in which the overall risk is lower than that of any of the assets individually; even, conceivably, to attain a theoretically 'riskless' profile of investments.

This remote possibility of hedging investments through perfectly negative correlations exists because a shortfall here can be offset by a surplus there. That is not true of credit risk itself, since unexpected defaults cannot be compensated by other obligors paying more than what is legally due. Here again we see the distinction drawn in Chapter 2, between two-way price risks and one-way credit risks.

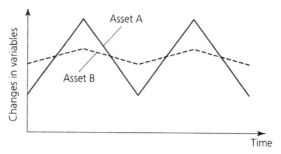

6.2 Positive correlation.

In practice, however, most assets in a credit portfolio will tend to be positively correlated to some degree, as illustrated in Fig. 6.2.

The correlation gives us only a limited picture of the risk consequences of combining assets in a portfolio. To understand their interaction more fully, we need to combine their correlation with the risk profile measured by their *standard deviations*, thus:

$c \times sA \times sB = cov$

where c = correlation, s = standard deviation, A and B are the assets, and cov = covariance.

The term just introduced, covariance, goes beyond correlation in reflecting not only linkage of movement but volatility of each asset around its arithmetic mean. For simplicity's sake, the example above is confined to a portfolio of only two assets. Once the number of assets exceeds three, the number of covariances increasingly outstrips the number of individual asset variances: thus a four-asset

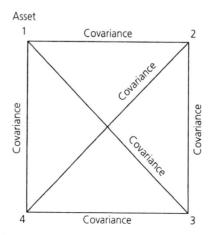

6.3 Covariances in a four-asset portfolio.

portfolio has four variances and six covariances (see Fig. 6.3), whilst a six-asset portfolio has six variances and fifteen covariances. This makes for complexity of calculation, but the basic principles are the same throughout.

One further ingredient is needed to determine the effect of combining these risks in a portfolio: their respective proportionate *weights* (granted that measurement, by present value or other means, can present a theoretical problem). Weight corresponds to degree of 'lumpiness' in vulgar parlance, and too much of it is not normally a good thing for risk limitation. Modern bankers prefer a 'granular' consistency to their portfolio.

Perhaps the most common application of these techniques is to ascertain the proportionate contribution of an item (or class of items) to the loan loss uncertainty of the portfolio as a whole. Components of a portfolio should be risk-assessed by their influence on the portfolio, not by their own individual standard deviations. This is a statement with far-reaching consequences, refuting as it does the notion that each division of a banking group can behave or be judged as if it were an independent business. Here is a case where common sense would do well to pay more attention to mathematics.

As this is a general introduction to the subject and not an instruction manual or a mathematical treatise, we can content ourselves with one more equation answering the question of how an individual asset affects the overall risk of the portfolio (as measured by its variance). The following formula will serve to illustrate simple loan loss:

$$wA \times c \times \frac{sLA}{sLP} = \text{Proportionate contribution to portfolio variance}$$

where w = weight proportionate to portfolio, c = correlation, s = standard deviation, L = expected loan loss, A = specific asset, and P = portfolio.

If the asset in question weighs in at 3% of the portfolio size, if the correlation is 0.5, and if its standard deviation of loss is 0.4% compared with the portfolio's standard deviation of 0.3%, the calculation works out as follows:

$$0.03 \times 0.5 \times \frac{0.4}{0.3}$$

$$= 0.02 \text{ (i.e. 2\%)}$$

Thus our illustrative 3% contribution to the size of the portfolio represents only 2% of its overall loan loss risk.

This example has addressed *gross* loan loss experience, which bankers will probably find the most accessible and useful building block in the early stages of portfolio analysis. Strictly speaking, however, portfolio risk calculations should address total net return – not just losses but offsetting revenues as well. First, this gives a more complete picture on which to base decisions. Secondly, it is only to the extent that losses exceed related income (mainly interest) that bank solvency is threatened. The more comprehensive formula, also discussed in Chapter 3, would be:

$$wA \times c \times \frac{sRA}{sRP} = \text{Proportionate contribution to portfolio variance}$$

where wA = weight of specific asset (size proportionate to portfolio), c = correlation, sRA = standard deviation of return on specific asset (including net losses), and sRP = standard deviation of return on portfolio.

Having established the theoretical foundations of portfolio management, we can now take a look at the analytical tools which translate the theory into practice.

6.2 Industry sector analysis

Before the advent of credit grading and scoring (covered later in this chapter) the scope for portfolio management was largely in the sectoral dimension. Banks sought diversification through geographical and sectoral spread, and through 'granular' as opposed to 'lumpy' consistency of book (to mix a metaphor).

Sectoral analysis always made eminent sense, but was largely shaped by regulatory reporting requirements. In the UK, the Bank of England established its Standard Industrial Classification (SIC) Codes, comprising 39 categories of borrower. To the layman, this may sound like a generous amount of slicing, yet it resulted in:

- A Code 251 which combines agriculture of all kinds, forestry and fishing.

- A Code 393 covering all manufacture of food products, beverages and tobacco.

- A Code 397 combining manufacture of wood products with publishing and printing.

● A Code 381 which groups aerospace with shipbuilding, motor cycles, handcarts, trolleys and horse-drawn trailers, pedal cycles and invalid carriages, amongst other things.

Whatever macroeconomic purpose these broad classifications may have served at governmental level, they are far too imprecise for discriminating portfolio management. Revision/expansion is under discussion between the banks and the regulatory authority, and at least one bank has designed a new template multiplying the number of classifications almost tenfold. Provided that due care is exercised, the increased precision of definitions should ensure that there is actually less misclassification than of old.

Given a comprehensive and accurate information system, a bank can manage its sectoral exposures with proper selectivity and start to measure correlations between different sectors in its portfolio. The most obvious positive correlations reflect industry affinities (such as manufacture of vehicles and of vehicle components), but regional dependencies should not be overlooked (for example, the linked fate of coal mining and of retail trades in the neighbouring community). Despite their upbeat name, 'positive' correlations, remember, impede diversification of risk. An in-house economics department can make a major contribution here, in analysing the book if need be, in conducting continual surveys of trends in industry and the economy, and in identifying risk factors and scenarios for stress-testing. Credit policies will take their cue from these findings.

Table 6.1 illustrates the beginnings of such a sectoral analysis, based on the old SIC Codes. It is of interest to compare the half-yearly standard deviation of the portfolio with the weighted average of the individual industry standard deviations: 0.15% versus 0.29%. This demonstrates once again the risk-reducing effect of diversification. Similarly, the portfolio peak write-off of 0.67% compares with a weighted average of 1.23% for the individual sectors. The sensitivity column on the right-hand side gives an indication of particular sectors where extreme risks may be realised in generally adverse economic conditions. Times change, of course, and such judgements must not be fossilised in terms only of past outcomes.

In the light of such internal analysis, the bank should specify its own exposure appetite and prudential limits (short, medium and long term) for each sector or grouping of sectors. As far as possible, the sectoral goals should be established and reviewed together

Table 6.1 Industry sector risk analysis (one large bank: December 1976 to June 1990, half-yearly data)

Industry	Write-offs as % advances				
	Weight	Mean	High	Standard deviation	Sensitivity factor[1]
	%	%	%	%	
Agriculture, Forestry, Fishing	11.4	0.11	0.34	0.14	0.15
Mining and Quarrying	0.7	0.32	5.50	1.03	1.79
Food, Drink and Tobacco	3.7	0.09	0.38	0.08	0.27
Chemicals and Allied Trades	2.3	0.15	1.15	0.26	0.15
Metal Manufactures	1.1	0.11	0.62	0.15	0.22
Electrical & Electronic Engineering	3.1	0.24	0.75	0.22	0.81
Other Engineering	7.0	0.31	1.43	0.35	1.27
Shipbuilding etc	0.5	0.70	3.90	1.08	3.21
Motor Vehicles	1.4	0.20	2.19	0.42	1.57
Textiles etc	3.2	0.12	1.78	0.43	1.76
Other Manufacturing	6.0	0.30	1.22	0.28	1.23
Construction	9.8	0.42	1.36	0.29	1.38
Property Companies	10.0	0.53	3.65	0.78	2.29
Transport and Communication	2.9	0.40	1.30	0.45	1.02
Retail Distribution	10.0	0.38	1.05	0.27	1.06
Other Distribution	7.6	0.24	0.59	0.17	0.63
Other Industries	19.5	0.31	0.59	0.16	0.80
Total	**100.0**	**0.30**	**0.67**	**0.15**	**1.00**
Weighted Average		**0.30**	**1.23**	**0.29**	**1.03**

[1]Change in write-off % for a 1% change in total write-off %.

(Source: Professor H B Rose, London Business School)

rather than in isolation from one another. Limits and targets will be set with an eye to:

- Optimising risk/reward.

- Avoiding undue concentrations of risk.

- Diversifying away from strong positive correlations towards weaker ones or zero correlations.

- Seeking natural hedges through negative correlations.

With the help of techniques now available, the benchmark for each sector should ideally be set by the amount of economic capital that the bank is prepared to allocate in that area – i.e. to risk losing in the period concerned. This measure ties in credit grade (see section

6.5) as well as industrial classification. A capital rationing approach of that kind should prevent a repetition of the catastrophic losses incurred on property-related lending in many countries in the past decade.

Once agreed, prudential limits should be strictly monitored and respected, not breached or expanded *ad hoc*. There is no point in going to great trouble and expense to install the machinery of modern portfolio management if the precepts that drive it are then going to be flouted; an observation which could serve as a watchword for this chapter as a whole.

6.3 Exposure ceilings on individual names

As mentioned in Chapter 2, the Johnson Matthey Bankers collapse of 1984 featured two large exposures equal to 76% and 34% respectively of JMB's own capital. These were seen to breach a canon of prudent banking and caused the Bank of England to introduce new reporting requirements for all UK registered banks.

By way of a monthly return, each bank is required to report its 20 largest exposures and any other exposure which exceeds 10% of its capital base. No individual exposure amounting to more than 25% of the bank's capital base is permitted, and the total of all cases above the 10% reporting threshold must not exceed 800% of the bank's capital base. Notable exemptions from these rules are exposures to other banks (under one year) and to overseas governments (any term).

Aimed at limiting concentrations of name risk, these regulations are pragmatically sensible. A prudent bank would probably not wish to exceed the 25% barrier for any one counterparty, would think twice about exceeding 10%, and would ration its use of the *carte blanche* given for other banks and overseas governments. Furthermore, a credit grading system affords the opportunity of setting an absolute appetite limit, grade by grade, for any one name. Although this is scarcely scientific in terms of expected default rates, portfolio correlations and risk contribution, the applied science itself is fallible and a gut feel of 'enough is enough' has humanly much to commend it.

The obvious alternative to limitation by exposure is limitation by amount of economic capital allocated to any one name. This automatically takes credit grade into account (see section 6.5).

6.4 Credit grading: evolution

Now recognised as an engine of change in the credit process, and perhaps the single most powerful facilitator of modern portfolio management, credit grading appears to have had its modest origins in regulatory and auditing practices developed in North America.

The prototype may well have been the 'criticised assets' model employed for many years by the Office of the Comptroller of the Currency in the USA. This divides a bank's weaker credits into a deteriorating progression summarised as follows:

Other assets especially mentioned	Currently protected but potentially weak.
Substandard	Actual weakness that jeopardises liquidation of the debt.
Doubtful	Pending further developments, strong possibility of partial loss.
Loss	Considered uncollectible.

Assets which are not criticised are simply deemed 'pass' credits. The purpose of the OCC system is to draw attention to vulnerable advances requiring remedial treatment or write-off, and to assess the comparative quality and trend of the book as a whole (including grade migrations in between bank examinations). Legitimately, the approach is that of the 'watch-list', focusing on distress rather than success. Accepting these precautionary criteria, banks followed suit and modelled their own internal grading systems accordingly for self-protection.

During the 1960s, not dissimilar thinking in one Canadian bank led to an internal audit practice of grading the lending book in tiers from A to D at each branch inspection. 'A', however, was a strong grade and not the top of the watch-list.

Another of the early models was *country* (or *transfer risk*) grading, which became increasingly common practice in large commercial banks from the 1970s onwards. Perhaps because it addressed a separate issue, and was administered by specialist 'international' departments, this tended to be a free-standing system and did not act as much of a catalyst for change on the domestic lending front. Country grading is discussed later in this chapter.

Whilst having an eye to likelihood of loss, the early credit grading evaluations of all kinds were word-based and essentially subjective, without statistical validity. This is also true of most of the increasingly elaborate internal systems which banks developed during the 1970s and 1980s, as they realised the necessity for fuller analysis and formulation of policies at the stronger as well as the weaker end of the book. Statistical science was thought to apply, if at all, only to credit scoring of consumer lending.

Driven by competitive pressures and the search for profits, and under recurring criticism for their bad debt records, banks wanted to manage their portfolios better, whilst lacking some of the tools to do the job. To this day, systems exist with up to 10 'descriptive' credit grades ('superior', 'average', etc), but without intrinsic numerate linkage to the principles of risk and reward, expected loss, equity capital allocation, hurdle rates of return and differential pricing as outlined in Chapter 1. In the absence of such linkage, 'market forces' (consisting largely of volume-driven competition for its own sake) have filled the philosophical void on appetite and pricing.

The definitive conceptual breakthrough (though it took some time to be recognised as such) came from the rating agencies in the USA, notably Moody's and Standard & Poor's, with their credit ratings which specifically addressed the probability of default on public corporate and institutional debt. As these rating systems gained growing acceptance in national and international markets, banks, academics and financial consultants began to cross-compare, to develop and to integrate the statistically-based theories of credit grading, portfolio management, and risk and reward that hold sway today.

If banks (and their regulators) have been slow to come to terms with statistical techniques, this reflects the traditional view of lending (indeed, banking) as a craft rather than a science. Somewhat of a sheltered profession until recently, banking has not been in the habit of recruiting significant numbers of mathematicians and statisticians to supplement its 'liberal arts' ethos.

6.5 Credit grading: today's model

Grafting a statistically coherent set of cut-off points on to an existing description-based grading system is a contortion scarcely worth the effort, and for practical purposes it is advisable to start again. Besides, we as bankers have learned to expect that sooner or later words and figures will differ, and what do we do then? It is better to dispense with descriptive words for grades, and concentrate instead on statistical prediction of behaviour in the form of *expected default rate* (EDR).

A bank creating a modern grading system from scratch will need to concentrate first on its corporate and institutional credit portfolio, working downwards from the largest exposures to the medium or small businesses. In a 'universal' type of lending book, there will come a point of diminution where comprehensive and reliable financial data are less readily available, or where the predictive criteria found valid for the large corporates start to apply less well, or simply where different handling arrangements demand a different approach within the bank. Where that cut-off point lies (turnover below £x million, facilities of less than £y million or whatever) is something that each bank will have to discover for itself. Below the upper business slice, banks generally are experimenting with 'expert systems' technology capable of generating automated grades tailored for the middle market, and with credit scoring for small business and personal sector sanctioning; we shall touch on these methods later.

The first task in the corporate and institutional grading exercise is to examine representative samples of successful and 'failed' credit cases, probably numbering in the thousands for a large bank and going back over a history of five to ten years if practicable. Intensive examination of customers' financial and other data available prior to success/failure will help to identify (with hindsight) what factors were predictive of repayment and of default respectively. The answers will differ in relativity for each bank and for each customer community, but by rigorous testing and regression analysis it is possible to narrow the field from hundreds of characteristics to a handful of quantitative indicators such as:

- Balance sheet strength, by size and by specified ratios.

- Profitability.

- Reserves.

- Capital gearing.

- Debt service.

By the use of scoring matrices, a borrowing customer can be rated against each of these criteria and thence in total. Some lesser scope may also be given to qualitative factors like:

● Management.

● Financial reporting.

● Industry standing of company.

● Industry sector prospects.

Whilst these are important considerations in the credit process, their main sphere of influence lies outside credit grading but rather in sanctioning and in sectoral management of the portfolio.

Once each borrowing customer in the book has been scored, we can calibrate the results to produce the grade stratification that is most relevant to the bank. Five grades may be too few for sensitive portfolio management, whilst more than ten may be an over-complication. Ten is, in fact, the most popular choice, with grade 1 consisting of the strongest (highest scoring) names whose EDR over the next 12 months is considered minimal. With careful calibration, the top grades can be given rough equivalence to rating agency grades for publicly issued debt. As we descend the scale, the EDRs increase exponentially, and the bottom four grades constitute degrees of 'watch-listing' similar to the OCC categories. Table 6.2 depicts a hypothetical grading model illustrating these principles.

As explained in Chapter 1, the expected default rate is an arithmetic mean standing for the credit cycle as a whole, and is surrounded by a field of uncertainty or variability comprising

Table 6.2 Hypothetical credit grading model

Grade	Range of expected default rates, next 12 months %	Equivalent long term debt ratings	
		Moody's	Standard & Poor's
1	0.0–0.15	A3 and above	A– and above
2	>0.15–0.3	Baa1/Baa2	BBB+/BBB
3	>0.3–0.6	Baa2/Baa3	BBB/BBB–
4	>0.6–1.2	Ba1/Ba2	BB+/BB/BB–
5	>1.2–2.5	Ba3	B+/B
6	>2.5–5	B1	B–
7	>5–10	B2/B3	CCC
8	>10	Caa/Ca/C	CC/C
9	Provision raised	—	—
10	Partial/total write-off	—	—

unexpected default rates (and therefore risk). Expected default rate is the building block from which we can go on to calculate *expected loss*, an actuarial cost of doing the business. Expected loss consists of expected default rate × anticipated exposure × severity.

Anticipated exposure (at time of default) takes into account the limits marked for the customer, the likely drawdown as the position deteriorates, versus the bank's compensating efforts to manage down the position.

Severity estimates the offsetting value of security realisations and other recoveries, less any related costs. It is worth noting here that security is an input only into severity (what we stand to lose) and not into grade (probability of default). Whilst that distinction is strictly correct, there could be some undervaluation of behavioural side-effects, in that (for instance) a sole proprietor who has mortgaged his house in support of the business is less likely to default in the first place.

Be that as it may, history shows that realisation of security in distressed circumstances typically yields much less than its formal valuation even a short while before the default. Severity calculations must therefore include firmly realistic (and thus sizeable) discounts reflecting the bank's own experience with different types of security other than cash. This merely points up the folly of 'pawnbroking' in banking (lending in undue reliance on security), one of the prime lessons from the 1980s lending boom.

Credit grading and severity estimation can be done together for each counterparty name, and reviewed regularly thereafter. The account officer is probably best entrusted with this formality, although most banks will want to build in some sort of double-check via normal sanctioning, supervision and auditing routines. The process calls for a good deal of participative devolution, but with technical standards and policy remaining tightly centralised.

6.6 Uses of credit grading

Credit grading as described above provides an analytical framework dedicated to the calculation of expected and unexpected loss. It therefore furnishes an economic discipline in the credit area for meeting the canons of risk/reward management specified in Chapter 1, namely:

- Costing the business (expected loss).

- General provisioning (expected loss).

- Equity capital planning and allocation (unexpected loss).

- Setting hurdle rates, business selection and rejection, marketing appetite.

- Pricing policy.

- Risk-adjusted performance measurement.

. . . In brief, a major part of portfolio management.

Depending on perceived freedom of manoeuvre, revision of pricing policy alone may recoup the cost of the exercise in a matter of a year or two. Typically, the initial finding is that there is little correlation between existing pricing and the assigned grades: indeed, there may prove to be closer linkage between pricing and *size of facilities*, based on a false analogy with 'wholesale' versus 'retail' pricing in the trading of physical goods. Thus the bank may discover that it has been overcharging some few top grade borrowers, but substantially undercharging in most other grades measured against statistically demonstrable risk. This is all of a piece with the banking industry's record of poor returns and neglect of shareholder value in an age of overheated and undereducated competition (graced, naturally, by public incomprehension).

In the revision of its pricing policies, however, the bank must be careful not to trigger a self-fulfilling wave of defaults on existing debt, since studies have shown that 'high' interest rates increase the incentives to default.

At a very practical level, grading provides a master scale on which to plot credit quality and migration between grades, and thence to devise strategies for improvement. The lower grades can be accorded watch-list status, with prescribed policies for safeguarding the bank's position. Graduated sanctioning can be introduced, featuring streamlined processing for top graded credits and more restricted approval powers for middle and lower grades; with less single-minded regard than previously to graduation by size of facility, which is a poor proxy for risk.

Finally, it should be emphasised that credit grading is a *portfolio* technique: the larger the actuarial base of borrowers and counter-parties, the more valid the classifications are likely to be. At the

6.4 Credit grading as the hub of portfolio management.

level of *individual* credits, there are always exceptions to the rule: the grade should be treated as a guideline for policy purposes and not as any kind of substitute for the rigours of normal credit analysis, approval and control.

Figure 6.4 summarises the potential gains from a credit grading system. This technique promises something of a renaissance for many banks, but realisation of the full benefits may require several years of intensive effort.

6.7 Country grading – transfer risk

'Country risk' is an umbrella term covering three distinct issues: *transfer risk* (referring to the willingness and/or ability of a government to allow its country's cross-border obligations in foreign currency to be met); *sovereign risk* (the credit risk of the government itself); and *national credit risk* (the domestic economic setting which affects the credit risk of all obligors in that country). Clearly all three considerations are interrelated, but the second and third are probably best treated as part of the normal credit judgement and credit grading processes. The management of transfer risk, however, can be greatly enhanced through the construction of a country grading system aimed at transfer risk alone.

By definition, transfer risk is ultimately a narrow question, but its assessment is necessarily based on a broad range of factors that go to make up a country's willingness and ability to provide foreign exchange to its citizens for the servicing of their external obligations. A bank engaging in cross-border transactions will want to examine those factors very carefully, so as to establish its own marketing appetite and prudential limits (short, medium and long term) for exposures emanating from each foreign country. To complicate matters further, these principles also apply, in either direction, to cross-border exposures between different branches/subsidiaries/associates of the same bank.

Transfer risk poses many special problems and technical challenges. Its chief distinguishing feature is its *exceptional volatility* compared with ordinary credit risk. The relative lumpiness of the transfer risk portfolio (of countries, not customers) induces a tendency for expected loss to be low and unexpected loss to be uncomfortably high. Moreover, different credit product types may be differently affected by defaults and reschedulings, so credit exposure values may need to be mathematically adjusted to reflect consistent transfer risk equivalence (which might be termed 'transfer risk equivalent exposure', or TREE) across the board. Further risk adjustments may need to be made for differing maturities.

Transfer risk scrutiny is in parallel with, and not in substitution for, the normal credit appraisal system: both are necessary where cross-border credit is in contemplation. If the credit risk is deemed acceptable, the transaction has to be accommodated out of transfer risk limits marked for the country concerned, and if these are exhausted the request must be reshaped (e.g. by substituting a guarantor/obligor in a different country) or declined. Conversely, no amount of advocacy of the transfer risk capacity of a particular country can turn a bad credit risk into an acceptable deal. It is important that the two approval processes should be run independently of one another.

Bankers have continually sought a disciplined framework for assessing country/transfer risk, and the quest for comparability and consistency leads naturally enough to thoughts of league tables and grading. Early models tended to be wordy and subjective, with too few grades, and short on predictive indicators and valid links to the bank's own capital at risk. However, following the adoption of statistically-based credit grading systems, banks are finding, somewhat to their surprise, that much the same methodology can be brought to bear on country transfer risk grading.

Large numbers of national economic and social indicators can be tested, going back over twenty or more years, to find out which types are most predictive of transfer risk default. These distillations in turn can be used to calculate country default frequencies. As with credit grading, the concept of severity (determining loss in event of default) also comes into play, albeit in a more complex form. The bank will have to assess in advance which countries are likely to receive the 'Brady treatment' of maximum international support in the event of default/rescheduling, and which will be left to their own devices. These two polarities make for wide variation in potential outcome.

As a result of such an exercise in classification, an internationally oriented bank with a sufficient actuarial base should be able to dispense with its old 'descriptive' system, and emerge with a calibration of up to 10 statistically-based country grades for purposes of policy formulation, 'appetite' and limit-setting, pricing, and watch-listing at the bottom end. *Mutatis mutandis*, the benefits of credit grading (as shown in Fig. 6.4) apply similarly to country grading.

A counterparty's 'grade' in these circumstances is the *credit* grade and not some combination of credit and country grades. It just so happens that a graded credit has been accommodated out of limit capacity of the (graded) country concerned. Both dimensions, however, must be considered in determining the total risk and the correct pricing.

In addition to grade, country limits should take account of portfolio correlations arising out of common economic dependencies, the most obvious example of which is oil production.

As should be clear from this brief account, transfer risk grading is a young science with an unfinished agenda.

6.8 Expert systems

Expert systems, also widely referred to as 'knowledge-based systems' and 'rule-based systems', are part of the wider families of 'decision support systems' and 'artificial intelligence'. Expert systems attempt to codify the quantitative and qualitative knowledge of one or more experts (e.g. expert lenders) into a computer software package incorporating rules, policies, procedures, norms and advice for the user. The system enhances the user's own skills, and promotes training and a consistent approach across the organisation, unswayed by passing fashions, boom and incentive psychosis, or other emotional aberrations. The system advises and the user/sanctioner takes the final decision (e.g. to lend or not to lend); which he must be prepared later, if need be, to defend and to reconcile with the recorded advice that he received.

In the credit field, expert systems are mainly harnessed to processing advances applications and reviews. The bank can build its own system from scratch, or alternatively can buy and customise one of the branded products (known as 'shells' or 'kernels') available on the market, such as Lending Advisor. Using reference tables controlled by an 'inference engine', a sophisticated system will:

- Compare a particular corporate customer with its industry peers and rank it in terms of sales and margins, cash flow and debt service, liquidity, gearing and other balance sheet ratios.

- Require the lender to input subjective views on management competence, industry sector risk, competitive position, and financial management.

- Automatically produce financial projections which can be flexed by the user.

It will also raise pointed queries and comments where appropriate, such as: 'In this period, the borrower paid its trade creditors more rapidly. For subsequent analysis, it may be useful to determine the cause for this change . . .'

The system will highlight strengths and weaknesses and provide the user with a form of overall rating of the customer. Indeed, it will have the facility to incorporate automated credit grading, derived from logic tree methodology with assigned weights leading to an expected default rate.

Finally, a well-furnished system provides a backcloth of industry data, credit policies within the bank, portfolio priorities and 'no go areas'. It is an invaluable storehouse of credit portfolio information.

Expert systems, as applied to credit assessment and grading, are best suited to the 'middle market' – characterised by medium size of customer, a fair amount of analytical complexity, and moderate volumes of applications. For credit grading purposes, this size band needs its own criteria for predicting default rates, as distinct from the indicators developed for the large corporates and institutions. The end result is the same, however: placement on a common grading scale according to EDR.

Expert systems reinforce 'best practice' and help reduce volatility in the portfolio. For many banks they will also offer the most practical means of implementing credit grading over a large part of the commercial lending book.

6.9 Credit scoring

Credit scoring is a statistically derived artificial intelligence technique which may be used for either decision-taking or decision support (advisory only). It is most effective where there is a high volume of cases and low analytical complexity: specifically, in the areas of small business and the mass retail market of personal loans and credit cards.

Application scoring applies essentially to new customers, and *behavioural scoring* to existing customers. Both of these subsets of credit scoring address expected default rate in their separate ways: behavioural scoring, having the advantage of direct relationship data over a period, is not surprisingly the more powerfully predictive of the two. A hybrid approach, combining both techniques, can be employed in many cases and is known as *performance scoring.*

Credit scoring has been around for many years, but came into its own in the 1980s with the rapid growth of consumer credit. At this point, traditional methods of credit assessment proved too cumbersome to meet the volume demands. Given also that the mass market was more impersonal than the banking relationships of old, lenders had to find new yardsticks to replace the first rule of 'know your customer'. To illustrate the volumes we are talking about, the largest credit card operation in Britain currently has over five million cardholder accounts, receives 30 000 new applications per month, and considers 10 000 requests per month for increases in credit limits. Highly automated systems and computerised records are the only solution.

This impersonal trend can be viewed by traditional bankers and customers as inflexible, unsubtle, robotic: 'lending by numbers' and courting disaster. People also question the need for heavy expenditure on artificial intelligence in an age of cost cutting. However, the evidence of recent times surely is that the banks have spent too little, rather than too much, on the credit process and thereby incurred unwarranted bad debts. The dictum of General George S Patton, Jr is pertinent: 'an ounce of American sweat saves a pint of American blood' (a British Army addendum ran 'and brains save both'). The new artificial intelligence systems will prove themselves and repay their cost many times over.

Apart from being more scientific than traditional appraisal methods for the mass market, credit scoring is demonstrably objective and offers protection from charges of bias; provided, that is, that the scoring criteria steer clear of a minefield of social legislation banning discrimination on grounds of sex, race or religion. In Britain, by virtue of the Consumer Credit Act 1974, the Office of Fair Trading monitors consumer credit practices and issues periodic guidance to lenders and borrowers – including, for instance, the standards (increasingly adopted) that disappointed applicants should be told why they have been turned down and should have a right of appeal. Consideration of appeals, and of other rare marginal cases, is ultimately a matter of human judgement within the bank and not an automated process.

The approach to designing a credit scoring system is similar to that for credit grading. Representative samples of good and bad accounts have to be examined from past history, together with records of applications declined. From the basic information categories (known as 'characteristics') and their variants ('attributes') a picture can be built up. For example, one characteristic might be 'age of applicant', of which the attributes might be bandings by decades: '20–29', '30–39', etc. Other characteristics could be 'length of residence' and 'time in present job', with respective attributes split into time bands. When such attributes are plotted against good and bad experience, some sort of message may start to emerge as to who, on average, are the better and the worse risks. Points can be allocated according to statistically proven predictive power of the various attributes, and thus a complete scoring system (known as a 'scorecard') built up, with a high point count representing a good risk and a low point count a bad risk.

In addition to its own application form, a bank will normally wish to consult one of the credit reference agencies for external information on the applicant: adverse events like county court judgements can be reflected in the point count. In Britain there are four credit reference agencies, which collectively also own the bulk of the 'generic' scoring systems available to banks lacking the 'surface' or the historical database to build their own.

It is accepted wisdom within the industry that a scorecard needs a complete redevelopment based on fresh sampling every few years to keep abreast of economic and demographic changes; otherwise predictive accuracy starts to deteriorate. It may be, however, that the use of *neural network* technology can help to obviate the need for these overhauls. A neural network is a computer simulation of the way the human brain is assumed to work. Through a mathematically complex ('heuristic') process of sifting and combining information, the program continuously updates itself and learns from experience. However, the technology is new and has yet to show its paces in banking.

Having acquired a scorecard (or as many different scorecards as it chooses to cover market subsegments), the bank can do its sums and decide on an *acceptance rate* that satisfies its risk/reward requirements. The higher the acceptance rate (i.e. the lower the threshold or cut-off point), the higher will be the risk and the expected default rate/expected loss on the portfolio, as illustrated in Fig. 6.5. This consideration must be set against expected revenues, which in the special case of the credit card industry will depend on how many good customers borrow as opposed to paying off their balances monthly.

Figure 6.6 shows this matrix of concerns. Credit cards are intrinsically unprofitable in their first two years anyway, taking into account delinquencies and startup costs, so the profit projection needs to look about seven years ahead. This is a striking manifestation of a universal truth that ageing of a credit book tends to benefit portfolio quality. A mature and economically viable credit

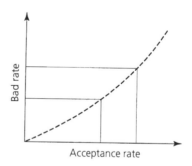

6.5 Target bad rate sets acceptance rate and vice versa.

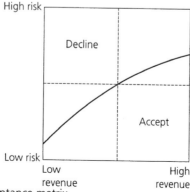

6.6 Risk–reward acceptance matrix.

card operation will usually have a book aged on average 10 years or more.

The foregoing operational principles apply equally to application scoring, behavioural scoring and performance scoring, albeit that each will have its own distinctive scorecard. A common approach also covers credit cards, other mass market finance, and small business lending – although, again, each of these categories will need a different scorecard (or family of scorecards) developed for its particular population. As mentioned earlier, credit scoring can be a technique for decision-taking or decision support. Results in the personal sector have shown that human intervention in the decision too often compromises the integrity of the system: the trend therefore is towards full automation as the norm. In the small business field, however, scorecards are in a more experimental phase, and it may be some time before bankers are willing to transfer the final say to a computer.

To summarise, the virtue of credit scoring lies in centralised selection guided by statistically-based prediction of revenues and delinquencies. The acceptance rate (cut-off point) can be moved up or down at will according to recent experience. Because the scoring system focuses on expected default rate, the book can be graded within the bank's greater portfolio if that is deemed necessary. By way of a spin-off, the computerised databank is a powerful platform for cross-selling of other goods and services.

At its most developed, as in the field of credit cards, credit scoring is a dynamic and satisfying paradigm of portfolio management in banking.

6.10 Artificial intelligence models presaging corporate failure

A number of proprietary packages exist which monitor public companies (mainly in the manufacturing sectors) and attempt to identify those most likely to default on debt or go bankrupt in the next one or two years. These software models are no substitute for a bank's own credit appraisal and grading processes, but can be used to stimulate, supplement and cross-check internal judgements. The two best-established systems are the Z Score and KMV Credit Monitor, and banks in the USA and the UK are subscribing in increasing numbers to both of them.

The Z Score, as applied to company solvency, was developed in 1968 by Professor Robert Altman, using *discriminant analysis* to identify a shortlist of variables which, in combination, were statistically predictive of a corporate bankruptcy in the manufacturing sector. The final distillation consisted of the following ratios:

- Working capital/total assets.

- Retained earnings/total assets.

- Earnings before interest and taxes/total assets.

- Market value of equity/book value of total liabilities.

- Sales/total assets.

A weighting is prescribed for each of these ratios, and the weighted answers totalled to produce a 'Z Score'. If the Z Score is lower than 1.8, the company is in 'bankrupt profile' – that is, likely to go bankrupt within, say, two years. If the score is higher than 3.0, the company is likely to continue trading. The band between 1.8 and 3.0 is conceded to be a grey area or 'zone of ignorance'.

Whilst this scoring system has a high success record on average, there will always be exceptions to the rule: companies that look bankrupt but are not, and others that go under without exhibiting the warning signs (having, perhaps, gone to the trouble of concealing them from the public eye). Apart from that caveat, the main drawback is the dependence on published accounts: updating of a company profile can be many months behind events and too late for a subscriber to react effectively. The same is true of a conventional bank spreadsheet, of course, and subscribers have to look to other information sources for their early warnings. However, the Z Score package offers not only hindsight but also the facility to model future trends.

KMV Credit Monitor addresses the probability of a quoted company defaulting on its debt within one year. This system, by contrast, is market-based, and assumes that a company defaults when the market value of its assets falls below the value of its liabilities. The model uses the volatility of the share price as a basis for projection of the volatility of asset values, and hence short term debt coverage.

Thus far, user banks have limited experience of the predictive accuracy of the KMV system. To the extent that it works, its merit is that the company picture is always current in terms of today's share price.

6.11 Summary

Successful portfolio management begins with an understanding of the principles of risk and reward and diversification of risk. Sectoral analysis identifies correlations and concentrations of risk by industry and region, and thus guides marketing appetite. The imposition of exposure ceilings for each sector and for any one customer is prudent practice.

Further analysis of portfolio quality, and thence risk and reward, is achieved by the use of credit grading, country grading, and credit scoring, all statistically-based on expected default rate. This scrutiny can be enhanced by other artificial intelligence techniques.

Above all, portfolio management is a discipline of conviction and not of going through the motions: it is therefore highly dependent on credit culture within the bank.

This chapter has described the theory of portfolio management, the measurements, and the framework of management information and control. The next chapter will cover the means by which a bank can reshape its book and thus complete the cycle.

CHAPTER SEVEN

Credit risk: changing the portfolio

This chapter debates the merits of:

- Marketing entries and exits.

- Other traditional approaches.

- Asset trading.

- Asset securitisation.

- Capital markets alternatives.

- Swaps vehicles.

- Floating off part of the bank.

- Possibilities for hedging.

In the previous chapter we examined portfolio theory and diversification of risk, and looked at the principal techniques for analysing the risk/reward profile of the book. Having identified scope for improvement, how do we make the desired changes? The choices revolve around the following manoeuvres:

- Turning marketing taps on and off.

- Allowing unwanted exposures to run off without renewal.

- Intensive care and debt recovery operations.

- Asset trading.

- Asset securitisation.

- Directing customers towards the capital markets.

- Use of special purpose vehicles for swaps business.

- Retaining the 'good bank' and floating off the 'bad bank'.

- Finding ways of hedging undesirable imbalances.

7.1 The traditional methods

The first two options mentioned above are reminiscent of regulating the temperature and level of bath water by the use of taps and plug. At the 'tap' end, positive and negative marketing initiatives may be taken in order to expand, maintain, or shrink classes of exposure so as to achieve targets or observe portfolio limits set in accordance with the principles discussed in Chapter 6. This is the mainstream approach of entry, adjustment, and exit traditionally employed in commercial banking, as well as in credit scored consumer lending operations.

Ejecting unwanted exposures by enforcing repayment, or by allowing them to run off at expiry without renewal, is equivalent to 'pulling the plug', usually a rather more *ad hoc* arrangement. Corporate exposures are not usually self-liquidating in these circumstances and may have to go somewhere else, to another financier such as a bank or a factoring or leasing company.

Again, intensive care and debt recovery activities, aimed at cleaning up the delinquent end of the book, have been with us since the beginning of banking. These days, every large bank will have its own dedicated work-out team, as distinct from the normal lending function.

These traditional methods form the core of portfolio adjustment practice in most banks and will doubtless continue to do so, albeit guided increasingly by statistical science. If we devote little space here to describing them, it is not because they are unimportant (on the contrary) but because they are obvious and self-explanatory. They are indispensable, but their disadvantage lies in the length of time entailed in effecting any significant shift through such honest toil.

7.2 Asset trading

Asset trading comes in many different guises, and has grown up through a variety of influences: the packaging practices of the syndicated lending market, the increasing overlap of bank credit and paper-based public or private financing, the spread of investment banking, the extensive sales of Third World debt following the reschedulings of the 1980s, and the resourcefulness of dealers everywhere.

Banks wanting to sell good quality debt, for reasons of capacity or portfolio balance, are free to do so if the loan agreement permits; equally, they are free to buy. As in the securities markets, the striking price is only sure to be face value at or near initiation, and thereafter should fluctuate in line with current interest rates (if the debt is fixed rate), current 'spreads', and changing perceptions of credit quality (grade/expected default rate). Most trades, however, take place early on, through the now standard practice of large banks winning mandates and then selling down some or all of the lending to other banks; thus expanding the service base without inflating the balance sheet pro rata. This sort of secondary trading opens up the debate on 'transaction banking' versus 'relationship banking', which veers one way and the other according to fashion but is never finally resolved: banks find it expedient to pay homage to both.

An interbank market also exists for selling and exchanging distressed commercial debt, and it is not uncommon for a large bank to have a dedicated (usually part-time) trading desk for this purpose. Some banks are even prepared to supplement their own problem-solving enterprise by acting as brokers and intermediaries. However, this market has shown slow growth because banks have a propensity to be on the same side of the trading fence – for example, all wanting to offload surplus real estate exposure at the same time.

Hovering on the fringe of banking circles are the private speculators and the so-called 'vulture funds'. These players publish newsletters and lists of going prices for well-known cases of distressed debt, but in London trading is very thin owing to the unrealistic discounts demanded by the vultures for their trouble. Only a naive or nervous bank would be tempted to exit at such a cost. This market also drives a coach-and-four through the 'London approach' sponsored by the Bank of England, whereby bankers to a distressed borrower are enjoined to stay with the problem, exercise patience for the common benefit and commit themselves to putting up fresh money if necessary: selling out at panic price to a non-bank speculator who is not party to any consortium agreement is the antithesis of such good citizenship.

One of the most effective secondary markets for adjusting existing portfolios has undoubtedly been that for Third World, or 'emerging markets', debt. This has grown from an estimated $1 billion of trades in 1984 to $5.3 trillion (i.e. $5300 billion) in 1996. A big expansion took place after 1987, when banks came under regulatory, competitive and shareholder pressures to increase their provisions for non-performing country exposures: the discounts thereby created removed former inhibitions against selling (at a loss) in the secondary market. Following the Brady Plan of 1989, many countries have converted their debt from loans into standardised, easily tradable, bonds. As a result, new investors have come forward, not just banks and fringe speculators but also insurance companies, pension funds, mutual funds and the like. In the wake of much trauma, we now see one of the few proven success stories in the history of the banks' efforts to realign their lending portfolios.

The future tendency must surely be for these three debt trading operations – good domestic, bad domestic, and cross-border risk (good or bad) – to be increasingly co-ordinated within each bank in the interests of cross-fertilisation, flexibility and liquidity.

7.3 Asset securitisation

Asset securitisation is a form of *disintermediation,* whereby a bank can continue to provide credit facilities for its customers whilst transferring (or diverting) the direct financing and risk away from its own balance sheet onto that of a non-bank securitisation vehicle. To the extent that credit risk to the bank is reduced (compared with direct lending), the regulatory and prudential capital requirements decrease pro rata, without a compensating capital requirement in the securitisation vehicle.

This process 'unbundles' not only the credit risk but also some of the other traditionally merged functions of the lender, i.e.:

● Business development and loan origination.

● Credit assessment.

- Loan administration and servicing, payments and collections.

- Risk-bearing.

- Funding.

Such division of labour facilitates choice and focus, and spreads the load by bringing more players into the market.

From a banking perspective, the possible benefits of securitisation may be seen as:

- Freeing up the bank's capital, improving ratios.

- Leveraging credit service on the same amount of bank capital, and thereby earning extra fees.

- Offering corporate customers cheaper finance as a result of taking the cost of bank capital out of the equation.

- Shedding low margin senior debt that fails to meet the bank's rate of return objectives.

- Enhancing the bank's reputation for service and innovation.

- Improving the bank's liquidity by encashing assets.

- Adjusting the portfolio mix.

The validity of the capital benefit in particular calls for close scrutiny and careful structuring.

Like so many other innovations, asset securitisation was conceived in the USA. Mortgage-backed securities were issued in the 1970s, and were later joined by other types of securitised receivables. The public market has grown to well over $1 trillion in outstandings, with mortgages still dominant. A much smaller private market exists, using special purpose vehicles or conduits established mainly by the banks.

Securitisation in the UK began in 1987 with the issue of mortgage-backed securities by National Home Loans Corporation. The public market, at some £15 billion of outstandings in 1996, is tiny in comparison with the USA but is the second largest in the world. Bank-sponsored securitisation began to appear in the early 1990s.

Elsewhere, public issues have been completed in France, Germany, Italy, Spain and Sweden. Private transactions have also taken place in Belgium and the Netherlands.

Assets suitable for securitisation are those which form a homogeneous 'pool', with clearly defined cash flows and performance characteristics amenable to statistical risk analysis. In the USA such asset pools include:

- Residential and commercial mortgages.

- Credit card receivables.

- Instalment credit.

- Automobile loans.

- Trade receivables.

- Leases.

- Other rental payments.

- Insurance premiums.

Bank-sponsored securitisation can take one of two forms: (a) providing the means for a corporate customer to sell off its receivables (in substitution for obtaining conventional bank finance), or (b) selling off receivables from the bank's own balance sheet (corporate loans, mortgage loans, personal loans, credit card receivables, etc).

It is best to describe each of these separately.

7.4 Securitisation: customer as seller

Arrangements in each country will differ according to applicable law and market practice. A typical British banking securitisation structure contains the following cast of characters:

- The originator, customer.

- The seller, customer.

- The servicer, usually the customer, which administers the sold portfolio and collects the receivables when due.

- The securitisation vehicle, which buys the assets and funds itself by issuing asset-backed commercial paper.

- The ultimate owners of the securitisation vehicle, usually charitable institutions unconnected with the sponsor bank.

- The investors in the commercial paper, usually corporate and institutional participants in the money market.

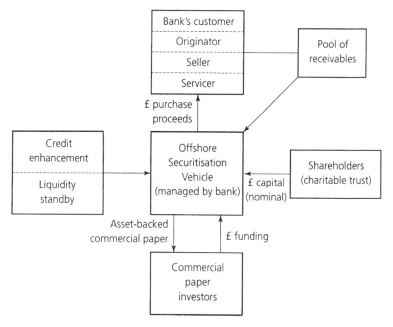

7.1 Typical securitisation structure with corporate customer as seller.

- The credit enhancers and liquidity backers, which may include the sponsoring bank and/or others.

Figure 7.1 illustrates the interaction of these parties. The bank establishes the securitisation vehicle with minimal capital, usually offshore and owned by a charitable trust. The vehicle purchases the receivables from the customer, and funds itself by issuing asset-backed commercial paper. In order to be acceptable to the market, the commercial paper must be rated A1/P1 or better by the rating agencies. That in turn depends on the paper being *credit-enhanced* and supported by a *liquidity standby line* from a bank or banks.

Credit enhancement is achieved by a primary tier, or 'loss reserve', consisting either of 'overcollateralisation' (assets over and above those sold to the vehicle) or of an element of direct recourse to the originator (or to a third party credit insurer, or to a bank providing a letter of credit). The loss reserve is set at a generous (typically three or four times) multiple of historical loss experience (representing expected loss) on the types of asset in question. A second tier of enhancement may also be required, in the form of a line of credit, for the unlikely event of the loss reserve being exhausted. This double depth of defence is intended to withstand even a disaster scenario.

The liquidity standby line is needed in case the securitisation vehicle has temporary difficulty in reissuing its commercial paper when tranches mature. Although such an event is no more than a remote possibility, the rating agencies require 100% coverage for a rolling programme of short term commercial paper. If the liquidity standby line is drawn, the bank will have a prior secured claim ahead of other creditors of the vehicle.

The securitisation vehicle, managed but not owned by the establishing bank, handles a succession of different deals. It can also market its facilities to other banks and their clients. Those banks must, however, be carefully chosen because the vehicle incurs various seller/servicer risks, such as:

● That the bank will fail to perform adequately as servicing agent of the vehicle.

● That the bank will 'commingle' (mix up) cash flows belonging to the vehicle with the bank's other cash flows.

● That the bank will not honour recourse to it under credit enhancement facilities or liquidity standby lines (i.e. the vehicle is exposed to credit risk).

We may pause here to review the pay-offs and the driving forces at work in such an exercise.

For a start, the sponsoring bank earns fees from its role as manager of the securitisation vehicle. There are also commitment fees on the support facilities. More to the point, the bank can satisfy its customers' need for finance without taking on drawn credit exposure and incurring the regulatory capital requirement that would go with it.

Offset against that relief are the credit enhancement facilities, which may amount to as much as 10% of the exposure sold and which do incur the normal capital requirement. Then there may be interest rate swap lines, possibly even forward exchange contracts, to enable the vehicle to manage its positions. The bank may try to syndicate some of these facilities, but is likely to end up as the main risk-bearer.

Most importantly, there is the liquidity standby line which, at 100% backing for short term commercial paper, might appear at first sight to kill any benefits of securitisation stone dead. However, under the Basle Accord rules, lines of credit committed for less than one year *attract no capital requirement as long as they remain undrawn.* This regulatory concession (noted in Chapter 3) may be said ultimately to sum up the entire 'advantage' to a bank of securitisation: namely, substitution of an undrawn facility for a drawn one, which enables the originating bank to mark its liquidity line for 364 days (and subsequent 'evergreen' rollover) and thereby escape any formal capital requirement.

Seen from the business community's point of view, bank-sponsored securitisation gives the seller an image boost by public association with a commercial paper programme of investment grade. It also allows more corporate financing to be done, more cheaply, with the same quantum of bank capital (*ergo* 'banking without capital', as it has been dubbed). However, before ringing any alarm bells, commentators should note that in practice all bank-sponsored securitisation vehicles have to receive prior approval from the banking regulators, even though the vehicles are not licensed banks and are thereafter outside the regulatory net of capital requirements.

The regulators, it appears, are satisfied as long as the Basle rules are not flouted by the sponsoring bank. Realistically, the authorities recognise that the securitisation market exists and will continue to grow in one form or another, with or without bank-sponsored participation. It is also arguable that, unlike a bank's depositors, the corporate and institutional investors in the commercial paper issued by the securitisation vehicle are sophisticated enough not to need regulatory protection . . . at least until such time as this becomes a mainstream form of banking with systemic implications, at which point there might be second thoughts.

Furthermore, there is no doubt that a properly structured securitisation programme represents a very low credit risk to investors in the asset-backed commercial paper. It is good for them, and good for the seller of receivables. Is it as good for the banking system as proponents claim? A devil's advocate might ask:

- Are these programmes always properly costed, and is the true risk/reward ratio demonstrably advantageous for the bank?

- Has the bank weighed up the consequences of losing high quality credit from the banking system, and thereby weakening the overall quality of banking assets?

- Does the bank want to become typecast as a lender of last, rather than first, resort, which is what the credit enhancement and liquidity standby lines imply? Admittedly, if the worst comes to the worst, any exposure that crystallises should be exceptionally well secured by the underlying assets.

● Who will be held accountable if, against all the odds, the securitisation vehicle becomes insolvent? The legal answer is that the bank does not own the vehicle, and therefore walks away (apart from direct recourse under its support lines); but at what cost to its reputation? In a litigious era, what is to stop aggrieved creditors from suing the bank for mis-representation or for mismanagement of the vehicle?

Any such misgivings have not been borne out by market history to date, granted that experience of securitisation in banking is short and narrowly spread. Enthusiasts take a far more positive view: indeed, some visionaries see securitisation, disintermediation, and escape from the tyranny of bank capital ratios as the natural progression from balance sheet banking as we have known it.

7.5 Securitisation: bank as originator, seller and servicer

Here the motivation is more directly in tune with the aim of centralised portfolio management, namely to shed unwanted exposure. A collection of receivables on the bank's books – e.g. residential mortgage loans, personal loans, or credit card receivables – is sold to a securitisation vehicle with minimal capital, owned by a charitable trust, managed by the bank and established for that one deal alone. Where residential mortgages are concerned, an intermediary 'receivables trust' may also have to be set up for tax purposes.

The securitisation vehicle funds its book by the public issue of medium term asset-backed bonds, which need to attain investment grade. Capital and credit enhancement for the vehicle come partly from the pricing 'spread' in the sale and partly from a subordinated loan from the selling bank (which will count as a deduction from the bank's capital base under the Basle rules). In most cases a further layer of credit enhancement (up to 10% in the case of personal loans) will be obtained from third parties, who either issue a letter of credit or subscribe to tranches of subordinated securities issued for this purpose by the securitisation vehicle.

The selling bank will provide a liquidity back-up line, purely to cover arrears in the collection of interest (unlike the funding standby for commercial paper rollovers described in section 7.4 above). This liquidity support facility is most needed in the case of residential mortgages, and gives the bank secured priority even over senior investors (i.e. purchasers of the bond issue).

This more introverted form of securitisation (where the bank is its own customer) may be seen to lack some of the revolutionary glamour attaching to the first kind. The issues it raises are those of prudent housekeeping, regulation and compliance, rather than the challenging and controversial questions of 'whither banking?' found in the previous section. On the other hand, it is more directly relevant to the subject matter of this chapter.

At time of writing, National Westminster has broken new ground by securitising £3.2 billion worth of corporate loans (to some 300 high grade borrowers) already on the bank's balance sheet. If deemed successful, this exercise could stimulate a significant restructuring of existing corporate credit exposures in many other major banks.

7.6 Capital markets alternatives

The capital markets offer a disintermediation alternative without the complications of securitisation. One attraction, again, is the chance for the borrower to economise on financing costs by doing away with the need for bank capital: hence capital market financing has grown faster than bank corporate lending since the Basle Accord capital adequacy rules were formulated in 1987. Banks themselves have abetted this disintermediation through the parallel growth of investment banking. Long term questions arise as to the ability of conventional bank lending to survive in the corporate area, faced with such competition.

A bank wanting to reduce or contain its exposure to an individual corporate customer may therefore persuade it to turn to the capital markets, where the choices of funding include not only equity but domestic bonds and eurobonds, floating rate notes, and commercial paper.

To obtain a premium rating some short term issues are underwritten, and commercial paper in particular requires back-up liquidity facilities. If the bank provides such support, its role is not dissimilar to sponsoring a securitisation programme: a 364-day liquidity line attracts no regulatory capital requirement. The customer's cost of finance usually remains lower than it could obtain direct from the bank.

The bank's true risk, however, is rather worse than under securitisation. While the customer performs strongly all is well, but if it hits a sticky patch the capital market investors are intrinsically less supportive than a bank and are apt to destabilise the company's finances. When the company can no longer roll over its short term paper, the last resort liquidity line, which the bank hoped would never be drawn, comes into play without the specific asset backing and earmarked cash flows that accompany the disruption of a securitisation programme. Moreover, the bank may find itself simultaneously in conflict with a multiplicity of unco-operative bondholders in its efforts to save the situation.

In the recessionary conditions of the early 1990s, many banks found to their cost that diversification of a customer's funding sources complicates life in ways that were never anticipated. Given that the corporate switch away from bank finance and towards the capital markets may prove to be a permanent phenomenon, the remaining question for banks is the extent to which they are willing to adopt the role of credit enhancers and lenders of last resort.

7.7 Special purpose vehicles for swaps business

Here we have another device for taking business off the bank's books, but any resemblance to securitisation ends there. The use of a special purpose vehicle (SPV) for swap contracts is aimed at obtaining and keeping the highest possible credit rating with the rating agencies – higher, typically, than the parent bank has been able to sustain.

Active engagement in the swaps business requires a large number of counterparties, but many governments, municipalities, and top grade companies will not themselves deal with a bank (or any other counterparty) with a credit rating below a specified level (e.g. AAA or AA on the Standard & Poor's system). This is especially the case for swap contracts above five years, which are perceived to be more risky. Few banks can muster such a rating for their general business, but they can achieve it for a favoured subsidiary by concentrating super-abundant capital resources on it: that subsidiary is the special purpose vehicle.

The motive, then, is to avoid disqualification for top grade swaps business, which is more important to some banks than to others. Unlike securitisation, this is no escape from the rigours of banking regulation, since the SPV has proportionately greater capital strength than its parent. By the same token, setting up a swaps SPV is a capitally draining exercise and not for everyone.

A bank which is, by definition, worried about its credit rating will think twice about diluting its solus capital ratio further in order to endow a swaps subsidiary, even if that endowment is reabsorbed in the (in this case, less relevant) consolidated capital ratio. It may be that this is the cautionary line of thinking that, together with some wariness of the swaps market in general, has caused the Office of the Comptroller of Currency to decline applications by Citibank and Continental Bank to set up their own swaps vehicles. Thus far, only investment banks have been granted this permission in the USA. Elsewhere, Japanese commercial banks in particular have been active in setting up swaps vehicles.

The two most prominent vehicles in operation anywhere to date are Merrill Lynch Derivative Products (founded in 1991) and Salomon Swapco (established in 1993), both rated triple-A by the rating agencies. MLDP's capital and reserves of $361 million anticipate future growth, being more than 10 times the Basle requirement to support the 1994 level of swaps. Swapco's initial capital of $175 million will increase in line with a proprietary formula measuring the size, concentration, and credit quality of the vehicle's counterparty exposures. Both operations are said to be legally ring-fenced so as to be 'bankruptcy remote' from their parent companies – i.e. the unlikely contingency of their parents' insolvency would leave them financially unscathed, although without the rationale to continue in business.

MLDP matches its book with other market counterparties at its own discretion; whereas Swapco avoids complexity by matching every deal back-to-back with the Salomon parent, which collateralises 100% of the net amount it owes to Swapco on a daily basis. Various constitutional provisions within each SPV govern the types of business conducted (interest rate swaps, currency swaps, commodity swaps, etc), the credit rating hurdle for counterparties, and how exposures are to be assigned if those counterparties are downgraded.

The corporate constitution also defines certain events (such as downgrading of the SPV or the demise of its parent) that would trigger the termination of the SPV, and how such termination would be administered. MLDP would have its book managed down in an orderly fashion over time by a third party bank brought in for the purpose. Swapco, by contrast, would simply cash up all its contracts as quickly as possible, leaving its counterparties to seek replacement contracts elsewhere in need.

To date no British bank has sought to emulate the example of these North American pioneers, and it is not certain whether the Bank of England would grant permission. The justification in risk/reward terms lies somewhere in the future, and the structures have yet to be stress-tested in crisis conditions.

All this seems a far cry from portfolio management as conventionally understood, but the connection lies in what credit risks a bank takes onto its own book and what it contrives to outplace in other entities. Such policy decisions play a part in shaping a portfolio.

7.8 Floating off the bad bank

This is sometimes referred to as the 'good bank/bad bank' solution, although that ambiguous expression means different things to different people.

The theory is straightforward enough. If a troubled bank can pack all its worst exposures (say, the four bottom grades) into an *alter ego* (the 'bad bank'), it will have cleaned up its book at a stroke – separated Dr Jekyll from Mr Hyde – and will be psychologically poised for a fresh start. Staff will then be specialised in what they do best: respectively, marketing in the good bank, and work-outs in the bad bank. The balance sheet will have to be split, and capital reconstruction will involve issuing separate share certificates for existing shareholders, or else a sale of the bad bank to outside parties. Unscrambling the good and the bad may unlock shareholder value on both sides.

Nothing can be quite that simple, of course. Staff and customers may object to being consigned to the bad bank, no matter what euphemistic name is given to it. Does it make sense to put all the marketing staff in one bank and all the recovery experts in the other? In practice, some good business will have to be injected into the bad bank to give it a sporting chance of respectability and success; thereby compromising the initial premise.

Then again, what happens a few years later when the good bank acquires a fresh portfolio of bad debts? Does it incorporate a second bad bank? Is it in fact a sound principle to allow bankers to walk away from their mistakes and recommence business as usual?

Viewed as an academic exercise, this solution seems to collapse under the weight of its imbalances and contradictions. In fact it is not merely academic, as versions of it deployed in a few instances in the United States, France, Italy, and New Zealand appear at least to have satisfied some short term objectives. What seems clear is that shedding the bad bank is drastic surgery, hardly repeatable within a generation, and not the stuff of normal portfolio adjustment.

In some countries there may also be insuperable tax obstacles. It is essential to subject all disposal propositions like this, and indeed all new ventures of whatever kind, to the scrutiny of tax experts.

7.9 Hedging possibilities

Chapter 6 touched on *natural* hedges, achieved by negative correlations (opposite and offsetting tendencies) within the portfolio. The taking of guarantees and other security may arguably be regarded as traditional hedging, to the extent that they mitigate expected loss flowing from possible default.

Natural hedges within the portfolio, however, are hard to find as credit exposures more often exhibit some degree of positive correlation with one another. That may also be one reason why the innovative derivatives market has trouble inventing artificial hedges for credit risk, which after all is crying out for treatment. Futures, options or swaps are readily accessible for hedging of risks in equities and gilts, commodities, currencies, and interest rates, but represent an as yet unattained ideal when it comes to credit, probably the greatest banking risk of them all.

Artificial hedging of individual corporate credit exposures is fraught with difficulty. There is enough controversy over spot prices, let alone forward deals. If a troubled name can be offloaded at all, why not sell it now, with future expectations discounted in the striking price, rather than complicate matters by taking out a derivative contract? 'Credit default options', which have recently made their debut, are really guarantees dressed in derivative clothing.

The role of artificial hedging in the credit area would seem to be best directed towards sectoral exposures and collective chunks of the portfolio which are destined to remain on the books to maturity or termination. That suggests the use of credit rating systems (like Standard & Poor's and Moody's) and other indices to create trigger points for synthetic instruments capable of hedging adverse trends.

One such example is the issue by Barclays Bank of £250 million of Property Index Certificates (PIC) in 1994 and 1995, linked to the £40 billion Investment Property Databank in the UK. If the IPD index rises, a premium will be paid in addition to principal on maturity of the certificates in two to five years' time: if the index falls, however, the repayment will be subject to a discount. In effect, the issuer is trading some of the upside potential of its devalued property lending portfolio for insurance against downside risk: all things being equal, further writedowns of that portfolio should be to some extent recouped from writedowns of the PICs on the liabilities side. Thus the bank is limiting future volatility in preference to betting on future trends in the property market.

A different kind of hedge might be created by linkage to a rating agency scale. If a particular public credit rating (say, A+) were to be assigned a notional expected loss rate (as distinct from expected default rate) for 12 months ahead, a suitable derivative instrument could perhaps be designed to enable a bank to fix a proportion of its forward losses on that basis and eliminate the surrounding volatility.

Yet another possibility, demonstrated already in California, is to seek external insurance cover for unexpected losses. This expensive solution must of course be affordable within the economics of the lending operation, from which it follows that self-insurance could well be the preferred choice in a bank with the actuarial base. That thought brings us full circle; for what is self-insurance but a formalisation of the cash flows, provisions and capital allocations implicit in prudent, self-financing, risk/reward management?

Hedging cannot magically dispose of risk. The best it can do, at a price, is substitute a more acceptable for a less acceptable risk; and if the hedge entails counterparty credit exposure, default will bring us back to the status quo ante.

7.10 Summary

The message of this chapter is that those looking for short cuts and quick fixes will be disappointed. Assets that we can most easily shift tend to be those that we might prefer to keep. There is no substitute for the traditional, slow, methods of reorienting a portfolio: selecting and controlling inflows and outflows, and working hard to clean up the substandard end of the book.

Asset trading and derivative hedging have a limited supporting role, and those markets offer scope for further development. The same may be said of asset securitisation off the bank's balance sheet. Encouraging corporate customers to use the capital markets is a double-edged sword, as we have seen.

The remaining devices certainly affect the shape of the credit risk portfolio, but they have a primary agenda of their own which puts them into a category of 'alternative portfolio management'.

Securitisation of customers' receivables is aimed by marketeers at turning over new business faster than would be possible if it had to be domiciled (by way of loan) on the bank's balance sheet.

Swaps vehicles are created to obtain a share of high grade business that might otherwise bypass the parent bank.

Floating off the bad bank is a form of escapism intended to free staff morale and the share price from the shackles of past disgrace.

Modern portfolio management offers no miraculous solutions, but has developed a powerful battery of analytical tools in aid of common sense practices. Finally, it remains to state the obvious: in shaping a portfolio, as in life generally, prevention is better than cure.

CHAPTER EIGHT

Interest rate risk: structural exposure

This chapter looks at:

● The nature of interest rate risk, and the distinction between structural and trading exposures.

● Choice of risk management objectives.

● Yield curves and associated risks.

● Strengths and weaknesses of: mismatch/gap management; duration analysis; simulation analysis.

Interest rate risk has been fundamental to the business of banking from the very beginning, and in most banks is the prime focus of attention for the asset and liability management process (ALM) and its supervisory committee (ALCO) – see Chapter 4. It is the classical two-way (or 'speculative') risk, commonly defined as 'exposure to loss (or gain) caused by changes in interest rates'. Those losses or gains may be incurred either in net interest income or in present values of financial instruments in which the bank has a position: both impacts hit bottom line profits (and possibly the bank's share price), but risk management approaches towards the two contingencies are largely separate and distinct.

The risk relating to net interest income is what we shall refer to as *structural exposure* (also known in the USA as *accounting* exposure): this will be the subject of the present chapter. The risk affecting financial instrument values, which we may term *trading exposure* (referred to in the USA as economic exposure), has grown in importance with the rise of the modern dealing room: that category will feature in Chapter 9. Readers may note in passing that the dichotomy identified here corresponds in some respects to the distinction between the 'banking book' and the 'trading book' delineated by banking regulators in the European Union and elsewhere (see Chapter 3). Curiously, there seems to be more regulatory concern about interest rate trading exposure than there is about the potentially greater hazards of structural exposure: new capital requirements have been prescribed for the former but not the latter.

The banking/trading divide also marks a common fault line in career experience which bedevils the discussion of 'interest rate risk': bankers on either side of the rift tend to mistake their own part of the picture for the whole.

8.1 Managing structural exposure: what is the objective?

How should banks try to cope with the swings and roundabouts of the interest rate cycle? What outcome would their shareholders prefer? There is no single right answer to these questions. Granted that changes in interest rates can alter a bank's net interest income (in ways that we shall shortly examine), a number of strategic choices present themselves. Management may, for instance, aim to:

(i)   Adopt interest repricing positions which hedge (lock in) the bank's net interest income so as to meet a constant revenue or rate of return target, irrespective of changes in interest rates; or

(ii) Adopt interest repricing positions which hedge the bank's present value, and hence tend to stabilise its share price; or

(iii) Anticipate correctly all significant interest rate movements, shifting rate sensitivities actively so as to outperform the market (in terms of both net interest income and share price) in all circumstances; or

(iv) Do nothing to protect or optimise either net income or the share price.

These are the obvious, though by no means the only possible, orientations. Strategy (iii) tempts everyone from time to time, and used to be the conventional wisdom with its own steering rules (as illustrated in Table 8.1). However, this opportunist mindset has fallen increasingly out of favour as its sheer riskiness (and its public relations downside) has come to be recognised. We may reasonably assume that neither regulators nor bank shareholders wish to see the management indulging in a series of punts.

Table 8.1 Opportunistic approach to interest rate structural exposure – interest rate cycle

Approaching peak	Approaching trough
❀ shorten funding maturities	❀ lengthen funding maturities
❀ begin to lengthen investment maturities	❀ begin to shorten investment maturities
❀ acquire investments	❀ sell investments
❀ expand fixed rate loans	❀ restrict fixed rate loans

Strategy (iv) implies blind faith that gains and losses will even out in the long run. In the shorter run, however, the bank risks extinction. At best, annual results are likely to be volatile and shareholders disaffected.

Strategies (i) and (ii) are geared, in their separate ways, to keeping the ship on an even keel: both are compatible with share-holders' best interests. Unfortunately, they are mutually exclusive. You cannot hedge net interest income *and* the bank's economic value simultaneously, but must choose between them: to stabilise one is to destabilise the other, to a degree. Why? Because strategy (i) requires the level of net interest income to be *insulated* from changes in interest rates, whereas strategy (ii) depends on net interest income being *responsive* to such changes.

To understand the latter assertion, it is only necessary to observe the way the stock market adjusts its sights in reaction to changes in the general level of interest rates (and sometimes ahead of the game, by 'discounting' expected developments). As a general rule, when interest rates rise, share prices fall; and when interest rates fall, share prices rise. Interest-driven price adjustments reflect the economic reality that the present value of an investment is the sum of expected future cash flows, discounted back at the applicable current rate. For an ordinary share, the discount rate is the cost of capital of that share (see Chapter 1).

The share price is disturbed when something happens to change either the expected cash flows or the rate at which they are to be discounted. This chapter is concerned with the latter circumstance. When interest rates go up, so does the discount factor, reducing the value of the investment (in this case, the bank's share); when they go down, the reverse applies. To express it another way, the market's required rate of return is amended and so, inversely, is the share price.

In order to hedge the bank's share price, we would therefore have to ensure that net interest income increases sufficiently to compensate for the higher discount factor resulting from a rise in interest rates; and thanks to remorseless symmetry, such hedging would equally dictate that when interest rates (and the discount factor) fall, net interest income also decreases. These checks and balances can be quantified, within a given range of scenarios.

Stabilising the bank's present value means forgoing rate-induced falls *and* rises in share price: this is not a 'have your cake and eat it' choice on the lines of strategy (iii).

Banks with an old-fashioned 'endowment factor' (where interest-free liabilities like demand deposits and equity capital substantially exceed non-interest-earning assets) have a predisposition favouring strategy (ii) – that is, an inbuilt tendency for net interest income to increase when rates go up, and to decrease when rates go down. However, current wisdom espoused by some banking strategists has done its level best to break the link between the interest rate cycle and the volatility of bank earnings. Where that is the case, management's ideas (and performance incentives) are likely to be closer to strategy (i), commonly perceived as 'risk-averse'. Stabilising earnings ought in principle to make the bank a less risky business and thereby reduce *either* its need for economic capital *or* its beta factor and hence its required rate of return on equity (see Chapter 3).

At any rate, these alternative strategies – stabilising net interest income *or* stabilising the bank's economic value and share price – represent the boundaries of a prudent range of conduct in managing structural exposure. In operational terms, this translates into the difference between a neutral interest repricing profile and a moderately 'asset-sensitive' position (where gross interest income is more sensitive than gross interest costs). By definition, compromise positions anywhere along the spectrum between those two paradigms (and thus only partially contributing to either) are pragmatically acceptable. Positioning much outside either end of this 'prudent range' will be unduly asset-sensitive or liability-sensitive, and tantamount to 'betting the bank' (or, at least, its most important category of annual income).

Finally, unless strategy (iv) is to be the order of the day, it should by now be clear that there is room for only one executive view within the bank on interest rate prospects and appropriate positioning (for each currency). In a multibranched or multi-operational bank, this means that all interest rate risk-taking must be centralised in a dedicated treasury department by means of a common funding pool and a standardised internal transfer pricing system, currency by currency. The treasury department in turn will follow the policy guidelines laid down by the ALCO.

8.2 Yield curves and associated risks

Interest may be said to consist of two components: a 'risk-free' rate representing compensation for sacrifice of liquidity by the lender (or rental for the hire of money, taking into account expected inflation rates); and a premium tailored to the credit risk of the borrower. Within an overall economic climate, these elements drive the conventional *yield curve*, which is a line joining the current rates of interest for like instruments or quotes with different maturities (e.g. London interbank offered rate, LIBOR). The yield curve displays the term structure of interest rates.

At most times the yield curve ascends 'positively' from left to right (see Fig. 8.1), but occasionally the pattern can wobble, flatten, or

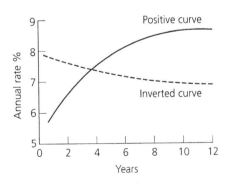

8.1 Illustration of yield curves.

become inverted (reflecting short term 'hiccups' in liquidity, or market expectations of a reduction in rates). By way of an aside, the tactic known as 'riding the yield curve' seeks to take advantage of a positive and static slope by holding a fixed rate instrument (e.g. a bond) for a period and then selling it at a lower yield on the curve, thereby realising a capital gain.

There are separate yield curves for different kinds of instrument (on either side of the balance sheet), but the rough parallelism of normal positive slopes explains the attraction to banks of 'borrowing short and lending long' in pursuit of enhanced interest turn (at the expense of liquidity, as pointed out in Chapter 4). This is just one of many reasons why the interest repricing propensities of a bank's assets and liabilities respectively may be mismatched, and hence why net interest income is at risk from changes in general or particular interest rate levels.

The yield curve is the best means of illustrating the varieties of interest rate movement that confront financial intermediaries. The first type, sometimes called 'open position risk', refers to the consequences of a simultaneous and parallel shift in interest rates (and therefore yield curves) across the board; e.g. a 1% rise or fall in all rates. Depending on the repricing schedules of its assets and liabilities, and its discretionary scope for manoeuvre on 'administered' (as opposed to market-determined) rates, the bank may find that its prospective net interest income is suddenly and materially altered for better or worse. We shall see exactly how in section 8.3 below.

A uniform change in all rates is, however, unlikely. In real life, the rates for different maturities may move by different percentages, reflecting a revised market perspective. The slope of the yield curve will change accordingly, exacerbating the effects of repricing mismatches that already exist. This threat, that a yield curve will not retain its shape, is commonly known as 'yield curve risk'.

A third, troublesome, category goes under the name of 'basis risk': this denotes the possibility that yield curves for different instruments or products may not move in parallel with one another – i.e. that rate relationships and differentials may change. Some retail rates, in particular, are less sensitive and more discretionary than others. Among the many potential consequences of basis risk is a narrowing or a widening of the interest turn between chosen forms of funding and the assets in which they are invested. A further significant aspect is that natural and artificial hedges (the latter constructed by means of derivatives) could become dislocated and thus impaired. Specific correlations are not necessarily guaranteed for life as we might have wished.

Having identified the principal types of rate shift likely to occur, we need measurement techniques to monitor our exposures, and remedial devices to keep these risks within bounds. Throughout the discussion which makes up the rest of this chapter, it should be borne in mind that each currency must be treated separately: no blended result is possible.

8.3 Mismatch/gap management

The most rudimentary approach to measuring structural exposure is to maintain an interest sensitivity ladder dividing assets and liabilities into time bands (or 'buckets'), according to when their respective interest rates are contractually due for review (i.e. 'repricing'). Derivatives should also be captured, as far as practicable, by splitting them into their asset and liability components. An interest rate swap, for instance, is treated as both a deposit and an equal placement, each banded according to its fixed or floating character. Futures and forward rate agreements are usually entered as a forward-starting deposit or loan. Options sold or bought can be inserted at the delta of the underlying instrument (see Chapter 9), although this does not reflect all of the risks involved.

The ladder format resembles liquidity analysis, as seen in Chapter 4, except that it focuses on interest repricing, not payment maturity. A simple interest mismatch table is illustrated in Table 8.2, converted into bar chart form in Fig. 8.2. Within each time band, there will be a net 'gap' or 'mismatch' position, constituting one of the following:

- *Positive gap*: volume of assets repricing exceeds volume of liabilities repricing.

- *Negative gap*: volume of liabilities repricing exceeds volume of assets repricing.

- *Zero gap*: equilibrium.

A positive gap in the near time bands (as in Table 8.2 and Fig. 8.2) denotes an asset-sensitive situation, in which a preponderance of assets will reprice and react first to a change in interest rates: net interest income should therefore show an early increase when

Table 8.2 Example of an interest mismatch table

	Interest rate repricing schedule by amount in £million							
	Up to 3 mths	3 to 6 mths	6 to 12 mths	1 to 3 y	3 to 5 y	5 y+	Non-interest items	Total
Assets								
Treasury bills/gilts	50	70	40	20	10	10	0	200
Interbank	150	140	10	0	0	0	0	300
Corporate loans	100	200	90	10	0	0	0	400
Retail loans	355	180	75	55	20	15	0	700
Securities	120	60	15	5	0	0	0	200
Other assets	190	40	20	0	0	0	50	300
Total assets	**965**	**690**	**250**	**90**	**30**	**25**	**50**	**2100**
Swaps						50		
Liabilities								
Interbank	180	155	15	0	0	0	0	350
Public deposits	500	400	100	50	50	0	200	1300
Other liabilities	175	75	50	0	0	0	0	300
Loan capital	0	0	0	0	0	50	0	50
Equity capital	0	0	0	0	0	0	100	100
Total liabilities	**855**	**630**	**165**	**50**	**50**	**50**	**300**	**2100**
Swaps		50						
Repricing gap	**110**	**10**	**85**	**40**	**(20)**	**25**	**(250)**	
Cumulative gap	**110**	**120**	**205**	**245**	**225**	**250**	**0**	

Note: Some banks vary this format to give a different perspective. For example, the column for *non-interest items* is sometimes placed on the left-hand side, thereby changing the short term gapping profile (and perhaps the proposed tactics). The *cumulative gap sequence* can also be run from right to left, instead of left to right as above.

interest rates rise and a decrease when they fall. The bigger the gap, the bigger the risk either way. The change in earnings is essentially temporary, until such time as the laggard liabilities catch up with rate repricing. Positive gapping of the rate-sensitive zone is the broad tendency required by a policy of hedging the bank's share price, as discussed in section 8.1 above.

A negative gap in the early time bands indicates a liability-sensitive position, in which net interest income temporarily stands to shrink when interest rates rise and to expand when they fall. Such gapping can be justified on tactical grounds if there is strong enough reason to expect an imminent reduction in interest rates, but in general it lies outside the 'prudent range of conduct' proposed in section 8.1.

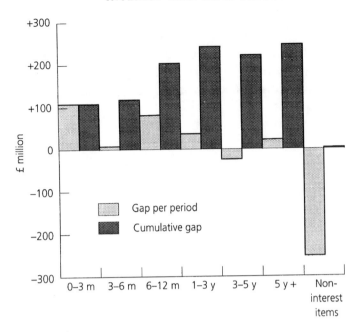

8.2 Gap analysis chart.

Zero (or neutral) gapping in the early periods suggests that the bank's net interest income is insensitive to general changes in interest rates in either direction. This is consistent with a risk-averse policy focused on stabilising net interest income, again as discussed in section 8.1.

On reviewing its mismatch report, the bank can seek to amend its gapping profile by changing its funding strategy (e.g. lengthening or shortening the term of new deposits solicited for the wholesale or the retail book), by changing repricing characteristics on the lending side (e.g. putting more, or less, emphasis on fixed versus floating rate mortgages), by switching out of some types of investments and into others, and by adopting other such policy revisions. Alternatively, the bank can enter into a variety of derivative contracts to hedge its positions. For example, swaps may be extensively employed to exchange interest streams on either side of the balance sheet, from fixed to floating rate or vice versa. Interest rate caps can be bought to limit any untoward rise in funding costs.

It hardly needs saying that all of these remedies require customers attracted by the new deposit and loan products, or counterparties willing to take the opposite view to the bank on interest rate positioning. In using derivative contracts to hedge open position risk, the bank increases its counterparty credit exposures and also its vulnerability to basis risk. These observations merely confirm the adage that, in risk management as in other walks of life, there is no free lunch.

Sizeable short versus long term mismatches can present a more intractable problem. A Savings and Loans institution which has a portfolio of 20-year mortgages funded by short term deposits (and is thus negatively gapped in the early time bands, positively gapped in the longer periods) may not have enough time to contrive an escape from its self-inflicted predicament before an interest rate crunch arrives.

Because of the evident perils of excessive mismatching, it is not uncommon for a bank to prescribe mismatch limits for each time band, and/or a ceiling on the percentage of expected net income put at risk for every percentage point increase or decrease in interest rates. Such controls are all the more necessary if the ALCO takes a 'sporting' view of risk management as a process of backing hunches. However, if it adopts the 'prudent range of conduct' recommended earlier, much of the difficulty falls away: the bank will consistently seek near-term gapping positions which are neutral to positive in line with the chosen policy, and will avoid creating potentially troublesome distortions for any future period.

8.4 Shortcomings of static gap analysis

Traditional mismatch/gap analysis embraces a number of valid insights, and fosters an instinctive feel for the macro risks being run. However, there are several weaknesses in the basic mismatch ladder represented by Table 8.2, which render it unsuitable for use by itself in a large or complex banking operation.

No matter how well chosen are the time bands for each particular type of bank, they will be insensitive to hidden internal mismatches. For instance, an apparently well-balanced position in the 3 to 6 months band may conceal, at the extreme, a substantial negative gap in the first day or two of the period which is not corrected until 'day 90'. At the longer term end, time bands spanning two or more years afford much greater scope for mischief, if there is any appreciable volume of business within them. The true vulnerability during most of a banded period may be the exact reverse of that depicted in the snapshot rendered by today's gap report. Subsequent daily snapshots will eventually correct earlier distortions, but may embody new falsehoods of their own.

The only thoroughgoing remedy would be to break down the bands into periods so small that such discrepancies do not matter: the ultimate logic being one time band for each day, defeating the object of the exercise by rendering it impossible for readers of the report to see the wood for the trees.

A pivotal and management-intensive problem in gap analysis (and, indeed, in all time-frame techniques) is the considerable number of items that defy easy classification within the grid. These include products with uncertain or 'sticky' repricing characteristics, like savings accounts and consumer loans and overdrafts. The contractual position needs to be weighed against behavioural expectations. Furthermore, the format does not cater for the imponderability of options sold or bought (whether/when they will be exercised), or of 'embedded options' such as a mortgage borrower's conditional right to repay the bank early.

A related limitation is that the gap report addresses only open position risk – i.e. the assumption that all interest rates will move together in the same direction by the same amount. It has nothing to say on yield curve risk or basis risk. Moreover, it takes a 'gone concern' rather than a 'going concern' view of the bank: that is, it features only existing assets and liabilities, and does not model future business development; for which reason it is often referred to as the 'static gap report'.

This static gap report is also mathematically naive in ignoring interest flows and the time value of money.

In short, compilations like Table 8.2 and Fig. 8.2 simply do not tell us enough of what we need to know.

8.5 Duration analysis

This more sophisticated approach, borrowed from the bond markets, takes account of interest flows and the time value of money. There are a number of versions, but the basic method aggregates the present value of all future cash flows (both principal and interest) within a portfolio, then weights them by their respective periods to maturity. The total of weighted values divided by present values gives a single number representing the *duration* of the portfolio, normally expressed in years.

Looked at the other way, duration is the weighted average life of the individual cash flows in the portfolio, where the weighting factors are the present values of those cash flows. In principle, the longer the duration, the greater is the interest rate risk.

One such calculation may be performed for the bank's assets, and another for its liabilities. Comparison of their respective durations will then give an alternative to a gap report. If the assets show a shorter duration than the liabilities (e.g. 1.5 years versus 2 years), the book is asset-sensitive: net interest income will tend to benefit from a general rise in rates, and to suffer from a fall in rates, according to the familiar gapping principles. Neutral or liability-sensitive profiles are similarly easy to interpret.

Duration analysis, with its single-number rendition, has several distinctive advantages. First, it provides a simple and accurate basis for hedging (or 'immunising') a portfolio, by taking a new equal and opposite position in a security with the same duration. Secondly, duration can be used as a prudential standard of comparison for alternative business development and funding strategies.

Thirdly, duration and yield to maturity provide the two essential elements for calculation of what is variously known as *interest rate elasticity* or *price elasticity*: this projects the approximate percentage change in the present value of a financial instrument (or a portfolio) that will result from a given percentage change (say 1%) in interest rates. We shall take a look at the relevant equation in Chapter 9. If the same modelling is applied to the bank's non-equity liabilities as to its assets, the difference between the two (assets less liabilities) will by definition be a projection of the expected present value of the bank's equity capital (and, in an ideal world, its market value and hence its share price). This computation is relevant to ALCO deliberations on the possible hedging strategies outlined in section 8.1.

Such notional revaluation of liabilities is a concept alien to most bankers. However, what is at issue is not the contractual obligation to repay at face value (which remains unchallenged), but the *economic worth* (or opportunity cost) of those liabilities from an objective standpoint. The reasoning is the same as that governing the present value of assets and of equity capital. If a depositor were able to sell his deposit account on the open market, the striking price would be not book value but the present value of expected cash flows.

Duration analysis can thus bring a different range of perspectives to bear on the interest rate sensitivities in a bank's book. Its main weaknesses lie in its very simplicity. The 'single number' may not tell the whole story, if it happens to be masking extreme mismatches within narrower periods which offset one another in the aggregate. What conclusion should we draw if both assets and liabilities show a duration of, say, five years? Primarily that this navigational information is too crude for comfort.

As with gap analysis, the conceptual emphasis remains on 'open position risk', the underlying assumption being that all interest rates move together, equally and in the same direction. Moreover, the focus is essentially 'gone concern', although the approach allows some scope for modelling.

Logistically, preparation of duration analysis is far from simple, requiring large volumes of data input. Outside bond market and other trading operations, most commercial banks are likely to conclude that duration methodology has a limited practical pay-off.

8.6 Simulation analysis

Those still in the hunt for a more comprehensive and less flawed technique will find their ultimate answer in simulation analysis. This entails modelling the characteristics of all the bank's asset and liability products, and subjecting them to a perpetual series of forward scenarios in which they exhibit likely and unlikely growth and behavioural patterns, interacting with an assortment of interest rate projections. The object of the exercise is to test what could happen to balance sheet structure, net interest income, present values and other financial targets up to three years ahead, under reasonable as well as unreasonable conditions. The choice of economic and environmental assumptions is limited only by the imagination, preferences and resources of the users.

Simulation analysis takes gap and duration analysis as a starting point, and additionally gives free rein to manipulation of future business mix and volumes, forecast and hypothetical interest rates, yield curve risk and basis risk, and exercise of options and embedded options. This 'dynamic' approach supersedes 'static' gap analysis and permits the most searching possible examination of a bank's interest rate sensitivities and strategies.

Corrective actions for open position risk follow the lines indicated in section 8.3 above. It is not possible to neutralise yield curve risk or basis risk but, with the benefit of greater awareness that comes from extensive simulation, the bank can take action to limit its vulnerabilities.

Simulation may be carried out on home-grown computer software, but the number of proprietary packages now on the market renders that unnecessary for any bank starting from scratch. Simulation is the most information-hungry of the analytical approaches we have reviewed in this chapter, and the user faces a balance of considerations regarding the level of detail to feed in. To track every single asset and liability is technically possible but scarcely practical in any bank large enough to want to engage in simulation. Aggregation by class of asset or liability is therefore in order; but to aggregate too far is to lose some of the power, flexibility and sensitivity that are the technique's chief attractions.

Operational decisions on level of detail and range of scenarios will be influenced by the appetite and capacity of the bank's top management. ALCO meetings should focus on a restricted selection of simulation reports, edited and presented by an elite team who understand both the number-crunching production process and the bank's business needs.

Simulation analysis demands a commitment of human and technological resources well beyond the requirements of other approaches to interest rate risk management. At its best, it can provide an unequalled information base for developing policy and testing the bank's strategic and financial plans; but given less than whole-hearted support, it is likely to be a waste of time and money. In that respect, it resembles many of the other modern banking techniques featured in this book.

8.7 Summary

Structural exposure revolves around the sensitivity of net interest income to changes in the level of interest rates. At stake is the single most important revenue contribution to a bank's profit performance. The bank can seek to stabilise *either* its net interest income *or* its share price but, by definition, not both at the same time.

However, either is a worthy target, and it is possible to mediate between the two.

An alternative ambition to 'maximise rather than stabilise' is a conceit not to be recommended. Equally hazardous is a policy of choosing to do nothing at all to hedge structural exposures.

Exposure management needs to take account of open position risk, yield curve risk, and basis risk, treating each currency separately.

Static gap management caters only for open position risk, and has a number of other rigidities. It may nevertheless suffice as a guidance system for simple banking operations with predominantly short term asset and liability maturities. Section 8.3 outlines some of the basic manoeuvres for adjusting and hedging gap positions.

Duration analysis offers advantages for modelling and hedging purposes; particularly where the book contains a sizeable element of longer term maturities, and the relativities of present values therefore assume greater importance. The approach also opens the way to interest rate elasticity projections. In other respects, duration analysis has much the same limitations as gap analysis.

Simulation analysis is the most comprehensive tool yet developed for the management of structural exposure. It builds on the insights of gap and duration analysis, but surpasses both in its multi-dimensional capabilities. Those who feel they need the extra risk coverage, and who are resolved to provide the financial and moral support that it deserves, should settle for nothing less.

CHAPTER NINE

Interest rate risk: trading exposure

This chapter addresses:

- The nature of trading exposure.

- Open position sensitivity analysis.

- Factor volatility.

- Value at risk.

- Stress-testing.

'Trading exposure' as described in this chapter denotes the sensitivity of *present values* of money market and capital market instruments to changes in current interest rates. This is one more of the treasury management concerns that fall under the supervision of a bank's asset and liability committee (ALCO). In the case of most banks we are talking about *asset* portfolios of treasury bills, government and corporate bonds, debt securities, certificates of deposit, commercial paper and other instruments held for purposes of trading, investment or liquidity; and possibly about *liabilities* in the form of 'short' (oversold) positions. Also included by association are 'repos' (repurchase agreements, akin to stock lending), 'reverse repos' (the same transaction, at the stock borrowing end), and interest-sensitive derivative contracts in general.

Where the interest rate on the principal or underlying instrument is fixed – i.e. does not float in line with current rates – the present value will normally adjust inversely whenever rates change. A rate increase induces a capital loss, and a rate decrease brings a capital gain. These losses or gains have to be recognised in the bank's books in respect of all tradable instruments that are marked to market (that is, regularly revalued at market prices): such treatment is increasingly the norm, although accounting conventions in most countries permit exemptions in respect of instruments identified as destined to be held to maturity (and hence categorised as 'not tradable').

Since interest-related trading exposes a bank to losses or gains due to price changes in the assets (or liabilities) concerned, the risk could arguably be classified as falling within the category of price risks to be covered in Chapter 10. The Basle regulatory regime merges them all under the heading of 'market risks' (see Chapter 3). However, this book follows a common usage in assigning to interest rate risk all impacts that are directly and solely attributable to interest rate changes. Chapter 10 will deal with other price risks that are not directly driven by interest rate movements; notably as affecting foreign exchange and equity share trading.

It should be observed at this point that a single financial instrument may well combine several different types of risk which are segregated in separate chapters of this book: for example, interest rate risk and foreign exchange price risk (not to mention credit and liquidity risks). The way to deal with such a case is to unbundle the risks, and manage each separately according to its generic norms.

Interest-related trading exposure can be measured and managed by a ladder and gapping methodology akin to that described at length in Chapter 8. However, this traditional approach carries with it similar problems of rigidity and imprecision: in particular, it does not cater adequately for zero-coupon instruments and derivatives. Modern banking prefers two superior and complementary techniques, profiled in sections 9.1 and 9.2 below. The first looks at the sensitivity of present values to movements in a benchmark interest rate, sometimes called a 'factor'. The perspective here corresponds to open position risk, as described in Chapter 8.

The second modern technique measures the statistical volatilities of the chosen 'factors' themselves. By combining an assessment of the volatility of the factor with the sensitivity of the instrument to changes in that factor, we can estimate, with a stated level of confidence, how much money is likely to be lost within a given timescale of holding the instrument in question. That monetary estimate is known as *value at risk* (or VAR). In the aggregate, at portfolio level, VAR renders a single number representing potential losses arising, over the chosen timescale, from the disparate levels of risk inherent in the bank's diverse trading positions. In theory, potential gains could also be plotted, but in practice the defensive focus of VAR is exclusively on losses.

VAR analysis implicitly recognises yield curve risk and basis risk (see Chapter 8), in addition to open position risk. The technique appears to be gaining increasing acceptance among regulators in Basle and elsewhere as a basis for determining bank capital requirements in respect of trading risks.

9.1 Open position sensitivity analysis

This discipline is accessible through the related calculations of *duration* and *interest rate elasticity*, as defined in Chapter 8. Interest rate elasticity measures the rate of change in the present value of a financial instrument or a portfolio in response to a specified change in factor interest rates. Trade vernacular uses the Greek letter delta to represent interest rate elasticity. The following is a basic equation to establish approximately the percentage by which the present value of a portfolio will fall if factor interest rates rise by 1%:

$$\text{Delta \%} = \frac{-\text{Duration}}{1 + \text{yield to maturity}}$$

Thus, if duration is two years and yield to maturity is 7% per annum, the equation works out as:

$$\text{Delta \%} = \frac{-2}{1 + 0.07} = \frac{-2}{1.07} = -1.87\%$$

In other words, for the purposes of this example, a 1% rise in factor interest rates will cause a fall of approximately 1.87% in the present value of the portfolio. Conversely, to ascertain the effect of a 1% fall in interest rates we simply change the minus sign to a plus, and the answer is a rise of approximately 1.87% in the present value.

Delta can be plotted as a trend line on a chart: sometimes it is constant and traces a straight line, which is consistent with the formula given above. In most cases, however, delta is variable and

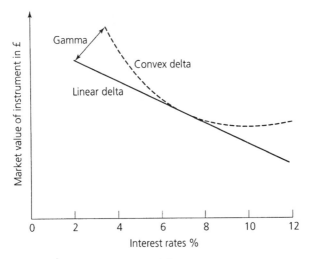

9.1 As interest rates rise, bond prices fall.

follows a curved rather than a straight path, owing to a mathematical effect known as 'convexity', dubbed 'gamma' by the market. Gamma measures any change in delta (i.e. in interest rate elasticity) as it moves up and down the scale – see Fig. 9.1.

Because delta is not usually linear (i.e. constant) – except for uncomplicated short term instruments – our simple equation can be relied on to give only an approximate answer. For some portfolios this will be good enough; for others not. It is beyond the scope of this book to delve into the finer points of convexity, beyond drawing the reader's attention to the phenomenon.

The duration-based formula provides no detailed information on the sensitivities of particular positions within the portfolio. A more precise methodology exists which uses zero-coupon pricing to value cash flows off the factor yield curve. The technique consists of flexing the factor interest rate by one basis point (one-hundredth of 1%) at chosen intervals along the curve (overnight, three months, six months, twelve months, and so on), one at a time whilst keeping the status quo on the remaining rates, in order to derive a series of notional revaluations of positions. This permits numerous modelling permutations on the lines of 'what if the three-month rate should rise by 20 basis points, the six-month rate by 10 basis points, and the rest stay as they are?' Industry practice is to express the sensitivity measurement in a convenient module known as 'present value of a basis point' (PVBP or PV01 for short): that is, how much present value the portfolio stands to lose (or gain) for each basis point movement in interest rates.

Having equipped itself with a satisfactory means of measurement, the bank will be concerned to contain the sensitivities within acceptable bounds. Duration-based methodology affords a precise framework for what is known as *delta-hedging*: that is, limiting the organic sensitivities by writing derivative contracts with opposite positioning. As noted in Chapters 7 and 8, all such artificial hedging is, however, bought at the expense of increasing the bank's counterparty credit exposures. Finally, the portfolio should contain a *spread of issuer names* (preferably twenty or more), so as to minimise *specific risk* (potential for decline in credit ratings, exacerbating the sensitivities).

9.2 Value at risk

Value at risk analysis provides the basis for an estimate of revaluation losses the bank can incur on a specified portfolio over a given time horizon. The technique involves compiling statistical distributions of daily movements in the factor interest rates that underpin the prices of the instruments in the portfolio, often going back as far as five years. By combining factor volatility with instrument sensitivity (the assessment in section 9.1), the bank can obtain a picture of the likely price volatility of each instrument that it is holding. Figures can then be aggregated to show the volatility of the portfolio as a whole. In the aggregation process, practitioners generally employ *variance/covariance matrix* methodology or alternative *historical simulation* to achieve a lower overall risk estimate than would otherwise emerge from a linear summation based on individual volatilities in isolation (see Chapter 6 on covariances). There are recognised technical problems in quantifying covariances in VAR analysis: suffice it to say that they are for specialists to debate, and beyond the scope of this book.

The end result, at any rate, may be charted in the form of a distribution curve on a histogram (as idealistically illustrated in Fig. 9.2) representing the volatility of the value of the portfolio. As we saw in the appendix to Chapter 1, in a 'normal' bell-shaped curve approximately 95% of the values in the distribution will lie within

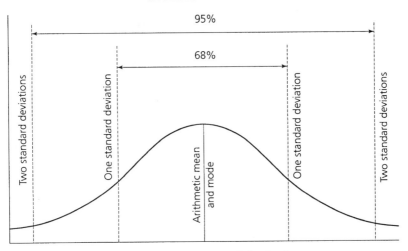

9.2 Volatility and standard deviations on a normal distribution curve.

two standard deviations on either side of the arithmetic mean (otherwise known as the 'expected outcome'), and over 99% within three standard deviations. However, as VAR in this case is preoccupied with loss rather than gain, and therefore confines its attention to the left-hand side of the curve, the mathematics are altered: 1.65 standard deviations will now cover 95% of the loss distributions, two standard deviations will cover approximately 97.5% of the loss distributions, and three standard deviations will account for nearly 99.9%.

Thus, subject to various caveats mentioned later, we have arrived at a point where we may conclude that within a chosen short period of trading (one day, one week, or whatever band we wish to derive statistically) we are 95% confident that losses in the value of the portfolio will not exceed £x, and 97.5% confident that they will not exceed £y, and 99.9% confident that they will not exceed £z, in an escalating series of amounts. The 'value at risk' in these formulations is the potential loss of £x or £y or £z (or the corresponding amount at any other confidence interval on the curve).

The corollary is that in one case out of twenty the losses probably *will* exceed £x, in one case out of fifty or so they probably *will* exceed £y, and in one case out of a thousand they probably *will* exceed £z. The problem is, the formula does not tell us by how much, let alone when; hence the need to probe the extremes by stress-testing.

9.3 Stress-testing

Thus far we have considered *historical volatility*, which may be regarded as an objective basis for purposes such as regulatory assessment of capital adequacy (see discussion in Chapter 3). In-house practice in the trading area of the bank will be to keep this computation rolling forward, reflecting daily revaluations of the asset portfolio. However, as we saw in Chapter 1, past volatility is at best a guide and cannot encompass all future possibilities. The point about risk is its capacity to surprise: hence, perhaps, what may seem to be a somewhat grudging attitude on the part of the regulatory authorities towards reliance on historical trading statistics.

Any bank which has taken the trouble to adopt a VAR approach to trading will want to go beyond the history and subject its portfolio to rigorous stress-testing. This involves simulating a continual series of unusual scenarios (and diabolical combinations) inspired by 'black Mondays/Wednesdays', civil and international wars, Japanese earthquakes and other sources of rate shift extremes. In effect, the bank has to ask itself: 'What is the worst thing that could happen to our book today?' Imaginative invention can be supplemented by 'Monte Carlo' techniques which generate streams of random rate projections and permutations. The results of stress-testing will have an important influence on portfolio management policies and decisions, and on the VAR sub-limits that are delegated to separate trading books or desks. Finally, a mature system offers a means of allocating risk capital and measuring trading performance in terms of return on that capital.

9.4 Problems with value at risk

In its present state of development, VAR is not without technical difficulties. For a start, there are many possible ways to measure volatility. What should be the 'moving window' of statistical distributions – 90 days, 5 years? Should all observations count equally, or should more recent experience be given extra weighting? There are arguments favouring the latter course, but it can produce big jumps in perceived volatility and VAR.

Secondly, professional opinion is divided on the mathematical validity of some aspects of the VAR aggregation process: are we

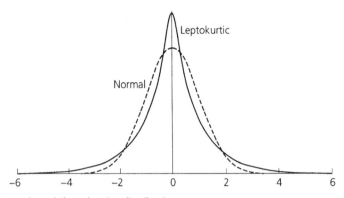

9.3 'Normal' and 'leptokurtic' distributions.

adding like with like, or is there an element of apples and pears? Moreover, the phenomenon of basis risk tells us that correlations are inherently unstable: they change over the course of time, and in extreme conditions may break down just when they are most needed. In a market crisis like that of October 1987, financial assets tend to become *more positively correlated*, which is bad news for portfolio managers (see Chapter 6). VAR analysis of a kind which invests great expectations in correlation science may therefore show an overoptimistic picture.

Thirdly, real life often fails to provide the 'normal' bell-shaped curve which best lends itself to standard deviation treatment. Where the statistical distribution is significantly skewed, alternative mathematical techniques will have to be employed in the estimation of risk probabilities. In the financial markets, the distribution tends to be not so much asymmetric as *leptokurtic*, as in Fig. 9.3: that is to say, it has longer/fatter tails and a higher peak than a normal distribution, reflecting a higher incidence of extreme values, particularly in short term intervals of measurement. This problem can be addressed, at least in part, by the use of a GARCH model ('generalised autoregressive conditional heteroskedasticity'), which assigns a weighting to current market volatility in relation to previous time periods.

Assuming we can solve these technical problems, should we centre our analysis, and our risk appetite, on a 95% confidence level or some higher standard?

Implicit in the chosen time horizon (usually one day in an active trading operation) is the assumption that any loss-making position will be liquidated or stabilised within that period, before it can grow to exceed the value considered to be 'at risk'. However, the potential loss represented by VAR is understated if (as is common) it omits the costs of liquidating and/or hedging that position. The act of liquidation might itself move prices further against the bank.

For the generalist reader, it is sufficient to be aware that technical and conceptual difficulties such as these exist. Value at risk is not an immaculate system, but it embodies the banking industry's best efforts to grapple with the challenge of volatility.

9.5 Summary

Trading exposure refers to the sensitivity of the present value of debt instruments and related derivatives to changes in interest rates.

Two measurement techniques are employed in harness, with a view to keeping revaluation losses within bounds. The first, sensitivity analysis, measures the change in present value to be expected as a result of a specified change in benchmark or 'factor' interest rates: this dynamic is known as 'interest rate elasticity', and is represented in equations as 'delta'. Delta itself is not usually linear (constant) but is subject to mathematical curvature known as 'convexity' and represented in equations as 'gamma'.

There is a general duration-based formula for calculating delta, but more specific answers to 'what if?' questions can be obtained by using zero-coupon pricing to value cash flows off the factor yield curve. The standard unit of measurement for instrument sensitivity is 'present value of a basis point' (PVBP).

The second, companion technique is to measure statistical volatilities of factor interest rates, as a basis for estimating the volatility of instrument values in the portfolio, and hence 'value at risk' within a specified trading time-frame at a stated level of confidence. Aggregation of individual values (allowing as far as practicable for degrees of correlation) produces a single VAR for a portfolio, or indeed for the whole bank. This technique offers a platform for stress-testing and formulation of portfolio policy, for delegation of trading sub-limits, and for capital allocation and performance measurement. It comes with a health warning, however, as it raises a number of technical problems and debatable issues. Nevertheless, value at risk now looks to be established as an indispensable tool of the trade.

CHAPTER TEN

Price risks

This chapter considers:

- The nature of price risks.

- Risks associated with foreign exchange trading.

- Dimensions of the foreign exchange market.

- Foreign exchange price risk.

- Banking industry involvement with equities.

- Equity price risk.

- Systematic and specific risk.

- Proprietary trading.

- Control of the dealing room.

- Basle Committee risk management guidelines for derivatives.

When a bank has any sort of 'open' (in this sense meaning 'naked' or 'unhedged') position – whether direct or derivative – in a foreign currency or an equity investment, it is exposed to a *price risk*: the risk that a change in the market price (quoted or otherwise ascertained) will occasion a loss (or gain) to the bank through revaluation or realisation. Price risks may also be incurred on open positions in commodities of all kinds (e.g. precious and base metals, crude oil, aviation fuel, grains, cocoa and coffee): these may be the subject of derivative contracts in a sophisticated dealing room, but they are not primarily banking risks and fall outside the mainstream focus of this book. And again, we shall not spend time on price risks associated with speculative investments in property and other physical assets, which are not specific to banking (although the exposure principle would be much the same).

Price changes in currencies and equities are caused by adjustments to supply and demand, which in turn reflect altered economic circumstances and revised market sentiment, sometimes linked with movements in the general level of interest rates. Price changes in fixed rate debt instruments, where revaluations are directly and solely attributable to interest rate fluctuations, are classified separately in this book as 'interest rate risk: trading exposure' (covered in Chapter 9).

Bank regulators in Basle, Brussels and elsewhere tend to merge all these price exposures under the heading of 'market risk' in the designated 'trading book' (see Chapter 3). The concept of the trading book has its problems, whilst an objection to market risk as a category is that the label is so broad as to confuse rather than assist analysis: all banking activities may be said to take place in markets of one sort or another. For the uninitiated or the insouciant, 'market risk' can become a convenient gloss for 'everything we don't really understand but pretend to'.

10.1 Risks associated with foreign exchange trading

Even 'foreign exchange risk' and 'currency risk', interchangeable terms with a longer pedigree, are themselves open to ambiguity or misinterpretation. This is because foreign exchange trading encompasses a microcosm of risks encountered in domestic banking; risks which can be managed in the ways described in other chapters of this book. The foreign currency cash flows, deposits, loans and financial instruments entail their own liquidity risks, credit risks, interest rate risks (both structural and trading), operating risks, and ultimately solvency risk.

Spot and forward exchange contracts, and currency swaps, involve separate types of 'presettlement' and 'settlement' credit risk (as outlined in Chapter 5). Crystallisation of foreign exchange presettlement risk through default unravels a hedge or a speculative position, and the resulting impact is the marginal cost of replacing the defunct contract at current prices (or the opportunity cost of possible gains or losses forgone): this entails an equivalent foreign exchange price risk, a category which we shall consider in section 10.3 below. Foreign exchange settlement risk is intrinsically a more dire affair, relating as it does to potential loss of the gross amount of the contract (not just the value change since it was written). A failed settlement inwards, after the point where irrevocable instructions have been given to pay away countervalue, becomes a conventional bad debt; in addition, depending on the circumstances, the bank may have to buy or sell an equal amount of the missing foreign currency to square its books, and in so doing it could incur a further loss on foreign exchange price.

The problem of settlement risk, which impinges directly on liquidity and systemic risks, has been examined earlier in Chapters 4 and 5. Suffice it to say that when people worry about the magnitude of foreign exchange risk in the market, they are often thinking of the ramifications of systemic settlement or 'Herstatt' risk (outlined in Chapter 2) rather than foreign exchange price risk *per se*, which is the proper subject of this chapter.

10.2 Dimensions of the foreign exchange market

The foreign exchange market is 'over-the-counter', and its communications are primarily telephonic or screen-based. Although every national banking system has its own opening and closing hours, the global market never sleeps: thus money can be lost (or gained) on overnight positions. In so far as such statistical aggregates are meaningful, the foreign exchange market lays claim to being the largest financial market in the world. According to the Bank for International Settlements' triennial survey (April 1995), daily turnover in global foreign exchange trading is estimated at $1230 billion (say £783 billion), with London the leading centre by a considerable margin (see Table 10.1). As this is something like eight times the daily turnover of international trade in goods and services, the question arises: what is the rest of the $1230 billion for?

Some of the gap is accounted for by the fact that each import/export contract can give rise to multiple foreign exchange contracts. A French importer who has to pay £10 million in three months' time for goods imported from Britain may cover his foreign

Table 10.1 Foreign exchange market turnover, largest world centres

Daily averages*	April 1992		April 1995	
	Amount $billion	%share	Amount $billion	%share
London	290.5	27	464.5	30
New York	166.9	16	244.4	16
Tokyo	120.2	11	161.3	10
Singapore	73.6	7	105.4	7
Hong Kong	60.3	6	90.2	6
Zurich	65.5	6	86.5	5

*Adjusted for local double-counting by country.

(Source: Bank for International Settlements, triennial foreign exchange survey)

exchange price risk by buying forward £10 million, to be delivered (and paid for) three months hence at a franc price determined now. The cost to the importer of that outright forward exchange contract is dictated by the spot price of sterling plus or minus a forward margin calculated by reference to the difference between franc and sterling interest rates for the period concerned (in this case three months). If the franc interest rate is the higher of the two, the margin will be a premium (will be added); if lower, the margin will be a discount (deducted). The rationale for the forward margin should become clearer as we continue this discussion: it is a net cost of carry and has no connection with any explicit forecast of exchange rates in three months' time, although such forecast may be implicit in the respective interest rates.

The French importer's bank, on furnishing the means of protection for its customer's foreign exchange price risk, may need to hedge its own position. This it can do by buying the sterling in the spot market and placing it on deposit to mature (together with interest) in three months' time, financing this transaction by borrowing equivalent francs for the same period. The opportunity cost or gain from the difference between the two interest rates (paid and received) constitutes the logical basis for calculation of the forward margin mentioned in the previous paragraph. However, such a manoeuvre increases costs by inflating the bank's balance sheet. Alternatively the bank can engage in an outright (and opposite) forward contract or (more commonly) an equivalent foreign exchange swap with another bank or corporate counter-party. A foreign exchange swap entails an exchange of currencies now and a reverse exchange at a specified future time: the spot leg is actually superfluous for the purpose under discussion here, and is therefore reversed out by a separate and opposite spot deal. The counterparty to the first bank's forward or swap contract may need in turn to write further swaps, etc, to hedge its own resultant positions. Thus the multiplication process is set in motion, abating only when the market as a whole has comfortably absorbed the risk arising out of the originating import contract: the ripple does not go on forever, because (at a price) there will always be customers and banks looking to square opposite positions.

A further multiplication factor arises if the French importer's bank buys the pounds (spot or forward) in exchange for dollars first, instead of for francs. Then it has two contracts (in addition to that with the importer): buy pounds in exchange for dollars and buy dollars in exchange for francs. This seemingly roundabout route is regular market practice stemming from the dollar's global dominance as a reserve or vehicle currency. The deutschemark has come to serve the same purpose as a regional vehicle currency for Europe.

Finally, since there are two parties to each one contract, there is always a possibility of double-counting in the statistical compilation. Readers may notice that some of the arguments here resemble those that revolve around the size of the derivatives markets (swaps in particular) and the inherent systemic risk (see Chapter 4). Forward foreign exchange contracts are essentially derivatives, although often excluded from that classification.

So risk absorption and structural features of the market make up some of the difference between import/export values and foreign exchange turnover levels. Other international cash flows not necessarily connected to import/export statistics include cross-border investments and eurocurrency financings where investors, lenders, or borrowers see attraction in particular capital or money markets. There is also bound to be an unquantifiable and highly variable element of foreign exchange speculation, unrelated to the financing or hedging needs of customers or banks: almost by the same token, there will be intervention by central banks seeking to stabilise or prop up exchange rates. These were the vested interests ranged against one another in the struggle that led to sterling quitting the European exchange rate mechanism (the ERM) in 1992. As already noted in Chapter 4, however, the distinction between hedging and speculation is not always as clear cut as might be supposed: in some circumstances, doing nothing or supporting the status quo could be regarded as speculation. The general issue of proprietary trading will be considered in a later section.

10.3 Foreign exchange price risk

Foreign exchange price risk relates to possible revaluation losses (or gains) on long/overbought or short/oversold currency positions, in response to movements in exchange rates. The argot expressions 'long' (for overbought) and 'short' (for oversold) introduce an unfortunate ambiguity, as the same terms are used to describe the *tenor* (original or remaining life) of financial instruments and contracts. However, which meaning is intended can usually be deduced without difficulty from the context in each case. A bank with a perfectly matched book (as to individual currencies, amounts, and maturity dates) has no overbought or oversold positions and therefore no price exposure – unless and until a counterparty defaults at the presettlement or the settlement stage.

From this brief description it follows that, no matter how widely foreign exchange services and dealing rooms are devolved in a large bank, ultimate control of policy and position-taking must be centralised within a treasury department under the auspices of the asset and liability committee (ALCO). That end is achieved by a combination of command structure, delegation of discretionary limits, and daily reporting of positions; and (in the absence of delegation) appropriate transfer pricing of exposures.

In the forward foreign exchange market prices are customarily quoted as forward margins for recognised 'forward value' dates, e.g.:

- Overnight.

- Tomorrow-next (starting tomorrow and maturing the next day, the latter coinciding with 'spot' date).

- Spot-next (starting spot date and maturing the following day).

- Spot-one week (starting spot and maturing a week later).

- Spot-one month, three/six/twelve months, etc.

Broken dates (e.g. spot-17 days) are available as well, sometimes at a less favourable price.

A bank's foreign currency engagements constitute a schedule of inward and outward cash flows, committed or expected, spread out over the calendar from today onwards. A 'ladder' of forward foreign exchange positions in each currency contains a number of different classes of risk which have to be split up and managed each according to its appropriate discipline. For example, within each future time band there needs to be a reasonable balance of inflows and outflows in each currency to meet liquidity needs (Chapter 4). Any mismatch between inflows and outflows will also give rise to interest rate risk (Chapters 8 and 9).

In the case of foreign exchange price risk, we are focusing on the spot risk in each forward position and separating it out from the embedded interest rate risk. The forward ladder in each currency tracks the cash flows in and out for every future date. If these flows are discounted back (at the appropriate currency interest rate for the remaining term) to present values, they can be summated to produce a net price exposure (overbought or oversold) for each currency. The Bank of England's basic reporting format for capital adequacy purposes is simpler, ignoring present value methodology and calling for a straight summation of net positions in each currency regardless of timing (see Chapter 3).

If the bank is overbought in a particular currency, it has a future asset which may lose (or gain) value compared with a contract price already fixed *or* compared with the value that the bank expects (e.g. on a dividend due from overseas). Conversely, an oversold position means there is a risk that the bank may have to pay for its impending liability at a significantly higher exchange cost than expected (maybe higher than the proceeds of its sale); or, of course, the luck could go the other way, in the bank's favour.

Once a bank has a picture of its price risk exposures (preferably discounted back to present values), it can adjust or hedge its positions by buying or selling additional currency amounts forward or writing new foreign exchange swaps (all, it bears repeating, at the expense of increasing counterparty credit exposures). In fact, this is too much of a rear-view mirror account of the way things work, since the bank would already have been applying these steering correctives as it went along, adjusting for constantly changing positions during the day, in accordance with delegated exposure limits reflecting the ALCO's tolerance for foreign exchange price risk.

How do we assess the extent of the foreign exchange price *risk* that the bank may be running, as distinct from the size of its *exposure*? Obviously by studying past and prospective exchange rate volatility of the currency concerned vis-à-vis the bank's base currency. The same considerations and caveats apply as for all other applications of this statistical approach. On the one hand, the more extensive the historical sample of daily rate movements, the more confident we may *feel* that we have pinned down the essential volatility of the particular exchange rate. But risk can never be confined in that way: we need also to look very hard at current economic and political trends, and to stress-test the extremes as well as the more likely scenarios.

The outcome of this assessment may be rendered as a probability distribution curve of the kind discussed in Chapter 9 (section 9.2). Again, in a 'normal' distribution two standard deviations on either side of the arithmetic mean will cover approximately 95% of the values, and three standard deviations will account for over 99%. Thus, in principle, we can read off the chart that over the given time horizon (one day, one week, etc) we are 95% confident that a particular foreign currency (say, the dollar) will not fluctuate against the domestic currency (say, sterling) more than $y\%$ above or below the mean, and 99% confident that it will not fluctuate more than $z\%$ (a higher percentage) above or below the mean.

Applying these volatilities to the present value of actual overbought or oversold exposure, we can then ascertain the *value at risk* (the likely range of loss, or gain, in sterling terms) from exchange rate movements in the bank's dollar book, over a stated time horizon, at 95%, 99%, or any other chosen confidence level. And of course we can repeat the exercise for every other foreign currency in which the bank has an open position, and aggregate the results by means of variance/covariance matrix methodology to show total value at risk from exchange rate movements.

An alternative to the variance/covariance matrix approach is to subject the bank's open positions to historical simulation of the daily profit and loss that would have been incurred in (say) the past five years. The results can be used to compute VAR for the bank's open positions, observing the chosen time horizon and confidence levels. This delivers the offsetting benefits of covariance (as outlined in Chapter 6) by means of a basically simpler mathematical technique.

On the same principles as expounded in Chapter 9, the application of VAR by one means or another affords a basis for quantifying the bank's risk appetite through the ALCO process, delegating daylight and (more restrictive) overnight open position limits for individual currency books and desks, allocating economic risk capital and measuring trading performance in terms of return on that capital.

The problems with, and objections to, VAR methodology remain as outlined in section 9.4, and we need not recapitulate them here. Most modern bankers feel that VAR, for all its flaws and uncertainties, is the best available tool for price risk measurement. No doubt the technique can be further refined as users gain experience. Achievement of consensus and full recognition for capital adequacy regulation appears to be only a matter of time (see Chapter 3).

10.4 The banking community and equity risks

Commercial banks in the Anglo-Saxon tradition have historically given equity investments a fairly wide berth, at least until the 1980s. They (and probably their regulators) felt that predominantly short term bank deposits should not be invested in assets characterised by unlimited maturity, volatile and unenforceable value, and uncertain liquidity. Moreover, when a company collapses the interests of its shareholders are subordinated to all other claims: share capital is risk capital, and shares are a more risky type of asset for a bank to own than conventional loans and overdrafts. This distinction between the rights of different classes of claimant also engenders conflicts of interest which it is uncomfortable for a bank to straddle.

In the rare instances where these commercial banks acquired shares for reasons of competition strategy, public policy, or happenstance, the investments were seen as being morally a deduction from the bank's own equity capital rather than a normal deployment of deposits: first in recognition of the riskiness of the asset, and secondly because it would be a false principle to gear up (leverage) the quantum of risk capital in the economy on the back of bank deposits.

British merchant banks, for their part, were better endowed with intellectual than with monetary capital, and there was no call for them to be big investors in an already well developed share market. Specialist jobbers and stockbrokers, outside the banking industry, were in business respectively as appointed wholesalers and matchmakers in the secondary market. The division of labour had its logic. In the United States, a different historical experience led to the roles of corporate financier, new issue underwriter, secondary market trader, jobber and broker being combined under one roof in large and strongly capitalised securities houses like Goldman Sachs and Merrill Lynch. However, the Glass-Steagall Act of 1933, enacted in the aftermath of the stock market crash of 1929, enforced a strict separation between the securities industry and the commercial banking system.

In continental Europe and Japan, by contrast with the UK and the USA, the stock markets developed more slowly, and commercial banks were consequently impelled to play a bigger role as shareholders in industry. There is a long running debate in British political, academic and journalistic circles as to whether the continentals have enjoyed a competitive advantage or disadvantage by reason of this structural difference featuring (in Germany and Switzerland at least) so-called 'universal banking': however, the rights and wrongs of this controversy need not concern us here.

The effects of such national divergences are still plainly visible, but with the globalisation of capital markets the tide is now beginning to turn towards a degree of *convergence*. Pressure of international competition caused the 'big bang' of October 1986 which swept away London's merchant banking/jobbing/broking barriers and the cosseted system of fixed dealing commissions. This led to the formation of comprehensive investment banks on the pattern of the American securities houses: in order to gain equivalent muscle, however, most of them eventually had to be taken under the wing of commercial banks, important among whom were German and Swiss giants seeking to adopt the new London model as a basis on which to globalise and compete with the Americans. In the USA, meanwhile, Glass-Steagall segregation of commercial banking from securities appears at last to be crumbling away.

Other contemporary influences for change include disintermediation and the migration of corporate clients to the money and capital markets in search of cheaper financing (see Chapter 7). In corporate rescue operations, there is also a growing practice of converting non-performing bank loans into equity shares in order to give more breathing space to the distressed company.

The combination of these trends, together with the pressures for diversification in pursuit of a more profitable business mix, explains how some banking systems (notably the British) have become more exposed to equity risks, against their earlier best judgement. Were those reservations merely mistaken prejudice? Not entirely. Whilst there may be increasing similarities between corporate credit appraisal and equity investment analysis, no responsible bank entrusts both areas of activity to the same staff. Apart from residual differences in market knowledge and skills, and in risk characteristics, there remains a fundamental conflict of interest between the roles of commercial banking intermediary on the one hand, and shareholder, market maker, etc, on the other; mirrored, perhaps fortuitously, in the capital adequacy directive's distinction between the 'banking book' and the 'trading book' (summarised in Chapter 3).

Probably the most common aspect of this conflict of interest is the danger of engaging in the criminal practice of 'insider trading'; that is, profiting, or enabling privileged others to profit, from inside knowledge (e.g. gained from the banker–customer relationship) unavailable to the equity market as a whole. Banks which are led by the profit motive or the survival instinct to diversify into equity underwriting, secondary market making, arbitrage and proprietary trading, stockbroking, investment advice, or investment management will have to run all those businesses separately and establish Chinese walls between each of them as well as between them and the banking side of the house. Further details of the problems and the administrative solutions are contained in Chapter 5 (section 5.10).

Equity and equity-derivative portfolios, of whatever kind, are subject to a variety of risks, including liquidity risk, credit risk (if the issuer becomes insolvent), interest rate risk (spasmodically), operating risks, and *in extremis* the bank's own solvency risk (witness Barings). In the case of cross-border investment, country risk and foreign exchange price risk assume great importance: suspension of international payments on the part of the country concerned, or erosion of the value of its currency, can wipe out any nominal returns or capital gains. Other chapters are dedicated to discussion of these various types of risk. The subject under consideration here is *equity price risk*, the risk of revaluation/ realisation losses (or gains) due to movements in quoted share price.

10.5 Equity price risk

The approach to management of this risk is not dissimilar to that outlined in Chapter 9 for debt instruments. That is to say, get a feel for the price sensitivity of each specific share in relation to 'the market' as represented by a relevant factor, namely a share index; then attempt to measure the past and prospective volatility of the index; then combine these steps to arrive at an assessment of the value at risk in each shareholding (or analogous derivative contract) and, by suitably adjusted aggregation, in the portfolio as a whole.

Share prices are driven by the relationship between supply and demand, which varies according to changes in economic circumstances and market sentiment, sometimes accompanied by movements in the general level of interest rates. Supply and demand achieve equilibrium at a share price which satisfies the market's required rate of return on the particular share for the perceived risk of investing in it. According to the standard capital asset pricing model (outlined in Chapter 1, section 1.10), the minimum required rate of return (also known as the 'cost of capital') is derived from the following components:

- A so-called 'risk-free' rate, usually represented by the yield on 90-day treasury bills in the short term, or a succession of projected treasury bill rates for a medium term view (or a medium term gilt for those who do not fancy forecasting treasury bill rates over such a length of time).

- A premium applicable to the equity market as a whole, representing compensation for its non-diversifiable risk.

- A beta coefficient, which is a historically derived measure of the sensitivity of the return on the share in question to a general change in the return on the market (as represented by a relevant share index, such as the Dow Jones Industrial Average or the Financial Times Ordinary Share Index).

For convenience, beta may also be tracked by reference to share prices instead of rates of return. If the share is of average price sensitivity (i.e. behaviourally identical to the index), its beta will be 1.0; if more sensitive than the average, it will be higher than 1.0; if less sensitive, lower than 1.0. By analogy with the method set out in Chapter 9, beta is the tool by which the bank may gauge the price sensitivity of its share portfolio to a share index: the sensitivity of each share is determined by its beta, whilst the sensitivity of a portfolio reflects the beta-weighted sum of holdings.

Having addressed beta sensitivity, our second step in this sequence is to measure the historical volatility of the 'factor' – i.e. the relevant share index – over a chosen timescale. By combining the volatility with the portfolio sensitivity, the bank may plot a probability distribution curve of value outcomes which, for the sake of illustration, we will assume to be 'normally' shaped. If attention is confined to the left-hand (loss potential) side of the curve, 1.65 standard deviations will cover 95% of the distributions, two standard deviations will cover approximately 97.5%, and three standard deviations will account for nearly 99.9%. These confidence intervals (or any others on the curve) may then be used to assess the value at risk (the likely limit of potential capital losses) in holding that share portfolio for a stipulated trading period (say one day or one week).

As in all its other applications, VAR may be used as a yardstick for quantifying the bank's risk tolerance (under the authority of the ALCO), setting trading limits and sub-limits for the dealing room, allocating notional capital and measuring profit performance.

Once again, it is necessary to enter all the caveats and disclaimers set out at greater length in Chapter 9. Historical statistics of beta and of share index volatility are not a guarantee of future behaviour: stress-testing is a necessary adjunct. Sensitivity correlations between different shares are somewhat unreliable, and may break down completely under extreme conditions. The mathematics of portfolio aggregation are disputed. The probability distribution curve is likely to be leptokurtic (characterised by a high peak and dangerous long/fat tails) rather than 'normal', calling for further specialised analytical techniques. VAR may be the most useful device for managing price risks, but it is by no means a complete solution.

10.6 Portfolio diversification: systematic versus specific risk

Section 10.5 has just explained things in terms of *systematic risk* – that is, the tendency for all share prices to move together (albeit by differing degrees according to individual or weighted *beta*) because the equity market as a whole is subject to a common set of economic, political and social influences. *Systematic risk* cannot be diversified away given that, for better or worse, we are stuck with the market and its environment.

The other element governing a share price is known as *specific risk*. This refers to strengths, weaknesses, and sensitivities unique to a particular company (and possibly to its close competitors) which may affect its share price *independently* of market movements. Finance theory tells us that *specific risk* can be virtually eliminated (cancelled out) as a component of share price by means of portfolio diversification, being negligible as a rule where twenty or more well spread stocks are held. This universal principle, recommending diversification of an equity portfolio (like any other risk portfolio), will not come as news to readers who have absorbed the message of Chapter 6.

For practical purposes, in a well-diversified portfolio only *systematic risk* remains, any divergence from the index being confined to weighted *beta* alone. For a portfolio with insufficient diversification, however, the methodology of systematic sensitivity outlined in section 10.5 would need to be combined with some measurement of the *specific risk* for each share, using variance/covariance calculations of the kind shown in Chapter 6.

10.7 Proprietary trading

Proprietary trading has had a particularly bad press since February 1995 when Barings, the London merchant bank, was brought down by losses of £830 million on what amounted to a massive bet on exchange-traded Nikkei 225 stock index futures. Rather than pursue that convoluted story, however, we shall confine ourselves here to a more balanced assessment of what proprietary trading involves. It is unfair to condemn a practice out of hand on the basis of one uncontrolled and untypical disaster.

Proprietary trading is open position-taking for the account of the bank, rather than a customer, in the hope of making capital gains out of price risks (including, for the purpose of this definition, the type of trading risks featured in Chapter 9). A variant is arbitrage, the squeezing of profits out of short-lived pricing differentials on the same instrument in different markets. These sorts of trading contrast with the more straightforward pursuit of income from the spread between the bank's 'bid' and 'offer' prices on currencies, shares, etc.

It is incidental whether a customer provides the initial material for proprietary trading (e.g. by way of a forward exchange contract which the dealer then refrains from hedging), or whether the bank goes into the market as end-user of an outright trade or a derivative contract. The result is the same either way: an open position, which is literally 'speculative' in as much as it stands to incur a gain or loss in value.

Seen in this light, proprietary trading might appear indistinguishable from customer-driven dealing which incurs a normal incidence of temporarily unhedged price risk. Thus the topic of proprietary trading can, and sometimes does, become mired in smudge and prevarication. The difference between 'normal' and 'proprietary' trading is simply one of degree and of speculative intention (passing up the opportunity to hedge). You may ask: so what? If the proprietary exposure is correctly assessed and understood, if it is adequately monitored, reported and controlled, if sufficient risk capital is available and allocated, what is the problem? These, as Barings showed, are big ifs, and there are other objections to proprietary trading as a way of life that bear thinking about.

Sustained profits from proprietary trading depend on the bank having a lasting competitive advantage – superior market intelligence, judgement, skills or resources – over the generality of other market professionals. Such advantage may possibly accrue from size and sophistication of operation, but logically it can benefit only a minority of players in any market at any particular moment; and the more efficient the market, the less likely it is that anyone will have an edge. For most traders most of the time, trying to outguess and outperform the market will be a frustrating experience.

Because markets are volatile, proprietary trading on any significant scale can also bring in volatile results. These are just what enlightened bank managements and most shareholders do not want, because they represent at best poor quality earnings: unpredictable and, even when handsome, unreliable and not regularly repeatable. Losses will be suffered too.

Proprietary trading which seeks to contribute a substantial revenue stream shifts the spotlight from serving the customer to indulging the 'star dealer' profile, the mega-bonus, the temptation to overtrade and to compound. It places a premium on communication and trust between the dealer and his management, and puts a strain on systems and controls. The Barings episode is replete with these lessons. A bank which is effectively in competition with its customers may have to recognise a conflict of interest by segregating the functions of proprietary trader and customer dealer.

The moral which suggests itself is that the ALCO must draw a psychological distinction between a normally fluctuating incidence of temporarily unhedged, customer-focused business on the one hand, and habitual target-driven position-taking on the other. Risk tolerance in most banks should be confined to the former; in which case exposure limits should be set at pragmatically modest levels, with trading positions (and their underlying motivation) continually open to supervisory questioning. Dealing room disciplines and performance incentives also need to be calibrated to the bank's appetite for risk.

10.8 Control of the dealing room

In the model so far described, the ALCO quantifies the bank's risk tolerance and delegates position limits for different purposes and sorts of exposure, in terms of value at risk or other measurements. The chief dealer in turn may break these up into sub-limits for each of the individual dealers concerned. At the same time, the dealing room must keep within the counterparty name limits established by the credit risk function.

Beyond that, extensive guidelines and operating rules are needed, to ensure not only observance of limits but also sound practice and compliance with regulatory and legal requirements. These may take the form, for instance, of a 'policies and procedures' manual; and a 'code of conduct' covering, e.g., ethical standards, social relations with clients, and the writing of business outside current market rates (historically often associated with cover-up or fraud). Matters such as these could equally be consigned to Chapter 11 on Operating Risks, but it is convenient to touch on the salient aspects here.

Perhaps the single most important principle is to maintain a strict functional separation of dealing from back-office processing. Neither function should be allowed to intrude into the other's area of operations, or to exercise authority over the other. Breach of this prudential rule sacrifices essential checks and balances and, as in the Barings case, invites concealment, falsification and fraud. All transactions, together with the time of day, should be logged by the dealer and communicated to the processing area by means of dealing slips (or electronic equivalent). The processing unit will arrange for settlement of deals on due date, and meanwhile will dispatch written confirmations to the counterparties: it will also verify confirmations received from counterparties. Each dealer's log of transactions should be checked against back-office records daily.

Dealer positions are monitored throughout the day, with excess exposures (to counterparties or to price risks) and corrective actions reported to higher authority. Mark to market revaluations should be undertaken at least once daily by the dealers concerned, and at prescribed intervals by back-office staff for the purpose of crystallising profits and losses according to the bank's accounting conventions.

It is normal practice in a modern dealing room to tape-record all telephone conversations, with external callers suitably put on notice. Each completed tape is kept in the archives for a few months, and only consulted as evidence in the event of a dispute with a counterparty. The mutual knowledge that a telephonic deal is being taped helps in itself to safeguard the professional standards of both parties.

Senior (non-dealing) executives responsible for supervising the dealing operation should have a daily overview of business done and positions taken. They should foster good relations and regular communication with their peers in other banks, as well as in financial exchanges and clearing houses, so as to keep close to market developments and pick up any hint of irregularities in their own back yard. All dealing room personnel should be compelled to take regular holidays (including at least two consecutive weeks in every year), so that there is no continuous opportunity to cover up and compound fraudulent activities.

A dealing room brings together a unique concentration of banking risks, handling so many of the transactions associated with liquidity and settlement risk, credit risk, interest rate and price risks; including the derivatives instruments that have introduced a quantum leap in financial flexibility, choice and complexity. A prudent bank will invest in the best available skills, systems and technology, and will take nothing for granted. Internal and external auditors should review front-end and back-office operations regularly and critically. Given the importance of what is at stake, it is imperative that there be business continuity/disaster recovery plans to provide for replication of records and continuity of dealing and settlement at alternative sites in the event of natural catastrophe or other disruption (see Chapter 11 for further discussion). In May 1996, the main Paris dealing room of Crédit Lyonnais was destroyed by fire, but the bank was able to resume dealing from substitute locations with little interruption.

Prudential rules for controlling derivatives follow much the same pattern as those mentioned above. In July 1994 the Basle Committee on Banking Supervision issued its panoramic 'Risk Management Guidelines for Derivatives', a document which is required reading for all with executive responsibility in that area: selected aspects are highlighted in the appendix to this chapter.

10.9 Summary

Price risks relate to changes in the value of assets or liabilities by reason of movements in their quoted price. Within the scope of this book, we are speaking of overbought or oversold positions in foreign currencies or equity shares, or derivatives thereof.

Foreign exchange price exposure is best measured by discounting future cash flows back to present values, currency by currency. Applying the volatility of the exchange rate concerned to the net exposure, we can deduce the value at risk within a chosen time-frame at a specified level of confidence. A similar picture may also be built up of the value at risk in the foreign exchange book as a whole.

Commercial banks which go into the equities business in one form or another need to take account of the conflict of interest thereby created: 'banking' and 'securities' activities must be strictly segregated in-house.

Each individual share has its own historical pattern of price sensitivity in relation to the applicable share index, known as its beta. Combining beta sensitivity with index volatility enables us to estimate the value at risk in a particular shareholding for a chosen period at a stated level of confidence. An aggregate answer can similarly be obtained for a whole portfolio, allowing for covariance offsets.

In all these applications, VAR provides a means of codifying risk tolerance, exposure limits, notional capital allocation and performance measurement. The technique has its critics and its limitations, as noted in Chapter 9.

Equity portfolios should be diversified with a view to minimising specific risk – the risk of particular price quirks in individual shares.

Proprietary trading, active position-taking with a view to capital gain, depends for its success on superior knowledge and skills which by definition can be available only to a minority. Moreover, it can turn profit performance into the sort of lottery that most banks and their shareholders would prefer to avoid. Practitioners should be sure that they can justify their stance (to themselves, their shareholders, the market, and the regulators) in the face of these caveats.

The dealing room is a focal point of banking risk: close attention should be paid to the checks and balances that foster a sound operation. Further risk management guidelines for derivatives are contained in the appendix hereafter.

Appendix: Salient points from 'Risk Management Guidelines for Derivatives', issued by the Basle Committee on Banking Supervision, July 1994

I Introduction and basic principles

'While some derivatives may have very complex structures, all of them can be divided into the basic building blocks of options, forward contracts or some combination thereof. The use of these basic building blocks in structuring derivatives instruments allows the transfer of various financial risks to parties who are more willing, or better suited, to take or manage them' (Para 1).

'The basic risks associated with derivatives transactions are not new to banking organisations. In general, these risks are credit risk, market risk, liquidity risk, operations risk and legal risk' (Para 6).

II Oversight of the risk management process

The board of directors should approve all policies relating to the management of risks, including derivatives. These should be consistent with business strategies, management expertise and overall willingness to take risk. The board should be informed regularly of the risk exposure, should regularly re-evaluate policies and procedures, and review risk tolerances. Discussions on these matters are to be encouraged between the board, senior managers and others (Para 2).

'Senior management should be responsible for ensuring that there are adequate policies and procedures for conducting derivatives operations on both a long-range and day-to-day basis.' This calls for clear 'lines of responsibility for managing risk, adequate systems for measuring risk, appropriately structured limits on risk taking, effective internal controls and a comprehensive risk-reporting process' (Para 3).

Entry into derivatives activities should be subject to a detailed internal approval procedure, as should any subsequent changes in, or additions to, such activities (Paras 4 and 5).

'As a matter of general policy, compensation policies – especially in the risk management, control and senior management functions – should be structured in a way that is sufficiently independent of the performance of trading activities, thereby avoiding the potential incentives for excessive risk-taking that can occur if, for example, salaries are tied too closely to the profitability of derivatives' (Para 7).

To the extent warranted by the bank's activities, risk management and exposure reporting should be independent of derivatives dealing. Compensation policies in the risk management function should be adequate to attract and retain personnel qualified to assess the risks associated with all the bank's derivatives activities (Paras 8 and 9).

III The risk management process

'The primary components of a sound risk management process are the following: a comprehensive risk measurement approach; a detailed structure of limits, guidelines and other parameters used to govern risk taking; and a strong management information system for controlling, monitoring and reporting risks. These components are fundamental to both derivatives and non-derivatives activities alike. . . . Accordingly, the process of risk management for derivatives activities should be integrated into the institution's overall risk management system to the fullest extent possible using a conceptual framework common to the institution's other activities' (Para 1).

'The risk exposures an institution assumes in its derivatives activities should be fully supported by an adequate capital position' (Para 2).

'Risk measurement standards should be understood by relevant personnel at all levels of the institution – from individual traders to the board of directors – and should provide a common framework for limiting and monitoring risk taking activities' (Para 4).

'The process of marking derivatives positions to market is fundamental to measuring and reporting exposures accurately and on a timely basis. An institution active in dealing foreign exchange, derivatives and other traded instruments should have the ability to monitor credit exposures, trading positions and market movements at least daily. Some institutions should also have the capacity, or at least the goal, of monitoring their more actively traded products on a real-time basis' (Para 5).

'Analysing stress situations, including combinations of market events that could affect the banking organisation, is also an important aspect of risk management. . . . These analyses should consider not only the likelihood of adverse events, but also "worst case" scenarios. Ideally, such worst case analysis should be conducted on an institution-wide basis by taking into account the effect of unusual changes in prices or volatilities, market illiquidity or the default of a large counterparty across both the derivatives and cash trading portfolios and the loan and funding portfolios' (Para 6).

'Such stress tests . . . should also include more qualitative analyses of the actions management might take under particular scenarios' (Para 7).

'An appropriate limit system should permit management to control exposures, to initiate discussion about opportunities and risks and to monitor actual risk taking against predetermined tolerances, as determined by the board of directors and senior management' (Para 8).

'The risk management function should monitor and report its measures of risks to appropriate levels of senior management and to the board of directors. In dealer operations, exposures and profit and loss statements should be reported at least daily to managers who supervise but do not, themselves, conduct those activities' . . . and more frequently as market conditions dictate (Para 11).

Management should ensure that the various components of the risk management process are regularly reviewed and evaluated. The risk management function should regularly assess the methodologies, models and assumptions used to measure risk and to limit exposures. Such internal evaluations may be supplemented by reviews by external auditors or qualified consultants (Paras 13 to 16).

IV Internal controls and audits

'Policies and related procedures for the operation of derivatives activities should be an extension of the institution's overall structure of internal controls and should be fully integrated into routine work-flows. . . . Reconciliation control is particularly important where there are differences in the valuation methodologies or systems used by the front and back offices' (Para 1).

Independent internal and external auditors should regularly review the institution's derivatives activities. 'Internal auditors should be brought into the product development process at the earliest possible stage' (Para 2).

'Internal auditors are expected to evaluate the independence and overall effectiveness of the institution's risk management functions' (Para 3).

'Especially for dealer operations, the auditors should check for adequate separation of duties (particularly between market-making personnel and functions of internal control and risk management), adequate oversight by a knowledgeable manager without day-to-day responsibilities in the dealer operation and the presence of separate reporting lines for risk management and internal control personnel on one side and for market-making personnel on the other' (Para 4).

CHAPTER ELEVEN
Operating risks

This chapter covers:

- The nature and diversity of operating risks.

- 'Operations' and 'business event' risks.

- A practical approach to managing operating risks.

- The limits of external insurance.

- Card and other fraud.

- Money laundering.

- Concentrated risks in dealing rooms and processing centres.

- Disaster recovery/business continuity planning.

- Key personnel risk.

- Co-ordination of operating risk management.

Operating (or 'operational') risks are defined in Chapter 2 as the diverse collection associated with potential failures in a bank's operational processes, or in the systems that support them. Possible adverse consequences of operating risk range from financial loss to reputational damage, hostile litigation, regulatory penalty, and even enforced closure of the bank. Occasionally, sheer luck may confer some random benefit as a result of missing a deadline or a departure, but that is no part of the risk manager's calculation.

There are, in fact, many different ways of looking at operating risks. For a start, we may as well recognise them as a residual or 'catch-all' category, reserved for those hazards that do not fit conveniently into other risk types as described in previous chapters. In any field of analysis, a sub-Parkinsonian law often dictates that the last category, headed 'miscellaneous', turns out to be the largest. Some thinkers simply classify as 'operating risk' all risk (or all profit volatility) not attributable to either credit risk or 'market risk' (the latter equating to the subject matter of Chapters 9 and 10). But such sweeping reductionism overlooks structural interest rate risk (Chapter 8), ignores other risk categories like solvency and liquidity assumed (questionably) to have no implications for profit volatility, and makes for an unwieldy residual pot at the expense of more helpful explanations.

Operating risks may also (usefully) be seen as essentially *non-financial* in origin: as those business risks which revolve around loss of efficiency, continuity or security of one kind or another. They mark themselves out as different because they are shared in part by all banking operations, whether or not those operations incur other banking risks; and they are the only kind of risk that a bank shares in common with all non-banking and non-financial enterprises. So experience of things that go wrong with operations and systems in other industries may help to supplement the banking industry's limited database.

Operating risks remain 'banking risks' for the purposes of this book, however, in view of the peculiar vulnerability of banks as society's main repositories and intermediaries at the heart of the financial system. Opportunities in banking for white collar crime are unparalleled. Fraud or loss of control can be extremely damaging and sometimes fatal to a bank with its highly geared exposures (witness BCCI and Barings), and in consequence to its counterparties and other stakeholders. Settlement failures can spread systemic disruption like a plague out of one bank into the market as a whole – as seen in the spectacular systems collapse in the Bank of New York in 1985, cited in Chapter 2.

11.1 A new impetus

Operating risks have been recognised and policed throughout banking history, albeit in a more disjointed manner than today.

Established disciplines like dual custody of cash and valuables (dubbed the 'four eyes principle'), tiered signatory powers, snap checks and internal audits testify to this traditional awareness. However, wholesale re-engineering of the business in recent years has forced bank managements to look afresh at the challenges of operating risks.

Foremost among the changes is the growth of information technology, harnessed both as an accounting and score-keeping system and as a marketing weapon. This has stripped the back office out of formerly self-contained branches and business units and concentrated much of the work in high risk processing centres; thereby necessitating a radical realignment of staff skills, responsibilities, and interdependencies. During this epoch too, we have seen the emergence of credit card subsidiaries, treasury departments, dealing rooms, and other power-houses of new professional expertise.

Gone are the old rigid structures and inflexible habits of mind. Geographical, linear chains of command have had to yield to degrees of matrix management. Recruitment, training and education policies in the industry have undergone a revolution. Inevitably, specialisation has brought about an increase in *moral hazard* . . . 'I no longer have to understand this: somebody else will pick it up.'

At the same time, progress in statistical measurement of credit and 'market' risks, leading to systems of capital allocation and risk/reward assessment (see, for instance, Chapter 3), has spread its influence into the operating sphere. Regulatory authorities have encouraged this migration, without as yet imposing any analogous capital requirement. The extent to which value at risk answers (as in Chapters 9 and 10) are achievable or even desirable in so complex an arena remains to be seen.

11.2 An immature science

Operating risk, seen as the remaining extensive *terra incognita*, is a subject prone not only to oversimplification but also, conversely, to a descriptive elaboration which contributes more to academic discourse than to practical counsel. This is merely to repeat a word of caution issued in Chapter 2: castles in the air never were a lot of use in dealing with the real world. What counts in the end is whether these visions help a bank to understand and manage the

Table 11.1 Subdivisions of operating risk

Operations risk	Business event risk
• Transaction risk – errors in processing, book entries, deliveries, settlements, contracts, etc.	Changes in taxation, law, or regulation, political or social threats and pressures, natural disasters, etc. Systemic risk.

• Operational control risk
 – breach of internal rules and trading limits,
   theft, fraud, money laundering, sabotage,
   key personnel risk.	

• Systems risk
 – errors in systems design, programming or
   methodology, systems failure, communications
   breakdown, etc.	

risks better, to pinpoint responsibility going forward, to cost operations, to allocate risk capital and measure reward.

Granted, the very act of drawing up exhaustive lists may serve to focus minds and ensure that important sources of risk are not overlooked. And, within reasonable bounds, there is an obvious incentive to work towards a communal chart of risk within each banking organisation.

Many banks and consultants subdivide operating (or 'operational') risks into two parts: 'operations risk' (adding to a confusion of terminology which pervades this area) and 'business event risk'. There is no exact consensus on which types of exposure go into each category, but the tendency is for operations risk to be focused on internal systems and business event risk to be externally oriented (taxation changes, natural disasters, etc). Table 11.1 illustrates a typical analysis along these lines. It is tempting, but erroneous, to associate the house-trained operations risk with expected loss, and the independent-minded business event risk with unexpected loss: in practice, each of these subdivisions will have its own pattern of expected and unexpected outcomes. Justification for the taxonomy seen in Table 11.1 rather lies in attempting to distinguish between those exposures that can be policed by internal controls and those that lie outside that scope.

11.3 Getting to grips with operating risks

Operating risks, being by nature more various than any other class of banking risk, do not admit of a single systematic treatment. They include, for instance, the possibility of cash losses (or robberies) from tills, automated teller machines, safes or vaults; loss or theft of payment instruments, securities and other valuables on bank premises or in transit; theft of equipment, records and trade secrets; communications and mailing lapses; credit and debit card fraud; accounting and administrative errors, delays, diversions and misappropriations; systems design defects; breakdowns and irregularities in dealing rooms and processing centres; sabotage; violent criminal attacks; physical destruction caused by hurricanes, earthquakes, etc.

Such events can have knock-on effects on other classes of banking risk. Information systems failures, for example, may increase a bank's exposures to liquidity, credit or price risks by impairing its ability to monitor them adequately. An earthquake in Kobe seems to have put paid to Barings' chances of recouping its trading losses in Singapore in 1995. But often there is only one loss, with two or more risk classifications sharing the blame.

Most operating risks have little or no apparent correlation with one another, or with the bank's other risks except where the one precipitates the other. Whilst a 'Poisson distribution' (i.e. a distribution of random occurrences within a given period) for each individual type of operating risk is likely to show irregular bunching of loss-making events, the aggregate of all such distributions will normally be a good deal steadier. By way of analogy, it may be hard to predict when a single light bulb (or series of light bulbs) will blow, but the failure rate of the totality of light bulbs in an office block should be comparatively smooth and predictable. Similarly, much of the financial volatility arising from operating risk as a whole may tend to be cancelled out by a 'portfolio' effect (basic principles of which are discussed in Chapter 6). This phenomenon lends itself to the estimation of expected losses.

We are thus in a position to simplify the issues underlying the bewildering diversity of operating risks, and to outline a broad strategy for dealing with them:

1   Identify the relatively 'small hits' that can be consigned to the portfolio effect just described. Search for individual ways (including insurance) of containing/reducing/eliminating these impacts, so long as the cost of prevention is not greater than the expected losses themselves. It is a truism that risk can nearly always be reduced *at a cost*, and risk reduction almost always costs.

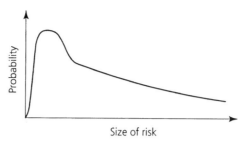

11.1 Long fat tails of operating risk.

2   Look out for the 'big hits', the rare events capable of causing great volatility in unexpected losses or of stopping the business in its tracks – a particularly apt metaphor when one recalls fires in the Channel Tunnel or power blackouts on the London Underground. Catastrophic exposures of this kind occur in the 'long/fat tails' of a distribution of possible outcomes (see Fig. 11.1). In a bank, they are likely to emanate from operations where large monetary values or transaction volumes are concentrated and processed, where key systems interconnect, or where important regulatory or reputational consequences are at stake. Again, the appropriate course of action is to seek preventive or palliative measures that are cost-effective (as opposed to eliminating the risk at all costs). In case prevention fails, the bank also needs to develop disaster recovery/business resumption/business continuity plans aimed at restoring normal service as quickly as possible after the event.

3   Use statistical measurements to estimate expected losses. Consider allocating capital to underwrite unexpected losses, thereby helping to fill out a picture of risk versus reward.

4   Subject all new services, products, and ventures to the same set of disciplines.

The sections that follow consider some practical aspects of this broad and admittedly imperfect approach, which takes note of, without always conforming to, the ideal world depicted in Table 11.1.

11.4 External versus internal insurance

First impressions might suggest that external insurance offers a ready solution to operating risks. In a large bank, however, the portfolio effect of quotidian events tends to generate a level of expected losses which can be economically absorbed via a deliberate process of self-insurance. The alternative appeal of external insurance then resolves itself into: 'premium arbitrage', access to independent expert advice (including perhaps a larger risk database), buying time pending better internal systems, administrative convenience and sharing the uncertainty.

Unexpected losses, for their part, are potentially so large – think of Barings' £830 million – that open-ended cover is unobtainable on any economically justifiable terms. At best, the bank may deem it worth taking out limited 'catastrophe insurance' up to a stated amount for any one event: this covers the type of accidental loss which, whilst falling short of threatening the bank's solvency, would make an unwelcome hole in profits. Such policies normally carry a hefty 'excess' or 'deductible' (first loss to be borne by the bank), and either exclude or charge a heavy premium for 'staff infidelity' (internal fraud). The moral is that external insurance does not offer realistic protection against truly crippling losses. No bank can afford to insure both its profits and its capital.

Niche insurance cover may be sensible and justified: for example, it is common practice to take out standard policies in respect of 'business interruption' (caused by computer failures, etc), and 'directors' and officers' liability' (for the protection and peace of mind of the individuals concerned).

External insurance, it should be remembered, is a form of hedging which does not eliminate risk but merely transfers it to a counterparty (the insurance company) who may, for a variety of reasons, fail to provide full or timely settlement of claims. Nor does monetary compensation do anything to restore a bank's good name, once lost: prevention is usually better than cure.

11.5 Card fraud

This term embraces credit and debit cards, charge cards and all similar plastic instruments, to which a common set of fraud considerations applies. In an active issuing bank, card fraud is likely to claim the lion's share of fraud experience in general, and could well dominate average operating losses as a whole. The main sources of card fraud may be summarised as follows:

Lost/stolen. Worldwide this combination causes the greatest losses, although its share is decreasing as other categories take up the running. Cardholders are seldom penalised for failure to keep their cards safe.

Intercepted/never received. Cards stolen in the mail, another proportionately diminishing category.

Counterfeit. The second largest source of loss, and the fastest growing (see Fig. 11.2). The fraudster finds a 'point of compromise' from which to reproduce authentic details onto a counterfeit card by one of the following methods:

- Re-embossing a genuine card by ironing the true number flat and punching on a counterfeit number. This is only effective at merchant outlets that do not have an electronic terminal.

- Re-encoding a genuine card by overwriting new details onto the magnetic stripe at the back. The newly encoded number will then differ from the embossed number on the front.

- Embossing and encoding blank plastic cards (termed 'white plastic') with fraudulent data. The plastics are either stolen from bona fide card manufacturers or forged.

- 'Skimming', i.e. electronically copying the contents of a sophisticated magnetic stripe and transcribing them onto a blank or less sophisticated card.

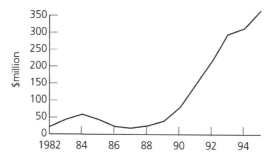

11.2 Worldwide counterfeit losses in the two largest credit card networks (Source: Visa and Mastercard).

The 'entry barriers' (particularly costs) to counterfeiting should certainly be raised by the imminent introduction of a new generation of 'smart cards', incorporating more formidable electronic safeguards.

Fraudulent application. Statistically a minor category. The applicant for a card assumes a false identity, real or fictitious. On receiving the card, he embarks on a brief spending spree and then absconds, leaving an unsettled card bill behind.

Mail order/telephone order (MOTO). This is the malpractice of ordering goods (typically hi-fi equipment) using another person's card details. The merchant is liable for any procedural negligence, which is almost a prerequisite for this method to succeed. After all, the delivery address and/or the identity of the recipient of the goods can and should be verified. MOTO poses little threat to issuing banks, and none to their honest customers (except perhaps for time spent on shifting a burden of proof).

When a card is reported missing, or when fraudulent activity is detected, a stop known as a 'status' is put on the account to prevent any further spending. Fraudulent misuse is therefore classified as occurring in two main time bands, 'pre-status' and 'post-status', with a narrow intermediate band of 'same day' (the day when the status was placed on the account). Not surprisingly, the bulk of losses to card issuers stems from pre-status activity. The principal weapons that can be deployed against card fraud, pre- or post-status, are:

Floor limits and authorisations. Historically, this has been the most effective safeguard. For transactions above the floor limit, authorisation is required from the card issuer. The merchant floor limit is set at an economically justified level, where the cost of the authorisation process does not exceed the level of loss experience in the retail area concerned.

Hot card files. These contain serial numbers of lost and stolen cards, with notices distributed in paper or electronic form. Modern electronic terminals at sales points can hold up to 800 account numbers. In addition there are independent service companies which act as intermediaries between card issuers and retailers, broadcasting over dedicated radio wavebands to special receivers in retailers' premises. A swipe unit by the retailer's till checks cards against the service company's hot card file, which can hold up to three million numbers. When this system was introduced in a UK supermarket chain, it cut fraud losses by 90%.

Secure delivery. In areas where the public postal system has been found to be unsafe, the issuer may have to resort to delivering new or replacement cards by courier services, or by customer collection from a local branch of the bank.

Application fraud file. By keeping a file of previous false applications for cards, the issuer may foil subsequent attempts, which tend to follow recurring patterns. Banks in the UK have pooled their files in the Credit Industry Fraud Avoidance System (CIFAS), which is estimated to save £3–4 million annually for member banks.

Profiling systems. These are pre-status monitoring systems aimed at detecting fraudulent misuse of a card, as suggested by aberrant transactions, before the customer reports it as lost or stolen. As card fraudsters become increasingly sophisticated, profiling systems provide an issuing bank with its main defence. The principal techniques are:

- Volume/value parameters. Based on average cardholder behaviour, the issuer sets a limit on the number and/or value of 'authorisations' (see above) permitted over one or two days. If the parameter is broken, the transaction is 'referred' back to the retailer and the identity of the card presenter is confirmed.

- Expert systems. These knowledge-based support systems are part of the family of artificial intelligence systems described earlier in Chapter 6. In this case, they work on a set of rules employing 'if', 'and', and 'then' commands: for example, 'If a transaction is over $1000 from a camera shop in Dubai and there have been no other transactions from Dubai, then refer.' Expert systems like Barclays' Fraud 2000 have proved invaluable in combating pre-status fraud.

- Neural networks. These (also described in Chapter 6) are at the cutting edge of artificial intelligence, as applied to card profiling systems. In mimicking certain processes in the human brain, they have the faculty of learning and identifying new behavioural patterns over time. Commercial packages are available on the market.

From this brief survey it should be clear that a card-issuing bank needs to equip itself with a strong fraud prevention and control department, featuring state of the art technology, excellent management information and investigative capabilities, and good liaison with other issuers and the police. Dedicated telephone lines should be manned around the clock, to allow for authorisation referrals and for incoming lost/stolen reports (which trigger the placing of an immediate status on the account, thereby blocking further authorisations).

11.6 'Phantom' cash withdrawals

This topic stands apart from normal card fraud, enjoying a high profile which reflects public anxiety rather than statistical importance. A so-called phantom cash withdrawal from an automated teller machine occurs at a time when the cardholder remains in possession of his card but denies making the withdrawal. Given that such a transaction requires entry of the card itself (or a replica) *plus* the cardholder's personal identification number (the PIN, which these days is often chosen by the cardholder and not written down), it follows that a fraudster would have had to avail himself of *two* 'points of compromise'. Issuing banks do not accept that this double compromise could emanate from their internally secure systems, and take the view that it is more likely to have occurred in the cardholder's home or work place; in other words, that the fraud (if there is one) has probably been perpetrated by a family member or a close associate. At time of writing, such claims and rebuttals have yet to be tested in the courts.

In one instance, an ingenious fraudster is known to have achieved a double compromise by installing a 'phantom cash machine' in a public place. When cardholders tried unsuccessfully to obtain banking services from the bogus machine, their card and PIN details were copied and later misused. Cardholders, as well as banks, need to be vigilant.

11.7 General fraud

In 1995 the British Bankers' Association reported general (i.e. non-card) fraud cases involving potential losses of some £316 million, whittled down finally to actual losses of £26 million. The principal recorded categories have a reassuringly familiar ring, although modern technology provides new ways of playing old tricks:

Forged cheques. These are genuine cheque forms stolen and fraudulently completed, bearing forged signatures.

Counterfeit cheques. Copies of genuine cheques or cheque forms.

Fraudulently altered cheques. Alterations to payee name or amount.

Forged authorities. This includes messages by letter, fax, telephone, telex, payment instructions on bank forms, etc. Measured by monetary value at risk, this is by far the largest category, as well as the most varied and interesting. However, very few of the perpetrators get away with it; partly no doubt because the instructions arrive and are scrutinised piecemeal, compared with the masses of cheques handled over the counter and in the clearing.

Conversion/fraudulent endorsement. Misappropriation of cheques and payment instruments, deposited or encashed by a thief.

Withdrawal against uncleared effects/crossfiring. Paying in worthless cheques and drawing against them before they can be cleared.

Miscellaneous. Includes counterfeit currency notes, borrowing on false pretences, staff defalcations on suspense accounts, etc.

Contrary to popular perception, staff misdemeanours and space age electronic scams (such as computer hacking) do not figure significantly in these statistics. The bulk of bank fraud boils down to external thievery by means of impersonation, forgery, misappropriation and alteration. The first and most important line of defence available to banks is *identification*: of new customers opening accounts, of persons subsequently claiming to be those customers, of presenters claiming payment, and so on. Identification procedures on opening of accounts have become very stringent, not least in response to money laundering legislation (see section 11.8 below). The identity of the applicant is confirmed by reference to documents such as a passport, national identity card (if applicable), or full driving licence. The applicant's address may be checked against the voter's roll, or against a recent public utility bill. In addition it is common practice to carry out a credit reference agency search, to ensure that no adverse financial record exists.

These precautions help satisfy the bank that it is dealing with a bona fide citizen of good repute, not an imposter, and thereby afford some legal protection against any subsequent charge of *conversion* (negligently collecting payment of a cheque or instrument for the wrong person). They also provide a template for comparison in case anyone else later tries to manipulate the account – e.g. by forged withdrawals, authorities or payment instructions. If borrowing is in prospect, the likelihood of it taking place under false pretences has been reduced.

Another line of defence is provided by scrutiny of cheques presented for payment, either at the counter or through the clearing. These may be subjected to a tiered series of tests according to amount; starting with basic examination of signature and other particulars, and progressing to ultra-violet light and damp/smudge tests which differentiate genuine from counterfeit cheque forms (UV light can also be used to detect counterfeit plastic cards). Where large amounts or suspicious circumstances are involved, the customer may be contacted to confirm the cheque.

When receiving letters of instruction (prevalent in the case of customers resident abroad), bankers need to use the full range of their common sense and their knowledge of the customer's affairs. Is the signature good, does the instruction exhibit characteristic behaviour? In such circumstances, it is often advisable to establish a codeword system whereby the customer's identity is tacitly confirmed, in a way that would not be obvious to a reader of intercepted mail. Faxed letters are particularly open to abuse, as a fraudster at the transmitting end (maybe an employee of the customer) can paste a genuine signature onto a deceitful message without fear of detection at the receiving end: if fax is to be the medium of communication, an indemnity should be taken from the customer absolving the bank of responsibility.

Similar considerations of common sense apply to payment instructions rendered on the bank's own forms: e.g. for standing orders, telegraphic transfers, and inland payments. Were the payment instructions delivered in the usual manner (by known representative, by mail, etc)? Does the payment conform to the customer's pattern of business or way of life? Is the payment from a company account to an individual beneficiary, perhaps to a building society account? This last is a common giveaway, particularly if it is not the method by which company wages are normally paid.

It is customary for a bank to maintain a fraud prevention section within its inspection or internal audit department. This squad will direct the investigation of live cases, render consolidated reports to top management, keep a databank, liaise with industry peers and the police, and generally co-ordinate the bank's fraud prevention efforts.

At the end of the day, it has often been said, the customer is a bank's best auditor; but, for the sake of its reputation, the bank will prefer to nip fraud attempts in the bud rather than rely on customer complaints (which are likely to leave the bank as the ultimate financial loser anyway).

11.8 Money laundering

'Money laundering' is the attempt to clean up dirty money so that it can be used in the light of day again. 'Dirty money' is the proceeds of crime: typically from theft of money or goods, fraud, narcotics trade, or terrorist activities. More often than not, national and international banking systems are used as the laundry. In the first instance, the proceeds may be deposited in one or more bank accounts, possibly in false names. The usual second phase, known as 'agitation' or 'layering', consists of a series of complex manoeuvres, breaking the money up, transferring it from account to account around the system, and mixing it with untainted funds so as to disguise its origins. The process of covering tracks, reconsolidating accounts and introducing some plausibility into their cover story completes the cycle: the money is now 'clean' and ready to be used by the criminals to finance fresh legal or illegal activities.

For many years there has been a growing consensus among governments (e.g. in the European Union) that money laundering must be stopped. It rewards gangsters and terrorists, and promotes their further antisocial crimes. Bankers in many countries now find themselves under a legal duty to notify the relevant authorities of any unusual pattern of transactions which leads them to suspect they are being used to launder money.

In the United Kingdom, financial institutions are required by the Criminal Justice Act 1993 and the supplementary Money Laundering Regulations 1993 (within the framework of a European directive) to maintain specific policies and procedures to guard against their businesses and the financial system being used for the purpose of money laundering. The Regulations lay particular stress on identification of customers, record keeping, internal reporting and control (to be co-ordinated by a money laundering reporting officer in each bank), and education and training of employees. Offences punishable with varying terms of imprisonment (up to a maximum 14 years) and/or fines include: failure to comply with the Regulations (irrespective of whether money laundering has taken place), wittingly assisting the money launderer, tipping him off that he is under investigation, and failure to report knowledge or suspicion.

In addition to national legislation such as this, regulatory authorities (applying 'best practice' principles first promulgated in 1988 by the Basle Committee on Banking Regulations and Supervisory Practices) are likely to take a stern view of money laundering, to the point of withdrawing a banking licence in extreme cases. The stakes are thus too high to admit of any complacency in the banking community. There is also peer pressure, in as much as no bank wants to be contaminated by slapdash practices among its counterparties.

11.9 Concentrated risks in processing centres

Processing centres handle high values and large volumes of transactions: such operations may include dealing room front and back offices, domestic and international payments (via CHAPS in the UK, CHIPS in the USA, and SWIFT internationally), interbank reconciliations, cash management services, cheque clearing, consumer loans, credit card operations, and branch accounts. In commercial banks, these relatively new centres represent bulk risks that formerly (to the extent that they then existed) were dispersed in the branch network. The industry has created new hubs of inter-dependent systems and lines of communication which are crucial to efficiency and continuity of service, and hence to the reputation of a bank.

These processing hubs are at the epicentre of internal 'operations risk' and its subsets as depicted in Table 11.1. The scope for *transaction risk* – mistakes of all kinds in processing – is clearly enormous. Wrong entries, duplications or omissions may upset a multitude of customers and cost money. Failure to settle contracts could cause disruption in the financial markets, or bring litigation on the bank. Intensive effort must therefore be expended on minimising the incidence of error.

In terms of *operational control risk*, such centres are exposed to fraud and money laundering as described earlier. They must keep watch for forged instruments and authorities, suspicious trans-actions, and manipulation of suspense accounts, and co-operate with others in bringing these misdeeds to light. Computer centres are inherently vulnerable to the depredations, or simple mischief-making, of 'hackers'. Computer viruses can also introduce malicious damage, so a virus checking program is essential.

Physical security is equally important. Personal computers, disks and related equipment have a ready market and must be safe-guarded from theft. Bank records and trade secrets need to be kept under strict custody, and in some cases duplicated at another site. Premises policy should be framed with a view to protection and resilience, bearing in mind the inconveniences or disasters which may occur but which cannot be allowed to prevail. Contingency plans should take into account the possibility of fire, flood, sabotage, bomb explosions, and indeed the proverbial jumbo-jet landing on top of the computer centre. We shall return to such considerations when we come to business continuity planning.

Thirdly, processing centres, as major systems users, are subject to *systems risk*. Systems breakdowns can interrupt banking services for hours or days on end. Processing centres will normally have *service level agreements* with their upstream suppliers and subcontractors on the one hand and their downstream clients in the bank on the other, specifying the standards expected of the servicing party and the penalties applicable for failure to meet them. At the end of the line is an external customer who may or may not have the benefit of that particular formality, but who on the strength of general assurances and codes of conduct could have a good claim for compensation. To the extent that service breakdowns cannot be entirely eliminated, they will need to be insured externally or internally as a cost of doing business.

Errors in systems design and programming cause much the same immediate effects as processing errors, but are more expensive: the damage will recur until the cause is diagnosed and corrected, which can take time. Chapter 2 cites the well-known trading mishap which practically incapacitated the Bank of New York over a period of days in 1985. Development of new products and systems also needs to build in some protection against hackers, 'cyber-terrorists' (who specialize in threats and extortion), and other saboteurs pursuing grudge agendas.

Logical fragility is an inescapable hazard in electronic data processing. Large systems comprise thousands of programs, of different vintage and authorship, which transact with one another. A slight change of computer hardware or software in one area can have unpredictable knock-on effects elsewhere; whole systems can suddenly go down. Such leverage is reminiscent of the apocryphal butterfly, which confounds weather forecasts by flapping its wings in the Pacific and causing a hurricane in the Atlantic. One legacy of short-sighted programming is seen in the universal failure to provide for the arrival of the year 2000: at time of writing, banks and businesses everywhere are struggling to disarm this 'millennium bomb' and avert a crippling systems crash.

The foregoing is just a taste of the variety of problems faced by an evolving and expanding banking industry employing mass-production techniques.

11.10 Dealing rooms

Much of what is said above applies equally to dealing room front and back offices, which generate high value/high volume processing demands. The question of internal rules and trading limits for dealers is considered in Chapter 10 on price risks (section 10.8 and appendix) as a matter of pragmatic convenience, although purists may argue that it belongs here as an aspect of *operational control risk.*

11.11 Business continuity planning

This expression is used interchangeably with 'disaster recovery' and 'business resumption planning'. Any bank which takes operating risk seriously will want to ensure that failures in its operational processes or supporting systems cause the minimum of damage and disruption to the business. In this world, disaster may strike despite all our efforts and prayers: a good example is the IRA bomb which wrecked many buildings in the City of London in 1993, causing the

NatWest Tower to be evacuated. Each business or supporting unit needs to make practical plans to survive the immediate aftermath of such an incident and restore normal service as rapidly as possible; the ideal being an unbroken thread of continuity. The distinction drawn in Table 11.1 between operations risk (internal) and business event risk (external) is not material in this context: a disaster could stem from either side of that dividing line.

The business continuity planners need first to determine the *scope* of their plan: what area of operations it covers, whether it is self-standing, whether it shares a common interest with an adjoining plan, whether it is subservient to other continuity plans within the bank. With those questions resolved, the next step is to conduct a *business impact analysis*: this looks in turn at each business function covered by the plan and assesses the impact of a temporary cessation, within a series of time bands: say, one day, one week, and longer than one week. Potential impacts include costs and loss of revenue, legal or regulatory problems, damage to the bank's reputation and loss of public or staff confidence. Using a weighted scoring tariff, the planners can arrive at a ranking to establish which functions are critical (must be restored within 24 hours of a disaster), which are necessary (must be restored within one week), and which are of lower priority (restoring full 'business as usual' as soon as possible thereafter). The first two rankings correspond to degrees of 'survival' and the third to full 'recovery'. In some cases, a business impact analysis may be used to arbitrate between the claims of different business units potentially in competition for limited resources (budget, computer time, etc).

Once a ranking of functions is agreed, the planners need to identify the resources (e.g. premises, equipment, services and staff) required to fulfil the plan's demands, in particular for the 'critical' and 'necessary' phases. At this stage they can also juggle with alternative options and costs for achieving recovery. In the case of dealing rooms and other processing centres, for example, consideration may be given to a combination of:

- *Hot sites.* Duplicate premises and equipment, owned by the bank and ready to operate comprehensively at a moment's notice.

- *Warm sites.* Potentially similar capability, but requiring several hours' notice to set up. Warm sites may be owned by an external supplier of recovery services who has a portfolio of clients, well spread as to geography and business type so that they will not be competing simultaneously for the same emergency space and facilities.

- *Cold sites.* Cheap empty office space, or even simple foundations reserved for quick installation of prefabricated buildings. These sites take up to a week to activate.

Having selected its recovery options and obtained approval for the budgeted costs, the business unit can draw up its formal business continuity plan, detailing roles, responsibilities, and procedures to be followed in the event of a disaster. A crisis manager should be appointed, to keep the plan under review and to ensure that all the necessary actions are taken if the occasion arises for it to be implemented. If the plan is dependent on external suppliers, it will be necessary to negotiate formal contracts or service level agreements with them.

The business continuity plan should be tested regularly to ensure that it works, is up to date, and is understood by all concerned. Large processing centres may conduct tests with live work in hot or warm sites several times a year: other operations should test their plans at least annually. Results of tests should be recorded and reported, and plans adjusted if necessary.

Figure 11.3 is a flow chart illustrating the sequence of planning steps described above. As a sign of our times, disaster recovery software is now available which will perform much of the analysis and propose a suitable plan.

11.12 Key personnel risk

Key personnel are highly valued members of management performing tasks critical to the bank's success. Business continuity requires that these people stay in place: the risk is that they will transfer to another employer, become chronically ill or die. These negative possibilities can be countered to some extent by good terms of service, rewards and job satisfaction; and by private health schemes and regular screening. Even then, key people need to go away on business trips, courses or conferences, and must take their holiday entitlements.

In passing, it is worth remarking that regular holidays and rotation of duties are important safeguards in the war against internal fraud. With due respect to modern specialisation, nobody

Step

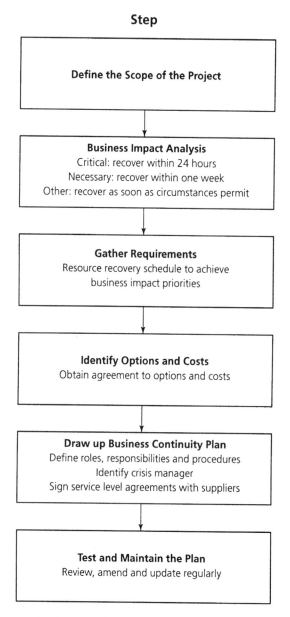

11.3 Establishing a business continuity plan.

should occupy one post for too long without a break; nor, indeed, should he want to unless he is up to something. Star performers can fall from grace, like the rest of us, and in banking there can be no second chance for anyone who abuses his position of trust.

Banking organisations, departments, and business units should earmark their critical job positions and ensure that there is qualified back-up available to cover for the absence of key personnel. Such contingency planning should have double depth, identifying a substitute for the substitute, to allow for instances of short notice when the nominated first reserve is also otherwise engaged. This interchange cannot work without staff versatility, which is another justification for rotation of staff duties.

There are, of course, a very few top executives who are deemed irreplaceable from within the organisation, by reason of their special business flair. Somebody can hold the fort for them in the short term, but for a permanent replacement the bank may have to go headhunting at the time of severance.

Key personnel planning may be regarded as part of business continuity planning, but it also has much in common with succession planning.

11.13 Co-ordinating the effort

Responsibility for risk management in a bank lies ultimately with the board and management. In the modern climate of heightened risk awareness, they will doubtless wish to impose a structured approach to managing operating risk, based on industry best practice and aimed at enhancing and protecting shareholder value, whilst satisfying regulatory and legal requirements. Such a pro-gramme should establish: clear accountability throughout; a level playing field in terms of a common risk model and common measurements; and controls matched to business impact, in terms of motivation and cost. There is a need for consistent bankwide reporting of risk events, big and small, and a rational methodology for estimating expected and unexpected losses. Finally, board and management will want to be assured that well-conceived disaster recovery/business continuity plans are in place throughout the organisation.

The detail of how the different businesses within the bank manage their operating risks is, up to a point, their own affair as long as they are accountable to the centre for their results. At the same time, there is an obvious case for a central resource to act as catalyst, facilitator, consultant and co-ordinator in the broad-brush implementation of the board's instructions. This unit can also be the channel of communications on operating risks, between the devolved businesses on the one hand and the board and executive management on the other. To this end it will convene or attend regular committee meetings and conferences of interested parties in the field, and will report back to the board or to an executive risk management committee on progress achieved. Finally, it will act as a secretariat for executive management dialogue with the banking regulator on the subject of operating risk.

11.14 Summary

Operating (or 'operational') risks may be defined in many different ways, but are essentially to do with failures in operational processes and supporting systems. The causes of these failures are non-financial in nature, and may be internal ('operations risk', which has further subdivisions) or external ('business event risk'). The main consequences to be feared are financial losses and damage to the bank's reputation. In banking, as has often been remarked, confidence is all.

Far-reaching changes in the banking industry have led to a new appreciation of operating risks, and a search for a more co-ordinated way of quantifying and managing them.

Despite the disconcerting diversity of operating risk types, bankers can take comfort from the lack of correlation between them, which tends to smooth out the lower level volatilities to a form of 'background noise' and assist in the estimation of expected losses. There are, however, rarer hazards capable of bringing the business to its knees. Some banks seek ways of allocating risk capital to underwrite these unexpected losses; others think there are too many variables to make the attempt credible. Preventive controls should be actively sought, within the bounds of cost-effectiveness, for risks of all sizes.

External insurance can play only a limited role in the management of operating risks. It can cover some special needs and help to cushion lumpy loss experience; but it offers no particular economic advantage with regard to expected losses, and cannot give realistic protection against the sort of catastrophe that overwhelms profits and threatens solvency.

Card fraud is the largest category of fraud in many card-issuing banks, and in some cases may even account for the bulk of average operating losses. Section 11.5 describes the main types of fraudulent activity (with counterfeiting seen as the fastest growing area), and the principal anti-fraud weapons (of which profiling systems offer an important way forward). A strong fraud prevention department is essential.

Section 11.7 surveys the most common kinds of general (i.e. non-card) fraud. Forgery, copying and alteration of cheques and other payment authorities dominate the statistics. Bank defences start with rigorous identification procedures for new accounts, for existing account-holders (in cases of doubt), and for payees and other beneficiaries where the occasion demands. Cheques presented for payment are subjected to prescribed tiers of scrutiny, including a battery of scientific tests depending on the amount and circumstances. Payment instructions of other kinds (e.g. letters, faxes and bank forms) need to be examined with bankerly caution; particularly those involving international transfers, or payments out of a company account to an individual.

A general fraud prevention unit is normally maintained within the inspection or internal audit function: this will co-ordinate fraud detection efforts, communicate standards guidance to the rest of the bank, collate fraud data, and be the bank's focal point for investigation and reporting on money laundering (see also section 11.8).

Processing centres and dealing rooms handle high values and large volumes of transactions; and thus embody a heavy concentration of internal operations risk, with its subsets of transaction risk, operational control risk, and systems risk. The implications of this risk management challenge are discussed in section 11.9.

Despite all precautions, disasters can strike a bank's operating processes from within or without at any time. All business or support units should maintain a business continuity plan with provisions for survival and recovery after any such disabling event. Impact analysis will determine which functions are crucial to the health of the bank and must be restored first (e.g. by moving rapidly to an alternative equipped site). Business continuity plans need to be tested for effectiveness at least annually.

Banks and their component units should earmark their critical job positions and ensure that there is qualified back-up to cover for absences of key personnel.

Management of operating risk needs to be guided and co-ordinated from the centre, albeit that the day to day detail belongs in the business units. A central resource can act as consultant in the methodologies of risk measurement and business continuity planning, and as general agent of the board and executive in ensuring that operating risk management is brought up to a common standard of awareness and professionalism to match the best in other areas of banking risk. There is some way to go because, as pointed out earlier, this is an immature science.

CHAPTER TWELVE

Conclusion: organising risk management

This chapter offers guidance on:

- The board's role, and its ultimate responsibility for risk management.

- Necessary attributes and disciplines in a risk-conscious bank.

- Co-ordination of risk management responsibilities.

- The role of internal and external audit.

- Staff: employment, deployment, incentives.

- Banks as managers of customers' risks.

The question of how to organise risk management makes sense only if approached from the top down. Risk management in a bank, as in any other business, is first and last the responsibility of its board and, by proxy, of executive management giving effect to the board's directives. Capitalist theory posits the board's prime task as maximising what has come to be known as 'shareholder value' (variously definable because different shareholders have differing long and short term perspectives). In so doing, the board must operate within constraints posed by the interests of other stakeholders: customers, employees, and the community (as

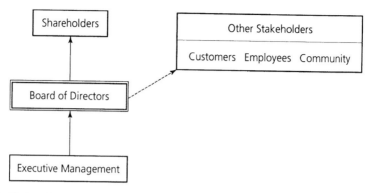

12.1 Chain of accountability for risk management

expressed in law, regulation and public opinion). Some readers might structure this hierarchy differently: preferring the claims of customers or society, for example, and relegating shareholders' expectations to secondary status. But the constituencies will be much the same whatever the case, as illustrated in Fig. 12.1.

The board's objectives must govern the way risk management is organised. So what does the board of a bank hope for from risk management? Fundamentally, it wants to take business risks in a way which optimally enhances, whilst minimising potential damage to, 'shareholder value' (say, the prospect of continuing growth in value of profits and equity); and which likewise fosters and protects the interests of its other stakeholders, in so far as those interests circumscribe or precede the owners' objectives. Risk management controls, however, should be economically and morally pro- portionate to the impact they are designed to ward off: there is no point in obsessionally spending pounds to save pennies, nor can we invoke the death penalty to deter pilferage of paper clips. The board will also seek assurance that, should disaster strike anywhere in the bank despite all reasonable precautions, a well-tried plan for survival and recovery is ready to swing into action in every case.

Pursuit of these broad aims leads to a shopping list of attributes and disciplines to be sought throughout the business. The following is a selection of desiderata that have appeared in and, to a considerable extent, linked previous chapters:

● A commonly accepted definition of 'risk' and of risk types, leading to a practical risk map for the bank (this book itself being one such extended attempt).

- Comprehensive and continual assessment of actual and potential sources of risk, internal or external.

- Clear risk management responsibilities (downwards) and accountabilities (upwards), to avoid confusion, duplication of effort, and things falling between stools.

- Transparency, a comprehensive management information, monitoring and reporting system, in which material exposures, gains and losses are fully disclosed, analysed and communicated to those who need to know, and stored for future reference.

- A common system of financial performance measurement, featuring expected loss (a cost of doing business), unexpected loss (a measure of risk), allocation of equity capital to risks as far as practicable, and adjusted reward for risk (return on risk-adjusted capital – 'RORAC', or the like).

- A market-related appreciation of the cost of capital, the minimum required rate of return, and the possibilities and limits of organic growth of risk exposures.

- A common understanding and employment of the principles of diversification of risk and portfolio management.

- A credit grading system based on expected default rate.

- Pricing of products and services which takes account of all these factors.

- In consonance with the foregoing, a means of assessing risk appetite/tolerance and setting exposure limits accordingly.

- A level playing field, on which to referee competing bids for scarce capital on the part of: different businesses within the bank, old and new products, and customer relationships (limit allocation).

- A consistent conceptual framework within which to set targets and measure performance: of business units, products, customer relationships, and members of staff.

- Disaster recovery/business continuity plans installed everywhere, up to date and regularly tested.

- Continuous analysis of risk management successes and failures, and adjustment of controls as necessary.

217

- Independent risk management control, separated from business origination, sales and trading.

- Professional, specialised, staff expertise in developing, hedging and controlling the different types of risk encountered in a banking business.

Historically, the last-mentioned of these requirements has been by far the best fulfilled, being in effect the banking sector's sub-conscious definition of 'risk management'. A modern conception of risk itself, comprehending all the ramifications set out above, has only recently begun to permeate the thinking of a traditionally craft-oriented industry. As noted in Chapter 1, however, national banking systems (and individual banks within them) are at different stages of progress on this evolutionary journey.

A board director's biggest problem is likely to be understanding the risks, the measurements and the controls; but this cannot be ducked as it is a duty laid on him or her by everybody from the Basle regulatory authorities downwards (see, for instance, the guidelines in the appendix to Chapter 10). An adequate level of understanding can only be achieved by studying explanatory papers and presentations, by attending relevant training courses and seminars, and by engaging in intensive discussions with experts, including on-site visits. If, after all that, the risks of a particular activity remain incomprehensible to board members, logic says that either they or the activity should go. The Barings collapse in 1995 shows, all too painfully, the dangers of not rocking the boat for fear of disrupting an earnings stream.

12.1 Co-ordination of risk management responsibilities

Day to day responsibility for risk management rests with the executive team, acting on behalf of the board. Risk management is not a peripheral concern, but is absolutely central to the management of a bank. Chapters 3 to 11 offer many practical, up to date approaches, tools and techniques to help accomplish this management task. Those chapters also address the structural issues of centralisation (co-ordinating policy, standards, aggregation, allocation, etc) versus devolution (application within business operations). Central co-ordinating bodies are seen as desirable in the management of:

- *Credit risk* (Chapters 5, 6 and 7). A credit committee to direct policy (including grading), strategy, portfolio allocation and review, sanctioning of large exposures (or *ex post facto* review).

- *Liquidity risk* (Chapter 4), *interest rate risk* (structural Chapter 8, trading Chapter 9), and *price risks* (Chapter 10). These interrelated risks come together naturally under the umbrella of an asset and liability committee (ALCO).

- *Operating risks* (Chapter 11). A central unit is suggested, to act as catalyst, facilitator, consultant and co-ordinator. There is a need for common methodology (particularly in business continuity planning) and co-ordinated reporting to the board.

- *Solvency risk* (Chapter 3). Capital planning and management is a shared responsibility of the chief executive and the chief financial officer.

Thus far we have identified a minimum of four central co-ordinating points for risk management; each with its own expert secretariat, planning department or 'think tank' to process its work, take minutes, maintain uniform standards, propose policies, and 'think the unthinkable'. This infrastructure takes care of the bank's outer reaches, but leaves fragmented reporting lines to the board.

Time and again, we have seen that the different types of banking risk do not exist in isolation but often have knock-on effects on one another. Liquidity and interest rate risks are interrelated; credit defaults can leave the bank with unwanted price risks; operational failures can cause credit, liquidity, and even solvency problems. Moreover, various of these risk types are potentially in competition for allocation from the same pool of scarce risk capital: the bank needs to ensure homogeneity and comprehensiveness without double-counting. Overallocation of capital can occur if single loss events in the past are attributed to more than one type of risk management failure. For example, a particular trading loss may be seen as stemming from either price risk or operating risk (or both), but it is a mistake to give full statistical weighting to both causes. After all, you can only die once.

The sensible way to keep things in proportion, therefore, is to create a top level 'risk management committee', which steers and supervises the work of the other bodies and provides a unified interface with the board. The chief executive, the chief financial

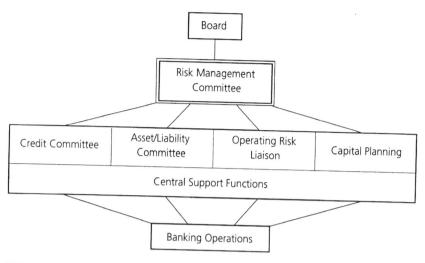

12.2 Co-ordination of risk management in a bank.

officer and others can help to supply an element of common understanding by sitting on all such committees. By the same token, it may be possible to bring together the various 'civil servant' support teams under one roof, if not single direct command. Figure 12.2 illustrates a reasonably unified risk management structure.

12.2 The role of internal and external audit

In addition to the operational framework of risk management, every bank should commission an internal audit function which will:

- Inspect the books and verify assets and liabilities in all locations of the bank, in stages over a prescribed working cycle (say, two years).

- Keep a running check on the effective operation of risk controls everywhere.

- Participate in the design of new risk controls (including all new products).

- Maintain the fraud databank, and investigate important cases of fraud and other untoward losses as they arise.

- Act as the bank's point of contact with industry peers and the police on intelligence matters and the state of the art.

The head of internal audit should report functionally to the chief executive of the bank, and should also have *ex-officio* direct access to the chairman of the audit committee (see below).

The bank's external auditors (a more or less universal statutory requirement) will perform a similar inspection role at the macro level, over an annual cycle. In the process, they will sample and to some extent rely on the assurance of detailed work carried out by the internal audit department.

As a normal aspect of corporate governance, the bank's board should establish an audit committee to conduct a regular dialogue with the external auditors, and to consider their reports and any remedial actions taken or proposed by the management. Ideally, a majority of committee members will be non-executive directors, one of whom will take the chair.

In the UK, Germany and Switzerland, the regulatory authorities have found it helpful to formalise demands for their own direct reports from external auditors of one kind or another (always at the subject bank's expense). The Bank of England has also opened channels of communication with audit committees, in addition to the usual meetings with bank managements. In these ways, the regulators can keep themselves informed without conducting their own full-scale bank examinations on the pattern seen in France and the USA.

12.3 Staff: employment, deployment and motivation

Three behavioural considerations warrant brief comment here: staff honesty; separation of risk assessment/limitation roles from business origination roles; and remuneration and incentives.

1   Given the unparalleled opportunities for financial theft and fraud, as pointed out in Chapter 11, bank staff are required to exercise the highest standards of integrity. This does not mean that Saint Peter himself keeps the gate, but simply that people do not get to work for a bank unless they are of good character. A bank employee with sticky fingers is like a pyromaniac loose in a gunpowder factory. Betrayal of trust is automatic grounds for dismissal, and there can be no question of a second chance for the miscreant (which would send the wrong message to all concerned). Duty to the

community also dictates that criminal incidents are reported to the police.

Every member of staff should take at least two consecutive weeks of holiday (and preferably the full entitlement) every year. It is not just a matter of the distortions caused by accumulation of entitlements: somebody else should occupy each position periodically as a check that nothing untoward is going on. Similarly, there should be rotation of duties every few years: leave a person too long in one post and he or she may come to be taken for granted and find easy ways to defraud the bank and cover the tracks. Long mutual familiarity can also breed *collusion* between members of staff, or between staff and customers, vitiating the normal checks and balances.

2 Separation of risk management assessment from front line business activity is called for in Chapter 4 in the shape of ALCO, and is thereby also implied in respect of Chapters 8, 9, and 10: a spread of concerns ranging from liquidity to interest rate to price risks. Chapter 10 further stresses the need to segregate front office from back office in the dealing room. Chapter 5 tells us it is a sound rule to keep sanctioning apart from credit origination. Without recapitulating the detailed justifications here, we may simply reaffirm that they are founded in human nature. No target-driven business originator can be expected to be not only advocate, but also objective judge and jury in his own cause: confinement to the first role sets him free from conflicts of interest.

The problem with this division of duties in the credit area is that it tends to promote confrontation, by assigning the final verdict (and thereby an 'obstructionist' image) to a credit sanctioner. Banks sometimes compound the difficulty by job-grading the business development role above the sanctioning role; as if to say the bows of the ship are more important than the stern. This has its psychological effect on both parties, making it harder for 'decline' decisions to be respected, and rendering recruitment for credit appraisal duties the more unpopular. Now that credit culture is being restored to its rightful place (having been mislaid for a while), there is no excuse for type-casting the credit officer as Caliban. And in any case, no one should be left in the credit appraisal/sanctioning job for too long.

Mutatis mutandis, similar considerations apply to the staffing of the independent internal audit (or inspection) function.

3   As regards performance motivation, it is clear that our age has bet heavily on an emphatically differentiated scale of financial incentives and bonuses; and that this trend has its drawbacks. As a general rule, business originators and traders can improve their substantial bonuses by taking on more risk exposure, by finding or creating market pricing anomalies which appear to overreward risk, or (alas) by doctoring the performance record. There is a built-in temptation to expand limits or to trade beyond them and manipulate the timing of transactions. Individuality is at a premium and teamwork comes a poor second.

The underlying assumptions are that entrepreneurial and trading talent is extremely rare (a proposition that deserves to be more rigorously tested), and thus has a bargaining advantage with employers; and that a bank can be sure of what an individual has contributed by his own efforts, unaided by colleagues or a fair wind. It used to be said that the only equipment a star trader needs in order to produce the goods is a telephone: however, today's better understanding of risk reveals that he is in fact dependent on the bank's good name, capital, infrastructure and support functions as well.

In defence of the mega-bonus, it may be argued that much is expected of the recipient, whose job security is also minimal. Dealers often burn out, or are dismissed without ceremony. Here we see another facet of the principle that high risk (employment risk in this case) merits high reward. These days, however, the less glamorous jobs in banking are proving equally vulnerable to hire and fire.

If we now shift the discussion away from front-line dealing and origination, it is worth repeating one observation from the Basle Committee's management guidelines for derivatives, already quoted in the appendix to Chapter 10:

As a matter of general policy, compensation policies – especially in the risk management, control and senior management functions – should be structured in a way that is sufficiently independent of the performance of trading activities, thereby avoiding the potential incentives for excessive risk-taking that can occur if, for example, salaries are tied too closely to the profitability of derivatives. (Part II, paragraph 7)

The vogue for heightened cash incentives may eventually wane, if and when the market changes its collective mind on the rationality of this escalating arms race. Meanwhile, a risk-aware bank will remain alert to the dangers.

12.4 Managing customers' risks

Banks have long underpinned society's financial risks in numerous ways. They safeguard cash and valuables; facilitate liquidity management via current, deposit and savings accounts, overdrafts, loans and leasing, and cash management schemes; collect commercial bills through factoring and international trade finance; provide forward foreign exchange cover; offer business advice; supply stockbroking services; insure homes, assure lives, act as executors and trustees, and so on. A generation ago, the treasury function grew a dealing room largely to service the bank's own money market needs; only to find the emphasis shift to meeting corporate customers' requirements.

Competition between banks has given birth to new sophisticated banking skills, ranging from guidance, training and support for small businesses to investment banking and 'financial engineering' at the large corporate end. The question arises: how much closer should the banks get to managing their customers' risks? From the small business market comes a frequent and widespread call for 'partnership'; which turns out on inspection to be more a plea for understanding, support and forbearance than a willingness to cede shares and a degree of control. But even if it were the latter, any joint venture comes up against the eternal conflict of interest between the roles of banker and shareholder, which both sides disregard at their peril (see Chapter 10). A few more steps towards 'partnership' of one kind or another, and banks could be into a minefield of dispute and litigation; a metaphor which, admittedly, could be pressed into service to describe aspects of the present situation.

At the larger end of corporate relationships, Bankers Trust has taken a lead in marketing derivatives to hedge its customers' risks.

To quote a shoulder-shrugging adage in the lending business, 'this is probably all right, as long as it stays all right'; but early corporate clients have proved not to be philosophical when swaps work out to their disadvantage. As mentioned in Chapter 4, Bankers Trust was sued by two customers for large amounts, and settled out of court. The same bank was also disciplined by three US regulatory bodies for deficiencies in derivatives controls. Over a short time span, these episodes look like a severe setback and possibly evidence of a wrong turning; but in history's long perspective, they may come to be seen as unfortunate teething troubles in a correct and inevitable reorientation.

Interim verdict: the banks now have growing risk management skills which could be more actively deployed in managing their customers' risks as well as their own, thereby introducing new streams of banking revenue. The latent demand may be there, and if so competition will sniff it out; but it remains to be seen how far banks can afford to abandon the arm's length style of banking relationship which has stood the test of time.

12.5 Summary

Risk management is central to corporate governance. The board of directors is primarily responsible for deciding on the criteria which it wishes to see fulfilled. Board members in a bank cannot escape the obligation (legal, regulatory, moral) to understand the risks over which they preside.

Risk management is also the responsibility of the executive team in fulfilment of the board's directives. Different types of risk interact with one another, so risk management needs to be co-ordinated at senior executive level by a steering committee.

In view of the opportunities for internal defalcation, unblemished standards of honesty are required in bank employees. Staff should be compelled to take regular holidays, and jobs should be rotated every few years to minimise any temptation to defraud the bank.

Separation of risk management control functions from business origination and trading is desirable in specified cases. A bank should be aware of, and take action to mitigate, organisational strains that may be caused by this segregation.

Heightened performance incentives can create a short-sighted bias towards excessive risk-taking. Compensation policies for those who can rein this in (risk management and senior management people) should not be directly linked to the short term performance of business origination and trading activities.

Bankers have acquired new and sophisticated risk management skills which could profitably be extended to managing more of their customers' risks. They must, however, avoid the trap of appearing so involved in a customer's business as to be deemed 'shadow directors', legally and morally responsible for its results. The normal role for a bank remains that of service counterparty, rather than joint venturer.

Bibliography and further reading

As already indicated in the preface and acknowledgements, this book is based predominantly on unpublished sources, first-hand professional advice, and the author's own work experience. There is, nevertheless, an academic literature underlying market practices which also deserves acknowledgement.

For example, some of the arguments in Chapter 3 (on bank capital gearing and cost of capital) originated in an article by F Modigliani and M H Miller, 'The Cost of Capital: Corporation Finance and the Theory of Investment', *American Economic Review*, June 1958. Similarly, the principles of risk diversification and portfolio management, summarised in Chapter 6, were first enunciated in an article by H M Markowitz, 'Portfolio Selection', *Journal of Finance*, March 1952. The ideas of these and other trail-breakers are conveniently accessible in an encyclopaedic modern work, *Principles of Corporate Finance* by Richard A Brealey and Stewart C Myers (McGraw-Hill, 1996).

Readers who simply wish to brush up on statistical techniques might like to consult *The Effective Use of Statistics* by Tim Hannagan (Kogan Page, 1990).

Those seeking technical depth and detail on derivative products, and their use in hedging risk, will find many answers in *Managing Financial Risk: A Guide to Derivative Products, Financial Engineering, and Value Maximisation*, by Charles W Smithson and

Clifford W Smith Jr with D Sykes Wilford (Irwin Professional Publishing, 1995).

Finally, for a coherent guide to asset and liability management (and especially to interest rate risk), see *Financial Risk Management in Banking* by Dennis G Uyemura and Donald R Van Deventer (Bankers Publishing Company and Probus Publishing Company, 1993).

Glossary of financial terms

Arbitrage Purchase and sale exploiting a price differential for the same product, instrument or security on different markets.

Buy-back See repurchase agreement.

Cap An instrument conferring an upper limit to a floating interest rate.

Collar An instrument conferring an upper and lower limit to a floating interest rate.

Derivative A contractual instrument whose value derives from another instrument, security, product, index or commodity.

Discounted cash flow The value of future cash flow from an investment discounted back to the present.

Exchange-traded Referring to financial instruments traded on an organised exchange (e.g. LIFFE – London International Financial Futures Exchange).

Exposure Maximum amount at risk.

Floor An instrument conferring a lower limit to a floating interest rate.

Forward exchange contract   A contract to buy or sell a stated amount of a foreign currency on a specified future date at a price fixed today.

Forward rate agreement   A contract whereby the interest rate on a specified future date, for a stated period on a notional principal amount, is fixed today. On settlement date, the contract rate is compared with a market reference rate: if the former is the higher, the contract buyer pays the seller the difference in interest; if market rate is the higher, the contract seller pays the buyer. No principal amount changes hands.

Future   An exchange-traded contract to buy or sell a specified amount of a commodity or other asset on a specified future date at a price fixed today. Contracts are in standard amounts and maturities. Contractual parties are required by the rules of the exchange to put up a margin (related to expected volatility), which is adjusted daily as the contract is marked to market.

Gearing   Proportion of debt incurred to expand the business and increase expected return on equity.

Hedge   The attempt to reduce risk by taking a position with mitigating or counter-balancing tendencies.

In the money   Position where a contract has positive value if exercised.

Interest turn   Interest rate (net of funding costs) earned on advances. This can be calculated before and after deduction of bad debt provisions (or expected losses).

Leverage   See gearing.

Net present value   The current value of the discounted cash flows from an instrument.

Option   A contract giving the right (but not the obligation) to buy ('call' option) or sell ('put' option) a particular asset at a specified exercise price on or before a specified date.

Out of the money   Position where a contract has negative value if exercised.

Over-the-counter   Informal market for financial instruments, not involving organised exchanges or standardised terms and conditions. This is the area of derivatives trading which is of most concern to regulatory authorities.

Regression analysis   Statistical technique for finding the line of best fit.

Repurchase agreement (repo)   A deal whereby one party sells securities to another, and simultaneously agrees to buy them back at a specified future date at a price fixed today. Also known as a 'Buy-back'.

Risk   Exposure to uncertainty of outcome.

Short sale   Sale of a security not held by the seller at the time. An equivalent purchase has to be made to square the seller's position.

Spot   A deal priced for immediate delivery.

Swap   A contract in which two parties agree to exchange specified cash flows for a stated period. In an interest rate swap, the parties may exchange fixed interest rate for floating rate, or one floating rate for another (e.g. three months for six months), on a stated amount of notional principal. Effectively they are notionally lending to one another, although no principal is at risk and only the net interest owing (either way) is paid across at prescribed intervals. In a currency swap, the parties exchange two different currencies today at spot rate, and agree to reverse that deal at a specified future date at an exchange rate fixed today.

Swaption   An option on a swap.

Index